# OMAN

For A.J. with best love.

In Memory of the late Sultan Said bin Taimour.

Dedicated to, and for, the People of the Sultanate of Oman,
so many of whom want this story to be told.

Awake! For morning in the bowl of night,
Has flung the stone that put the stars to flight. And lo!
The Hunter of the East has caught,
The Sultan's Turret in a noose of light.
*The Rubaiyat of Omar Khayyam*

# OMAN

## THE TRUE-LIFE DRAMA AND INTRIGUE OF AN ARAB STATE

JOHN BEASANT

Research by Christopher Ling and Ian Cummins

MAINSTREAM
PUBLISHING

EDINBURGH AND LONDON

First published in Great Britain in 2002 by
MAINSTREAM PUBLISHING COMPANY (EDINBURGH) LTD
7 Albany Street
Edinburgh EH1 3UG

ISBN 1 84018 607 0

Typeset in Apollo and Civet
Printed and bound in Great Britain by
Butler & Tanner Ltd, Frome and London

# CONTENTS

# Acknowledgements

The writing of a book such as *Oman* is rarely, if ever, the work of a single individual, a truth given a particular dimension when the significant 'cast-list' of those whose sustained endeavours brought the enterprise to publication is taken into account.

Of equal truth is that it is neither advisable, nor indeed possible, to pay public tribute to all those who, particularly during the research phase of the work, were provocatively brave, taking not inconsiderable personal risk to speak with both the researchers and myself about the life and times of the Sultanate of Oman.

The fact that so many, in taking such risk, made an invaluable contribution is the measure of their sense of conviction that the time had indeed arrived for the deceits of the past, which have so attended their country's occasions, to be brought into the antiseptic rays of the sun and subjected to public scrutiny.

While it is readily accepted that, in the face of a comprehensive deceit, the truth is revolutionary, this opportunity is taken to confirm that, contrary to peddled belief, there has been no conspiracy in the writing of this work. If, however, as some will doubtless claim, that such a record of Oman's past will generate bitterness, then let it be the bitterness of medicine, not poison. Those in Oman, and indeed beyond, who choose to fulminate, should be reminded that such conduct is but the rage of Caliban at seeing his own reflection in the mirror.

In paying tribute to the many of honour who have to go unnamed, I wish to pay tribute also to Christopher Ling and Ian Cummins, without whose research endeavours the book could not have been written. At Mainstream I mark my appreciation to Bill Campbell and Peter Mackenzie, and in the Editorial and Production teams to Jessica Thompson, Ailsa Bathgate, Kirsteen Wright, Deborah Kilpatrick, Tina Hudson, Sharon Atherton and Fiona Brownlee. I thank, too, Oliver Donachie for technical support.

In conclusion, I wish to record a debt of gratitude to Lady Hermione Grimston, Michael and Annete Davis, Kay Cummins, Claire Williams, Ern Tucknott, Peter Zedlewski and Raghuveer Shettigar, whose personal support has been pivotal. The burden of the book's conclusions and opinions are, however, exclusively those of my research colleagues and myself alone.

*John Wayland Beasant*
*May 2002*

# CHAPTER ONE

## The End of the Dream

As 1999 dawned and the final year of a blood-soaked century appeared on the horizon, the Western world embarked upon an orgy of millennium mania, casting its collective powers of speculation as to what lessons could be learnt from the preceding catalogue of human folly, with all the conviction of a fakir peering myopically at the entrails of a goat in order to divine the future, exciting itself to the point of tedium about what the new century would bring.

In Oman, however, as in other states of the Arab Islamic world, the year was 1419, so no such exercise in mass titillation was being indulged. Indeed, the State's manipulators of public opinion, the Ministry of Information, assisted by a 78-year-old, one-time British Intelligence functionary, Anthony Clayton Ashworth, the country's slayer of dragons both real and imaginary, continued its well trod and totally counter-productive route into a cul-de-sac with ever narrowing walls. Such a national journey 'to the broad sunlit uplands of international prestige and continuing prosperity' for its native population of 1.6 million people was to proceed under 'the wise leadership of His Majesty Sultan Qaboos'. This frequent description never varies in its insulting patronage of a monarch who in actual fact loathes sycophancy. Western expatriates in Oman, however, were contemplating with mounting unease their future in the country and were asking themselves the not-always-rhetorical question 'Is there life after Oman?' followed by the equally plaintive 'What, exactly, will life be like in the real world?'

Indeed as the year progressed, a sense of unreality in Oman was distinctly palpable for nationals and expatriates alike. Virtually everyone from Bedu to banker and back again, simply by believing the abundant evidence of their own eyes and ears, knew of the country's rapidly increasing economic woes as the oil price remained depressed. It was clear what effect this was having on the social fabric of society and everyone could hear in ever more strident tones constant calls for change from the increasingly educated constituency, even if only articulated in private. Indeed, the Government's principal effort to reduce the totally disproportionate levels of public expenditure for such a small population had, initially, as its principal target throughout 1997–8, a reduction in the number of civil servants through the expedient of early retirement. This policy began to meet with public resentment when in so many instances the full gratuity promised under the scheme was not immediately forthcoming. As so many Omanis, from within both the public sector and beyond, saw arms purchases and their attendant commission payments to powerful members of an oligarchy of businessmen continue, public anger and disillusionment rapidly increased.

But the power so well characterised by naked greed and spiteful jealousies within this oligarchy (not all of them Omani) besieging Sultan Qaboos, made itself felt in its opposition to any of the changes the Government attempted to make during the latter part of 1998. One senior Omani, the widely respected Ahmed Macki, the country's Minister of Finance and a man of sound integrity, recommended to the Sultan a whole range of cost-cutting measures, entailing a marked reduction in payments to Ministers, which all too often take the form of ludicrous 'perks' (one such 'allowance' being an absurdly high payment for fertiliser for ministerial gardens). Qaboos, initially, accepted this recommendation and other such measures but then the oligarchy moved to generate rumours that Macki had fled the country with much of the State's treasury, with which he had purchased an expensive apartment in the Trocadero area of Paris. This illicit pressure mounted, leading many diplomats and an influential banker in one case, to believe that the rumours had substance, particularly as they coincided with a heavy drawing down by the Government of its currency reserves. In the event, in a bid to end the speculation, a short, terse (and it should be recorded, effective) statement appeared in the state-controlled *Oman Daily Observer* newspaper, to the effect that Minister Macki continued to enjoy the full confidence of the Sultan and that he was currently on leave abroad and would soon return home. What the statement did not establish, however, was that all the 'allowances' the Minister had recommended be discontinued were quietly and promptly reinstated.

As 1998 drew to a close and under increasing economic pressure, a comprehensive range of taxes on consumer goods was introduced, increases which in some cases ran as high as 40 per cent and which, of course, adversely affected both Omanis and expatriates alike. On a scale and with an abruptness that shocked many, Oman, never an inexpensive place to live at the best of times (despite Omani salaries being considerably lower than in other Gulf states), began to be for many a very expensive place to live indeed, right across the social spectrum. As is ever the case, those least able to shield themselves against such a rise in the cost of living were having to bear the principal burden. There were token gestures towards taxing the affluent: imported marble, so beloved by Oman's new rich in the construction of their numerous 'palaces' (most of which are examples of an almost desperate vulgarity), was to be taxed. Such a measure did, at the very least, provide comic relief to an increasingly depressed community when the English-language *Times of Oman*, in reporting this state initiative, described it on the front page as 'A Government Tax on Marbles'.

But the relief was short-lived. During the early months of 1999 it became known that Oman was to engage in yet another round of expensive arms purchases, principally with funds hastily borrowed from a consortium of foreign banks and with the generous assistance of Sheikh Zayed, of the neighbouring Emirate of Abu Dhabi, to whom Oman had gone cap in hand. The purchases were 12 Pilatus training aircraft from America's Raytheon Company and the Rapier Air Defence System from Britain. As such deals involved huge commission payments by Oman, the sense of public anger and resentment grew even more intense among many Omanis (in the case of the Pilatus aircraft, payments were made to two Britons long close to Qaboos, much to the fury of the US Ambassador, John Craig, who apparently wailed 'Why are Brits involved in an American deal?'). One senior military officer was prompted to comment, not for the first time, 'This is equipment we do not really need and most certainly cannot afford.' In Oman such purchases are rarely, if ever, made public. This control of information only fuels speculation and disillusionment among Omanis not only with the Sultan's administration but with the Sultan himself, particularly as so many see such a process as making way for a return to national debt (and with it foreign dependence), which an oil-producing state with well under 2 million indigenous people should be able to avoid.

During the first quarter of 1999 it became increasingly apparent to a greater number of Omanis that the past was, indeed, returning to haunt them. On 19 March the Dubai-based English-language newspaper, *Gulf News*, reported that Standard and Poor's, the influential international credit rating agency, had affirmed its triple-B-minus status on long-term foreign currency and senior, unsecured credit ratings for Oman. It had furthermore changed the country's economic situation from stable to negative. The newspaper's report continued, 'The change in outlook reflects Oman's macroeconomic imbalances, coupled with an inadequate response by policy makers to undertake structural reform or corrective action of the economy. Government efforts to trim capital expenditure, or to increase corporate taxes on luxury duties are not likely to prove sufficient to restore balances. The authorities have elected to finance the deficit by drawing on the country's reserves.' The report also warned the Government to promptly reduce expenditure. While the Government, via the Ministry of Information, continue to exercise tight control of foreign news reports unfavourable to the regime, to those Omanis who read of Standard and Poor's assessment of their country's financial situation, it represented nothing less than the proverbial writing on the wall. Indeed, anti-Qaboos slogans daubed by senior school pupils had already served graphic notice that as the country became demonstrably poorer than an oil-producing state with a small population should be, public disaffection was going to be expressed increasingly loudly. This was despite the grotesquely large and varied branches of a security service designed to monitor and control public dissent, or indeed the overweening efforts at propaganda by the Ministry of Information with its mantra of 'ever onwards to the broad, sunlit uplands'. In any event, modern communications technology is increasingly making a nonsense of the Ministry's dubious best efforts. Reports banned from public gaze in Oman are promptly faxed or e-mailed by Omanis resident abroad. A related example of technology defeating such myopic practices occurred on 8 February 1999, when the *Oman Daily Observer* published a picture of Sultan Qaboos standing next to US President Bill Clinton at the funeral of His Majesty King Hussein of Jordan, which took place the day before. It was an example of image manipulation of which the Stasi, the former East German secret police, would have been proud. For on 7 February, many in Oman had clearly seen via live satellite coverage of the funeral in Amman, Sultan Qaboos with his customary self-effacement and dignity, standing well back in the line of state representatives, nowhere near the occupant of the Washington White

House. A dissenting Ministry of Information official commented that the picture was 'a public humiliation for Qaboos and Oman'. As is often the case in circumstances of such craven attempts at news management (and with it the absence of a free flow of information into the public domain), rumour and speculation continued to flourish.

Indeed, for many in positions of authority in Oman it must have seemed that in the spring of 1999 troubles most certainly did come, not as single spies, but as battalions. The rumour mills of Muscat spun mightily into overdrive, producing renewed speculation on everything from the nature of the Sultan's private life to a tale (true as it was, later, to be confirmed) that the Government had earned the disapproval of the Convention on International Trade in Endangered Species (CITES), for its refusal to accede to the Treaty; a refusal that ran counter to Oman's proud and continued boast that it is very much a state of the modern world. Such refusal was also a contradiction of the Sultan's acclaimed concern for the environment. As early as 14 December 1993, Jacques Berney, then CITES Deputy Secretary-General, had written to Dr Mahmood Al Zakwani, the Acting Director of Oman's Relations with 'International Organisation Affairs', urging the country's accession to the Treaty. But Oman's refusal, according to an insider, was because of its illicit importation of rhino horn, which is carved into handles for the traditional daggers worn by so many Omanis at the waist. This 'consumption' of a part of an endangered species would, again, not fit at all well with the country's 'modern' image peddled so furiously to the outside world.

The renewed speculation about the Sultan's private life in 1999 came at a time when Omanis were being increasingly obliged by the realities of the country's condition to peer down from the now illusory 'broad sunlit uplands' onto the ever more apparent plains of austerity below. The conjecture of these rumours centred on just how their ruler of 28 years plus was coping with the situation.

As such speculation gained an ever wider currency and many Omanis, some in positions of considerable authority, began to voice their hitherto private fears for the future to members of the expatriate community, one Westerner put the not altogether rhetorical question, 'Who will take the part of Rasputin?'

In all truth, Muscat's spring of 1999 did indeed have much of the flavour of the last days of the Romanovs: parties bordering on decadence; a Palace Garden assembly of Muscat's self-appointed 'great and the good'; the band not just playing on in tones of increasing stridency, but most effectively drowning out the cries for national caution and lawful dissent. Even the usually timid expatriate community from the Indian subcontinent, who actually get up each morning and run the country (many doing so on criminally low wages), began to voice their dissatisfaction when the country's Ministry of Health gave the order for Asian hospital staff to double up in their pitifully small government accommodation. For many of this long-suffering community, this proved to be a cost-cutting measure too far.

Yet despite such discontent, the arms purchases, just like the military bands, go on and on, now with borrowed money; a debt that the young, educated Omani generation will be obliged to shoulder. In fact given the scale of the expenditure, quite possibly their children will do so too. In the context of Oman and its 44 per cent expenditure of the national budget on the running of the exceedingly top-heavy defence and security establishment (with its consequent arms purchases), the influence of a small group of Omani and Western 'advisers' to the Sultan cannot be disregarded. Indeed, there are a rapidly increasing number who say it is virtually impossible to overestimate it. Particularly so given that this group's self-serving influence has distorted the very fabric of the state. They have permeated every aspect of its national life; grossly influenced that most crucial aspect of its economy, the sale of oil; have had a malignant influence on the state's foreign policy; drained much of its finances on 'deals' (principally on arms which as mentioned before 'the country does not really need and most certainly cannot afford'), with commissions permitting the chosen few to build up vast fortunes outside the country.

Indeed the cycle of history repeating itself, now believed by so many in Oman to be coming full circle, includes not just national debt and consequent foreign dependence, but the influence of a small, alien group on their leader, motivated by the creed of enlightened self-interest which, as is demonstrated in Chapter Three, was such a feature of Omani life in the nineteenth and early twentieth centuries. One of the principal reasons for this book is that it constitutes an attempt to illustrate just how a small group, with aims and priorities not compatible with those of the state on which it has descended, can come to exercise an adverse influence on major policy initiatives and in the process come to distort the country's very national life; a circumstance which in the case of Oman led directly to planned acts of violent revolt by some of its citizens.

In fact, so angry and so disaffected had a group of senior state officials become by 1994 that they joined together and hatched a plan to violently overthrow Sultan Qaboos of Oman, who for so long the world had been told was the very epitome of what a national leader should be. In the event they were detected, rounded up and the plan collapsed. Yet the embers of dissent continue to smoulder, with the result that the extensive state security apparatus collectively has once more turned the screw on the pressure cooker that is now Oman's social and political condition. In the spring of 1999 alone, the country's phone-tapping brigade took on an extra 40 eavesdroppers in a bid to keep track of dissenters. Until now, however, the plan to overthrow one of the world's two remaining Sultans has been veiled from public scrutiny. In this regard the plot was not unlike much of Oman's past, which for so long has remained a closed book, not only to Omanis, who have an inalienable right to know of the events which shaped their state, but to many beyond the country's shores, most of whom entertain a durable affection for this unique land and its people and continue to care very much for their future. Had the plan of revolt been successful then Sultan Qaboos would, without doubt, have been widely mourned, his many achievements well-marked. Yet the very fact that a significant proportion of Oman's professional classes exhibited such anger and frustration at what they saw as a debilitating, alien and malignant influence on their ruler was an important factor that led to a plan for his violent end. This, too, is essentially an integral aspect of the drama and intrigue which has for far too long attended Oman's history and which makes its story worth the telling, illustrating the strength of the dark shadows which fell across a land that many for so long have believed to be close to a paradise on earth. The Oman story is very much a modern-day parable, one virtually without equal given the melancholy consequences for the country today, as the state approaches full circle in its much-touted 'Renaissance Fairy Tale', a rags to riches story which held a very different promise to the one now being contemplated and which, in any event, clearly marks the end of an extremely well-crafted dream.

# CHAPTER TWO

## An Arabian Nightmare

'Tomorrow, tomorrow, it will all be over' – Dostoevsky

Arab coalitions are notoriously fragile affairs, with tribal affiliations, personal jealousies, unbridled ambition, artifice, avarice, financial considerations and the spoils of power all making their very own deleterious contribution, giving particular truth to the Arab self-observation that when ten Arabs assemble in discussion, eleven opinions will emerge, all on the same subject! Add to such social circumstances the ever present truth that few state or personal matters remain confidential and the nature of many state problems are all too apparent. Indeed in Arab society there are many 'secrets', most of which become public property well before breakfast. The nature of the problem is, without doubt, exacerbated by an absence of the free flow of information from the state into the public domain, a policy which the great majority of Arab rulers have yet to realise is counter-productive. In short, the policy of state control of information which, in effect, is based on the ultimately self-defeating assumption that the Government knows best what its people should be told, is one that can only make a considerable contribution to the culture of rumour and speculation, a fact of daily life so common in the Sultanate of Oman. One staff member of a Western Embassy was so irritated by this aspect of the social life of Muscat that he inaugurated an essentially harmless rumour in an attempt to demonstrate how damaging it could on occasions be. He was also trying to see just how long it would take for it to come full circle, being repeated to him as fact and what is more, repeated as being 'written on a tablet of stone'. It took just 20 short hours.

All the more surprising then that a coalition, joined together not just by spiritual concerns but bound by a sense of resentment at the constant draining away of so much of the country's finances by a small group of men close to Sultan Qaboos, conspired to unleash a chain of events that would have led to the assassination of the man to whom, in several instances, they had taken solemn oaths of allegiance. It was, essentially, a coalition for terror of a particularly pernicious kind, in that it would have swept away with the murdered Sultan the character of one of the Arabian Gulf's most liberal states along with many of the relative social freedoms with which both the Sultan and the country have become so well associated in the wider world.

Yet it is not enough (and it will never be enough) to speculate in splendid, appalled isolation about the consequences of this intended catalogue of death and destruction. The 'cause' is an essential factor to consider, every bit as much as a contemplation of what would have been the appalling 'effect' for the greater majority in Oman and in the world beyond her shores. Amazingly, a conspiracy of silence was maintained about the fateful occasion that the conspirators planned for the Sultan and Oman on 18 November 1994, a day celebrating both Qaboos's birthday and the National Day. There was no rumour, no speculation which would have alerted the country's extensive security apparatus and it was left to the intelligence service of a friendly Arab power to raise the all-important, life- and state-saving alarm.

There was, of course, rumour rife after the arrest of the coup leaders. But even then the State was silent, save for a brief statement in the state-sponsored *Oman Daily Observer* alluding to the detention of an implied small number of people, who were not identified, for activities prejudicial to public order. Indeed, there are many who will both dismiss and deny the account of the attempted coup given later in this book, for the denial of unwelcome, unpalatable news is essential to a maintenance of the policy of control which continues to serve such ill-credit and ridicule on Oman.

The people of the Sultanate demonstrably deserve better treatment and had they had universal access to the United States of America's *1994 Human Rights Country Report for the Sultanate of Oman*, issued on 1 February 1995, they would have received it. Its third paragraph reads:

> The Government continues to restrict or deny important human
> rights. In 1994 the Government detained 200 people in connection
> with an alleged plot to destabilise the country. The Government

charged 131 of these suspects with sedition and tried them in secret before the State Security Court. The detentions and secret trials raised serious questions about freedom from arbitrary arrest and the right to due process. Other human rights restrictions included infringements on the freedoms of expression and association. The Government does not guarantee full rights for workers and women. As a practical matter, the people do not have the right to change their Government.

The Report, under a section titled 'Denial of Fair Public Trial' commented:

> The Government tried 131 persons for subversion in secret before the State Security Court, which issued verdicts on November 12. The Court sentenced two defendants to death and the others to from 3 to 15 years in prison. The Sultan later commuted the death sentences to prison terms. The defendants did not receive a fair trial by international norms.

Under the heading 'Freedom of Speech and Press', the report commented, 'There is no legal protection for free speech or press. The law prohibits any criticism of the Sultan in any form or medium. The Government controls radio and television.'

The section regarding 'Freedom of Peaceful Assembly and Association' read, in part, 'the law does not guarantee freedom of assembly' and also observed under that section of the report titled 'Respect for Political Rights: The Right of Citizens to Change Their Government':

> Oman is an autocracy in which the Sultan retains the ultimate authority on all important foreign and domestic issues. The country has no formal democratic political institutions and its citizens do not have the ability peacefully to change their leaders or the political system.

It is this observation which, arguably, is the most poignant. It is certainly the most instructive point within the context of those imperatives which drew the conspirators together, their aim and purpose of bringing about change to a national climate which they manifestly regarded as intolerable. Such dynamics of political change are made virtually inevitable in a state where an increasingly expanding educated class reach out for some influence on the governance of their own lives and fortunes. This social grouping regards with dangerous exasperation the maintenance of a status quo in which influences all too often prevail that are perceived as not just alien, but fundamentally detrimental to the national good and to which it is legitimate to apply violent methods in order to achieve change. It is particularly instructive that even given the all-embracing practices of Oman's security services (which include the comprehensive use of telephone taps and the interception of mail), allied to the activities of an army of intelligence operatives, who mingle amongst all sections of the Omani and expatriate communities, that a plan which would quite literally have torn the heart out of the country, went undetected for so long. It also demonstrates the cruel mindset that change denied can engender, from which the most attentive of intelligence services can, all too often, fail to offer protection.

In the early spring of 1994 the President of Egypt, Hosni Mubarak, accompanied by his security supremo, Omar Suleiman, requested an urgent audience with Sultan Qaboos, subsequently flying to Oman for a meeting with the country's ruler at Al Hisn Palace in Salalah, capital of the Southern Province of Dhofar. The meeting had been prompted by Egypt's acquisition of important information.

In October, 1981, President Mubarak's predecessor, Anwar Al Sadat, who had earlier signed the Camp David Accords with the Israeli Premier of the time, Menachem Begin, was assassinated in Cairo by men of his own army as he sat watching a military parade, an assassination in which two members of Oman's military delegation were shot, one fatally. The assassination was to herald a long and bloody campaign by Egyptian fundamentalists who claim, then as now, that the Egyptian Government is corrupt and un-Islamic, a campaign which included the murder of some 61 foreign tourists at Luxor, in southern Egypt.

Once in secret counsel with Oman's ruler, the Egyptian President revealed that during police interrogation of some of the activists held in custody in Cairo, it had been established that a wider network existed to foment disaffection with other regimes in the Arab world, a network with tentacles that stretched into the very heart of Oman's establishment. Sultan Qaboos wasted no time in consulting with his security officials, who subsequently launched a comprehensive programme of surveillance. In May of 1994 they had enough evidence to act and in a series of raids arrested a large number of suspects, ranging from officers of the Royal Oman Police and the Armed Forces to civil servants (one of whom was an

Undersecretary of State in the Ministry of Commerce and Industry), to a crop of professionals prominent in the commercial life of the country. In one such raid a quantity of arms and explosives were found in a furniture showroom in the Muscat suburb of Al Khuwair. The total number arrested was always thought to be in the region of 200, a figure confirmed in the aforementioned American *Country Report on Oman*. A small number in the group, however, having got wind of imminent arrest, fled abroad. While, as we have seen, the American report confirms the belief that those subsequently sentenced to death were reprieved by the Sultan, diplomats accredited to the Court of Sultan Qaboos at the time continue to believe that those who had sworn oaths of allegiance to the Omani ruler, such as police and army officers, were summarily executed. It has to be recorded, however, that in a magnanimous gesture in November 1995, on the occasion of his 55th birthday, Sultan Qaboos decreed an amnesty for those who had been taken into custody 18 months earlier for, as it was obliquely termed, 'having been convicted of involvement in illegal activities and organisations'. A pardon was also granted to the small number who had fled abroad just before the arrests started.

The arrests had come as an unexpected turn of events for those for whom Oman remained what it had always appeared to be, a modern-day paradise on earth where every prospect pleased, with disaffection at the state of things non-existent. To such individuals the arrests came as a profound jolt. Their dismay can therefore be well imagined, if they had known that those arrested had a master plan which would have swept away all that most Omanis had come to learn was responsible for their progress from a mediaeval state to one enjoying all the material benefits that the late twentieth-century world could bestow; a national transformation which had been achieved in the lifetime of but one generation.

Essential to the plan, according to brave official sources in Oman itself, was the assassination by officers of the regime of Sultan Qaboos in the ancient, former capital of Nizwa, as he attended the country's 24th National Day celebrations. To cause maximum chaos in the capital, Muscat, during which the reins of power would have been seized, the plan also called for explosions in the city's three principal shopping malls, Sabco, the Al Harthy and Capital Commercial Centres. The action taken by officers of Oman's Internal State Security organisation and the Royal Oman Police thwarted such a bloody plan and with it relative calm descended once more upon the land. However, while the fire may well have been most effectively stamped out by the prompt, professional action of the country's security and intelligence services, the embers of dissent continued to glow and flare.

In the autumn of 1997, following a personal message to Muscat from the former American Secretary of State, Madeleine Albright, a further series of arrests were made, this time of Omanis who, it was alleged, had been making financial contributions to Islamic organisations outside the Sultanate. These payments were helping to fund Hamas, that most feared of Islamic action groups. This second wave of arrests sent an additional shockwave through much of Omani society and the expatriate community, with many in both camps finally acknowledging that while the Sultan remained firmly on the throne and the sun still shone in the sky above, there were now undeniable undercurrents of dissent which, if ignored, could well sweep away in a shockingly short time a lifestyle that was the envy of many in the Arab world. So the question came to be asked, initially in hushed tones, but as is the way of it with any emerging political point of view, with increasing clarity and indeed, stridency: what conviction, exactly, had ignited the blue touchpaper of potentially explosive, collective dissent in the Sultanate of Oman, a country that for a quarter of a century had been held up to the world as a paragon of virtue in all things which contribute to make a successful developing state and civil society? And, more to the point, what had prompted these Omanis, many of whom had been in positions of trust and authority, which they unquestionably owed to their Sultan? Similarly, what of those who had come from secure financial positions, which had been made possible by Qaboos's patronage? What had inspired them to actively conspire in the planning of his murderous overthrow? What coalition of concerns and interests had drawn together such a diverse band of conspirators in which all sorts and conditions of men were represented?

In a country with a tightly controlled press and broadcasting service, publicly putting such questions, which by their very nature demand increasingly urgent answers, is strictly forbidden, although there are many in Oman today, particularly those who wish to see the reign of Sultan Qaboos continue successfully, that now insist in asking them. It is a debate unheralded in the public domain and most certainly unreported but in which, in rapidly increasing numbers, both Omanis and expatriates now take part. In fact the existence in the Sultanate of a significant number of foreigners, given as some 500,000 at the time of the first (and last) national census in December 1993, is itself not without political connotations: the greater number are Asian, coming from India, Pakistan and Bangladesh, with a minority in this racial category hailing from Sri Lanka and the Philippines. The effect on the national character and social arrangements for the Omani people by having such a large number of foreigners in their midst has, as it was bound to do, taken a part in the drama currently being played out in the Sultanate, as does the presence of a minority of Westerners and, particularly, the British. For, as we shall see, Britain has long regarded Oman as a very special place indeed, one in which UK interests, both political and commercial, have been pursued with particular vigour and close attention. Many Omanis are only too eager to bear witness to the assertion that the prosecution by London and by a cabal of Britons of such interests has not always been beneficial to Oman. But when such commercial matters as those identified earlier and the country's relationship with Britain come under scrutiny and discussion, the prevailing, innate culture of secrecy and conservatism that has for so long inhibited and distorted legitimate public debate in the Sultanate, makes its very own contribution to its continued existence, an existence which is both morbid, counter-productive and ultimately culture-arresting.

All of this made free and open discussion of the background to the planned coup of 18 November 1994 quite impossible. So all the human attitudes struck by those who galvanised their sense of outrage into planned acts of open revolt and mayhem, the political opinions which allied to their individual social experiences were the essential currency of their inspiration, went unheard and therefore undiscussed and unheeded. Naturally enough, some of the opinions would have been universally unacceptable in both Oman and indeed elsewhere, but some would, undoubtedly, have been instructive; they would have had a greater relevance in both social and political terms and as such could have well made a positive contribution to Oman's commonwealth, on the shaping of public opinion and in turn, government policy. The failure to take such an opportunity to reinvigorate the national climate with a greater sense of realism, at a time when the dangers of maintaining the status quo are apparent to all those who are prepared to think for themselves, would leave the country without a sense of direction more in keeping with the national mood. To fail to take measures that would reshape the country's national institutions would all too soon be seen as a monumental dereliction of duty. The past will dictate the future, a universal process from which the Sultanate of Oman, however many in the country may wish it otherwise, is most certainly not immune.

In actual fact, it is this process that is already well underway. Should this be in any manner doubted then it is appropriate to recall the events of 1 September 1971, when Omani workers took industrial action against the mass arrival in their country of cheap, immigrant labour from the Indian subcontinent. Had they been listened to, instead of the Government having declared their peaceful protest unlawful, then a greater number of Omanis than is currently the case would now be in possession of vital, artisan skills. But as ever in Oman, the infamous, myopic greed of a small number of the country's powerful business community 'won' the day. The priority given by the Government to turn an apparent modern face to the world beyond its borders, through the rapid construction of contemporary edifices, proved a ready accomplice. It was a fundamental, structural error for which Oman now pays dear.

But the basic question remains. What exactly was the human chemistry that prompted men of previous goodwill and undoubted commitment to their ruler and country, men of considerable intellect, to plan to take up arms against a system from which, in the main, they had derived great personal benefit? Was it religious fervour alone? Hardly, for the facts fail completely to justify such a belief although this explanation was, of course, propagated in suitably muted and coded tones in Oman following the widespread arrests and trials of the summer of 1994. So what were the additional factors that prompted their dissent? Why should all that which has undeniably been achieved since the accession to the throne of Oman by Sultan Qaboos on 23 July 1970 have been put in very real jeopardy? That is very much the question, one that can, in part, be answered by telling the other side of the much-touted story of the Sultanate of Oman's 'Renaissance' from a backward, mediaeval country ruled from 1932–70 by a Sultan officially and interminably described as 'cruel', 'despotic' and a 'dictator', to a state which, in superficial appearances, assumed the style and character of the contemporary world. It is a story which for all its majesty, progress and undoubted achievement, is also one of human weakness and folly and as such is very much a modern-day parable of all our times.

# CHAPTER THREE

## A Place in the Sun

It was once described as the least hospitable land on God's earth, a judgement delivered by an early-nineteenth century British political agent. At a time before the salvation of an air conditioning system, he suffered so mightily in Muscat's long Arabian Summer, when temperatures of 50 degrees Celsius often prevail, that he took to sleeping on the roof of his residence, wrapped in a wet sheet in order to remain cool. It was a practice with only passing benefit, for not long into it he fell prey to pneumonia, not unexpectedly given his nightly-soaked shroud. He was forced to take to his bed, whereupon he promptly died. The agent was among the first recorded British casualties of his country's involvement with Oman, but was most certainly not to be its last.

Even given this understandable condemnation of its inhospitable climate, the Sultanate of Oman is in actual fact an Arabian Arcadia, with an indigenous people who are without any doubt the aristocrats of the Arab world, the gentlemen of the Arabian Gulf. The country they possess is often described in upmarket tourist brochures as 'The Jewel in Arabia's Crown', a portrayal which few people who have experience of the Sultanate would wish to disagree with, even when the excited hyperbole of the marketplace is taken into account.

It is a grand, gaudy country which casts its spell over all who visit it and for those fortunate enough to live there, quickly claims an allegiance which pulls at one's very heartstrings. The genesis of such a reaction is of course its people, who rank as the most courteous, dignified and intelligent in the Gulf, with an enormous capacity for kindness and hospitality. They possess too a culture and recorded history that distinguishes them from their neighbours on the Arabian Peninsula, from which a quiet, non-arrogant, non-aggressive self-confidence has been born. Indeed, while they share the unity of a common tongue (Arabic) and a spiritual faith (Islam), the Omani people have always stood well apart from their neighbours, seeing themselves with not a little justification as being really rather different.

In terms both concise and clear, that is exactly what they are. As is their land which, after the Kingdom of Saudi Arabia and the Republic of Yemen, is the third largest on the Arabian Peninsula, with a 1,700 kilometre coastline, running from the mountains of the majestic Musandam in the far north of the country, to the plains of the legendary southern province of Dhofar. It is from the latter that emissaries of the Queen of Sheba returned with supplies of precious Frankincense, which she gave as a form of tribute to King Solomon.

Away from the tourist trail, however, the harsh and unforgiving face of Arabia holds permanent sway. Indeed, out of a total land area of 309,500 square kilometres, 80 per cent is pitiless sand and gravel desert, with an additional 15 per cent being made up of rugged, bare, infertile mountain ranges, the MMBA or 'Miles and Miles of Bloody Arabia', in the fond parlance of so many of the country's Western expatriates. Arable land is confined, principally, to two areas: the 250-kilometre coastal Batinah corridor, running north from Muscat's environs, which with its cultivatable land varying between 2 and 30 kilometres in width has long been regarded as Oman's bread basket and the slimmer 70-kilometre Salalah Plain in the south.

The area under cultivation nationwide is officially given at 101,100 hectares, or about 0.45 per cent of the country's total land area. This is a marked improvement from the area of land being farmed at the time of Sultan Qaboos's accession to the Omani throne in 1970, which was then estimated at just 36,000 hectares, or just 0.15 per cent of the total land. While such an advance has been achieved principally through vastly enhanced systems of irrigation, further improvement is most unlikely, given the critical shortage nationwide of supplies of fresh water and insufficient funds to embark upon any major desalination project. Indeed, the situation has rapidly deteriorated during the last decade in the Batinah corridor, due to the unregulated digging of ever deeper wells. This has led to a high degree of salinity which, inevitably, is producing a decline in this most important agricultural region in cash crops such as dates, limes, tomatoes, potatoes, onions and lucerne. It is a situation which has been exacerbated in terms of fresh-water supplies because of the establishment in the area by the country's nouveau riche of 'Hobby Farms' during the past 20 years, so described by Kamal Abdulreddha Sultan, Oman's foremost intellectual.

But, in the past, the arid, unproductive nature of so much of the land that is Oman has been well compensated by the bounty of its seas, in which more than 150 species of fish and crustacean are to be found, with tuna, grouper, kingfish, sardines in abundance, together with significant supplies of lobster and abalone. For the traditional fishing fleets of Oman such a variety, in such abundance, was for centuries a veritable harvest just there for the taking. It fashioned a pattern of living and livelihood that gave marked emphasis to the people's long and proud tradition as seafarers. But with the arrival of oil, and with it the awakening in so many Omani breasts of the creed of enlightened self-interest, came the system of licensing foreign, industrial fishing fleets in the waters of the Sultanate. These fleets come most notably from Taiwan, South Korea and Japan, and their presence has taken its inevitable toll on fish stocks and with it an equally inevitable decline in the quantity of fish being landed by the country's traditional fishermen. Such a situation has been brought about by an arrangement under which just a very small number of local businessmen actually owned the fishing companies, whose catches under the licensing system were made by the Asian industrial fleets. In the words of a senior member of the Ministry of Agriculture and Fisheries such a system, ' . . . benefits the few at the expense of the many'. This became so blatantly obvious that by the late 1980s the Government was forced to act. In 1990 it restricted commercial industrial fishing to 15 per cent of the total catch, limited the season during which certain species can be fished (such as lobster and abalone), and regulated the size of nets and equipment. However, while the industrial foreign fleets are monitored by the Royal Air Force of Oman and coastal patrols of the Royal Oman Police, the belief persists among the country's traditional fishermen that the 'Big Men', the members of Oman's small but powerful business community who principally benefit from the licensing of the foreign fleets, continue to over-fish. The fishermen point to the continuing decline in the quantities of fish landed in their nets as proof.

While the country's traditional fishing community remains sceptical that the private interests of the few have really been curbed, the measures taken by the Government are proof enough that it can muster the political will to remedy a manifest national wrong. Equally importantly, and of no small interest, it further demonstrates an enduring sensitivity in the Sultanate to all things maritime, allied to an abiding awareness of the role the sea has played over the centuries in the lengthy distinguished history of the Omani nation and of the effect it has had on the State's many and varied fortunes.

Throughout its history it is to the open sea that the people of the country have looked, a national instinct and direction that took them away from their all too often hostile and ungenerous land and an instinct which entailed an abandonment of the securities of home and hearth. In short, the Omani people have a long tradition of turning their faces towards the world's oceans and it was in such a spirit that the early Omanis commenced an association with the world far beyond the shores of their own country.

As early as the seventh century, Omani vessels, the wooden dhows with their billowing, lateen sails, were to be seen in the ports of Persia, the Indian subcontinent and south-east Asia. In the eighth century the distinguished Omani seafarer, Abu-Ubaida bin Abdulla bin Al Qassim, completed a 7,000 kilometre voyage from Muscat to Canton, in the process laying the principal scientific foundations of maritime navigation. In 1498 the legendary Portuguese navigator, Vasco de Gama, was guided round the Cape of Good Hope and sent on his pioneering way to India by the celebrated Omani seaman, Ahmad bin Majid.

Not that the Portuguese were to show Oman much gratitude. Returning in 1507 they sacked Muscat, promptly occupied it and then went on to establish colonial settlements in nearby coastal areas, where they remained for almost a century and a half. The Portuguese fleet, under the command of Alfonso de Alboquerque, had initially anchored off Oman's eastern extremity, Ras Al Hadd, where the fleet's chronicler recorded:

> . . . and they found there 30 or 40 fishing ships which came thither to fish for bonitas and albeciras; for there is a great traffic in these fish to many parts . . . and they burned all these ships and on the following morning set sail with a fair wind and took the ships' boats with masts and sails.

The Portuguese fleet then sailed for Muscat, which was described in the following revealing terms:

> Muscat is a large and very populous city, surrounded on the inner side with very large mountains, and on the seaboard it is close to the water's edge . . . The harbour is small, shaped like a horseshoe and sheltered from every wind. It is of old, a market for carriage of horses and dates; it is a very elegant town, with very fine houses and supplied from the interior with much wheat, maize, barley and dates for lading as many vessels as come to them.

This latter observation is particularly revealing, suggesting that Oman in the sixteenth century grew significantly greater quantities of agricultural produce than later came to be the case.

While the Portuguese were the first harbingers of European influence to Oman, they were most certainly not the last, although they very soon met their match and did not stay long, as history is judged. The man destined to send the Portuguese fleeing to the winds was, without doubt, one of the most crucially important leaders, both in political and military terms, that Oman has ever produced.

Nasr bin Murshid bin Sultan Al Ya'Arubi had been elected Imam in Rostaq, yet another former capital of Oman. In 1624, at the time of Nasr's election and subsequent appointment to power, Oman was passing through one of its many well recorded periods of internal division, attended by intrigue, petty jealousy and, of course, petty rulers. These 'Kings', one each in Rostaq, Nakl, Samad, Ibra and Sumail were not the only significant rulers, with many brooding, fractious and increasingly resentful tribal leaders holed up in their respective forts. Consequently, the social fabric of the country was characterised by chaos and with it an inevitable state of national anarchy. Nasr quickly justified his election, promptly setting out to forge an essential sense of national unity by concentrating people's minds on the most urgent matter to hand, the expulsion of the Portuguese. A man of unrivalled courage, he was responsible for inspiring a quality and nature of leadership, principally through personal example, that oversaw by the men he led the application and so inspired of sustained military strategies of innovation and great daring. As a result, the foreign invaders were driven from the majority of their coastal settlements, back into the sea from where they had come.

But the task had been long, hard and arduous and it took an inevitable toll on this most remarkable leader of men. On 22 April 1649, with his soldiers laying siege to the rump of the Portuguese in Muscat, Nasr bin Murshid bin Sultan Al Ya'Arubi died. But his name has lived on in the annals of Oman's history and will continue to do so for as long as the people of the Sultanate respect the past.

Wishing to press home the military advantage, an immediate decision was taken to appoint a successor. By public acclamation one of Nasr's cousins, Sultan bin Saif Al Ya'Arubi, was proclaimed Imam. It proved to be not just a popular appointment but an inspired one. A man of singular mind and military talent, Imam Sultan not only expelled the enemy at his country's gate, driving the last vestiges of Portugal's colonial presence from Muscat in January 1650, but declared jihad (holy war) and in its name pursued the fleeing Portuguese into the Indian Ocean. There his fleet of wooden dhows, equipped for naval battle as best as he was able to achieve, chased the Portuguese as far as their colony of Goa on India's western seaboard, and bombarded their settlements on the east African shoreline. In a series of sustained naval battles, which were breathtaking in both skill and daring, Imam Sultan captured many of the better-equipped Portuguese vessels. The strategy enabled him to lay down, with his enemy's ships in his possession, solid foundations for the establishment of an Omani Navy proper. But that was not all.

This fleet of ships was superior to any that had previously been available to any Omani leader, particularly in terms of firepower, and it allowed Imam Sultan to continue to press home his advantage. Just as the Portuguese had done 150 years earlier in Oman, he laid the foundations for an empire, with colonial settlements on the East African coast, on the islands of Zanzibar and Pemba and also at Gwadar, on the south-western shore of present-day Pakistan. Oman's imperium had begun, an age which some 200 years later was to lead to a tendency towards foreign interference and influence in the affairs of the country, introducing unwanted change that was not just irreversible but launched the country into a long decline and foreign dependency.

It did not take long for the beneficial effects of Oman's new status as a colonial power to reach Muscat, with riches pouring into the national exchequer, permitting the construction of forts (including the fort at Nizwa with its magnificent drum tower), imposing government buildings and grand private residences. Of even greater significance, the new-found wealth prompted a nationwide programme of repairs to the country's ancient irrigation system, the Falaj, the foundations of which had been laid in the fourteenth century BC by the then dominant Persian influence. The renovation gave an enormous boost to agricultural production.

Capitalising on the resurgence of national pride and consequent unity his acts of derring-do had achieved, Imam Sultan wasted no time in consolidating his grip on power. In a series of far-sighted and politically adroit initiatives he established a strong central administration, the writ of which ran in unquestioned form in all the major centres of population. The watchwords of his administration were equity and justice; he appointed local governors and judges, the Walis and the Qadhis respectively, men of moral stature and probity who initiated a period of peace, progress and prosperity the likes of which had not been previously seen in Oman.

In his 1871 work, *The History of the Imams of Oman*, G.P. Badger wrote of the life and work of Imam Sultan:

> Oman revived during his Government and prospered. The people rested from their troubles, prices were low, roads were safe, the merchants made large profits and the crops were abundant. The Imam himself was humble. He used to traverse the streets without an escort, would sit and talk familiarly with the people. Thus he persevered in ordaining what was lawful and forbidding what was unlawful.

But, as humanity knows to its bitter cost, the past has an unwelcome and unpleasant habit of ambushing the present. Those national appetites and practices which were once deemed right and proper come to be regarded with a loathing of a particularly virulent and persistent kind. For the basis of much of the wealth which flowed from Imam Sultan's brilliant acts of naval warfare and his considerable, successful initiatives that gave the Omani people colonial possessions, was based on that internationally reviled practice of slavery. As with the entrepreneurs of Victorian England, whose constant cry of 'trade follows the Flag' had proved the principal agent of Empire, no sooner had Oman established its own colonial footholds on the East African coast than it began to engage on a very large scale indeed in that lucrative commerce of the trafficking of human souls. These were intended not just for use at home but for sale in the markets of the rest of the Arabian Peninsula. Oman's slave traders, who went on slave-acquiring safaris as far inland from the coast as present day Uganda, became some of the most feared of men by the villages of the hinterland, but not of course by the various and numerous African chiefs who were only too ready to barter many of their subjects into slavery, like their counterparts in the west of the continent.

Tippu Tip was one of the Omani slave traders who was particularly bold in the planning of expeditions into the far interior, with all the attendant risks of attack by hostile tribes and the ever-present possibility of succumbing to potentially fatal illness such as malaria. Even today his name is often invoked by African villages of the Great Lakes region as a ruse to inhibit the unruly conduct of their children.

This aspect of Oman's past can be seen across the face of the nation today and particularly in the town of Sur, the country's (and indeed Arabia's) eastern extremity. This was the port where the greater majority of the

African slaves were landed from the late seventeenth to early nineteenth centuries. But it has to be recorded that many of the slaves, who quickly converted from indigenous beliefs to Islam, became important parts of many of the households in which they worked. Aided and abetted by one of Islam's most liberating, eloquent ethics, the equality of all in the sight of God, they assumed positions of trust and responsibility throughout the land, often marrying into the most distinguished families. In this respect, slavery in Oman was devoid of the often wanton cruelty and racial exploitation with which the practice is indelibly associated, despite being relentlessly pursued for a period in excess of 150 years, principally because of its high profitability. But attitudes were changing and the national practice was recruiting the unwelcome attention of a European power, a country which was to have an enduring effect on Oman and its institutions. The British were most definitely coming.

In 1679 Imam Sultan died, his 30-year rule having beneficially transformed the fortunes of his people and country. A principal feature of his administration had been his own ability at statecraft with its undoubted, manifest success resulting in him becoming a cult figure among the great majority of his people. This status was a national development which led to a marked departure from the democratic process. For centuries an Imam assumed power with the consent of the governed. But Imam Sultan's successor, his son Bil'Arab, took the reins of power not by the acclamation of the people but by the nomination of his father. Fearful that his succession would be characterised by intrigue and bickering, during which the solid gains his rule had produced for the country would be frittered away, Imam Sultan paid off crucially important tribal leaders to sanction the appointment of his son as Imam. In the process the Omani people lost a basic, political right they had enjoyed and skilfully exercised for close on 900 years. Thus was the practice of hereditary succession inaugurated in Oman and the democratic principle abandoned, a national state of affairs which survives to the present day. Many historians have long regarded such a retrograde development as a serious blot on the otherwise distinguished rule of Imam Sultan, but it should be recorded that this truly remarkable leader acted so as to consolidate the national achievements of peace and prosperity that his long rule had forged. Where he undoubtedly erred was in failing to acknowledge that should ever the coffers of the politically powerful in the country become depleted and the leader of the day was unable to adequately replenish them, then the demand for a return to the democratic tradition would be stridently made. This was to happen frequently down through the generations.

Things did start to go seriously wrong right from the outset of Bil'Arab's rule. The departure from the democratic process attending the election of an Imam ushered in a long period of intrigue, greed, vaunting ambition and petty bickering which, in the event, brought about the very conditions which Imam Sultan had so greatly feared: civil war and with it the dissipation of the stability, prosperity and integrity of the Omani State. For much of Bil'Arab's rule, which ended with his suicide in 1692, he was obliged to ward off vigorous and persistent attempts by his brother, Saif, to gain control. With Bil'Arab's death Saif did just that and until his own death in 1711 did much to justify his own self-confidence. Indeed, during his 19 years of rule Saif paid particular attention to increasing the country's agriculture production, being principally responsible for the settlement of the Batinah corridor, through the digging of shallow wells on the 250-kilometre-long plain, which led to significant increases in the growing of dates, limes and vegetables. But his short rule was only a brief respite from the chaos and civil war which was, all too soon, to engulf and dissipate the country.

Following Saif's death the practice of hereditary succession continued, with his son, Sultan, being appointed Imam. He quickly proved to be an extravagant, flamboyant and wilfully aggressive figure, squandering much of his father's accumulated wealth on the construction of the fort at Hazm, an early indication of the warlike instinct which was to characterise his rule. The contruction was only completed with borrowed money. Such acts quickly filtered down to the Oman Navy, affecting their conduct on the high seas. They embarked upon a sustained chapter of aggressive tactics, not only in the country's own waters but in the Indian Ocean, where they attacked and plundered any vessel they fell upon with ever-increasing brutality. It was a strategy Imam Saif actively encouraged but which, given the regular passage by ships of Britain's East India Company through the Indian Ocean, was to lead inevitably to conflict, which, given the might of the British Navy, the will of Oman and its increasingly unruly leader, could not even hope to effectively counter. But before such a naval sledgehammer could be brought to bear on the Omani sea-captains directly responsible for this maritime carnage (officially classified by London as pirates), Imam Sultan died. The year was 1718 and his passing highlighted one of the basic, fundamental flaws in the hereditary process. For Sultan's heir, Saif bin Sultan II, was only 12 years old, with the inevitable and tragic result that he became a pawn, an instrument in the hands of the greedy, the ambitious and those who fostered disaffection and division for their own personal ends.

As a result of this catalogue of sustained, self-serving intrigue, Oman slipped back into the dark abyss of civil unrest and internal strife that tore the country apart, during which tribe was set against tribe, central power collapsed and the country became easy prey for foreign intervention. In 1737 the Persians crossed the Straits of Hormuz and became the occupying power, revisiting a land over which they had once held considerable influence, as early as the fourth century BC. But their return had one tangible advantage, for just as the uninvited arrival of the Portuguese 230 years earlier had eventually concentrated Omani minds, so did the unwelcome presence of the Persians galvanise the various warring tribal factions into a united response. Raising an army to his banner at Sohar in 1744, Ahmad bin Said bin Mohammed Al Busaid, a particularly vigorous tribal leader, led a highly effective attack on the Persians, which saw their defeat and with it their departure from the country. Just as Iman Nasr bin Murshid bin Sultan Al Ya'Arabi (and his cousin who succeeded him) had been able to unify their people and organise for the crucible of war that would expel the foreign invader in previous century, so did Ahmad bin Said bin Mohammed Al Busaid, gaining political advantage from his ability to unite the people and to wage a successful war.

Shortly after the routing of the Persians he was, with great public acclamation, elected as Oman's new Imam. But his political inheritance was bleak indeed. As a result of the locust years of internal division and civil war, the gains achieved during the decades of Ya'Arabi rule had been wantonly squandered. Agricultural production had all but ceased as a direct result of the destruction by one side and then another of the Falaj; such acts of inter-tribal spite were to lead the country's new Imam to consider how best Oman could not only prosper but govern itself successfully in the future. His initiatives towards such national ends were fundamental in the change they heralded and, in the event, had a profound effect on the subsequent political direction of the land he now ruled. Of equal significance was the enduring effect on the conduct of the State's religion, Islam, which these very same initiatives were to foster.

Oman was one of the very first adherents to Islam, converting to the faith during the lifetime of the Prophet Mohammed. As their agent of national unity it flourished and quickly became, then as now, the abiding foundation of the nation's very existence. Indeed Islam, which does not make distinction between the temporal and the spiritual, was particularly well suited to a people who, in the daily prosecution of their indigenous social arrangements, drew no distinction between the integrity of the state and the supremacy of the individual. They correctly judged the religion to be as much of a political force as a spiritual guide, governing their every waking hour. However, in the wake of the Prophet's death in 632 AD, conflict sparked between the people of his tribe, the Quraish, and a group which became known as 'secessionists' or the Khawariji, over the assumed right of the former to appoint a new Khalif who would be the world leader of Muslims. As a result divisions arose and with them came the birth of the Ibadhi sect. At the heart of their intellectual definition of what Islam's arrangements and due processes should be, was the democratic belief that any leader, an Imam, should emerge only through election. This was a procedure the Quraish vehemently opposed, realising that the adoption of an alternative to the hereditary system would inevitably lead to the considerable dilution of the centralised power and authority of the Khalifate administration. It was to this governing body that Muslims everywhere were obliged to pay tax, a consideration which brought its very own disinclinations to bear.

When news of the prolonged conflict over which procedures to adopt eventually arrived in Oman, it was that of election which won the greatest allegiance among the population, with its promise of independence from a centralised power many hundreds of miles distant on the far western reaches of the Arabian Peninsula. Of even greater significance still was the element of democratic rule, the consent of the governed, inherent and essential to the Ibadhi ethic.

Oman's adoption of the democratic and therefore independent spirit afforded by Ibadhism is of particular significance in that it demonstrates the attachment that the Omani people have to their national independence and with it the commitment and very considerable spirit, as we have seen, they have exercised in its defence down through the centuries. This secular version of Islam was so well incorporated into their new state religion, that it remains to this very day as a cherished principle, even if not in actual use with regard to the appointment of the country's ruler. The attachment to Ibadhism not only demonstrates an innate, natural instinct for maintaining the integrity of the state but a shrewd assessment of the nature of social cohesion that can come from the mechanics of democratic rule; rule by election which was, and remains, very much the cardinal principle of the Ibadhi concept and purpose. What is more, democratic rule is regarded by the Ibadhis of Oman as being in even greater concert with the essential liberating principles of Islam, as enshrined in the Holy Koran, than the other variants.

As such, Omanis do not regard themselves in any manner as a people who, in being adherents to Ibadhism, have deviated from the founding ethics of the Islamic faith, but a people who are, in actual fact, believers of the faith in its purest form. During the days of the Omani Imamate, the election of an Imam — 'one who sets an example' — was not in any way a formality or charade. A candidate for the job was identified by a council of tribal elders, constituted of men of proven wisdom and probity. He was then presented to the people for their scrutiny and due acceptance or rejection. Indeed, there are recorded instances of candidates being rejected; acceptance was achieved only through the acclamation of the assembled public. If successful the new Imam would publicly commit himself to upholding Ibadhi principles and maintaining the integrity of the nation. In return the assembly, made up of people who had gathered from near and far, pledged allegiance to their new Imam. Should he subsequently be seen to fail in such high office, it was accepted that the nation's allegiance would be promptly withdrawn. This process first took place in 750 AD when Imam Rashid bin Al Walid was selected; he was to become known as 'the first of the rightful Imams of Oman'.

When the Persians had fled, the land was once more free of foreign domination, but its problems remained. Just as the need to expel the invader had concentrated the mind of Imam Ahmad bin Said bin Mohammed Al Busaid, so the urgent need to repair the country and restore its institutions and industry commanded the attention and energies of Oman's new leader. In his consideration of such national imperatives Imam Ahmad, it would appear, came to the conclusion that the elective system of leadership, from which he had so recently benefited, was not altogether satisfactory. It laid itself open to abuse through the well-practised dark arts of bribery, nepotism and intrigue, for which in his opinion, his people had a particular appetite. While the democratic system of leadership was a cardinal principle of Ibadhism, apparently the new Imam came to believe that in so many Omani quarters it served to encourage the fickle and the self-seeking, and promoted the unholy creed of enlightened self-interest. Such human appetites were clearly entirely incompatible with the long-term national interest. In the event, this leader of men who had been tested in the heat of battle and consequently won the trust and gratitude of the nation, took a decision that marked a radical departure from that very core belief of Ibadhism. In short, he proclaimed that in future the hereditary system of rule would prevail, a system that survives to this very day in the Sultanate of Oman.

Whether Imam Ahmad meant it to endure, or whether he regarded its imposition simply as an expedient for the time, a temporary arrangement to be abandoned when civil institutions were again strong, we shall never truly know, but endure it most certainly has. Having taken such a fundamental decision of state he then turned his attention to the measures needed to restore the country's devastated economy. The years of civil war had, as we have seen, most effectively destroyed the means of agricultural production and the nation's coffers were virtually empty. The Imam was also concerned about the nature of agriculture as a means of not just providing sustenance for the nation, but as the basis of the economy. As we shall see later, this had an echo in the late twentieth century, when Sultan Qaboos expressed concern over the dependence of the country on oil revenues.

While riches of a sort had been raised during the rule of Imam Sultan bin Saif through the dubious practice of plunder and piracy on the high seas, it was hardly a satisfactory means of recruiting reliable revenue for the national exchequer, although at the very least it had demonstrated anew the skill of the Omani people as seafarers. So, in practical recognition of such a national attribute, Imam Ahmad made yet another fundamental decision of state, one that was to become the hallmark of his rule. He would promote, foster and actively encourage the people he now led to utilise their proven maritime skills and put to very best use their geographical position, turning both aspects of their circumstance to a singular advantage. In short, Imam Ahmad turned the face and the intentions of the nation towards the open sea and the noble, peaceful traditions of trade.

It was a policy that transformed the fortunes of the nation, with his 39-year rule witnessing the ascendency of Muscat as a regional centre for trade, from which great national prosperity arose. In 1775 an Englishman, Abraham Parsons, visited the city and recorded in his diary:

> Muscat is a place of very great trade, being possessed of large number of ships which trade to Surat, Bombay, Goa, along the whole coast of Malibar and to Mocha and Jeddha in the Red Sea. It is the great magazine and deposit for the goods which they bring from these parts; it is resorted to by vessels from every port in Persia and Bussera and all the parts of Arabia within the gulph . . . as far as the

> River Indus . . . There are at present such immense quantities of
> goods in this town as there are not enough warehouses to contain
> half of them . . . they are piled high in the streets.

Now there were surplus finances with which to repair the country's irrigation systems, with the satisfactory result that farmers of the interior saw a return to modest wealth, based on the activities and entrepreneurial energies of the trading community in the country's ports and on the high seas. With peace and prosperity reigning once more, Imam Ahmad was able to reinvest in the state's institutions and, although contrary to the spirit of Ibadhism which expressly forbids militarism, he organised the establishment of a standing army and navy. While such arrangements marked yet another radical departure from Omani beliefs, Imam Ahmad was essentially a pragmatist. With the nation's experience of having been invaded in the sixteenth century by the Portuguese and more recently by the Persians, he obviously saw it as a national duty to take measures that would contribute towards the prevention of any further such national traumas. Not that his rule was without personal challenge. By the time of his death in 1783 he had fought off not only several rebellions against his governance, but also an attempted coup by two of his sons, Saif and Sultan. This was yet further evidence, if such were needed, of the Omani appetite so prevalent at the time for intrigue and, with such machinations came the creation of a divided house. With the passing of Imam Ahmad the hereditary principle prevailed and while Saif and Sultan were disqualified for having conspired for their father's overthrow, Ahmad's second-born son, Said, became Imam. The brothers' act was a grave transgression in Arab eyes which, given Sultan Qaboos's overthrow of his own father in 1970, is a particularly poignant fact to ponder.

Sadly, Said proved to be a weak and indecisive ruler, quickly surrendering the day-to-day running of the state to his son, Hamad, who with political control in his grasp, moved from Rostaq, the seat of his father's administration, to Muscat. There he assumed the title Sayyid, 'Lord', which has remained in use to this very day among members of Oman's ruling Al Busaid family. Now cut off from the centre of political control in Muscat, Imam Said withered on the vine, alone, frustrated and apparently, increasingly ignored. Indeed, such was his isolation and consequent slide into obscurity that even the year of his death was not recorded. However, it is believed to have come to pass some time during the first quarter of the nineteenth century, although his exit from the national stage was not marked by an election of a new Imam and neither did his son, who continued to rule in Muscat, attempt to assume the title.

The rule of Sayyid Hamad, unlike that of his father, was characterised by a firm grip on power, with the result that no challenges of any significance were made against him. Consequently the country remained at peace and with it prosperity reigned unchecked. However, such a rule of calm and continuing progress was not without what can now be seen as a serious political miscalculation: it heralded a national divide which only the coming to power of Sultan Qaboos bin Said Al Said put to rights.

Even to this day it is not absolutely clear as to why Sayyid Hamad would have run the risk of inspiring division by renaming the country 'Muscat and Oman' but that is precisely what he did. The most likely reason is that like land-owning, conservative traditionalists the world over, the men of the interior, those of Oman's vast hinterland, spurned the very idea of trade as a way of life and as a means of livelihood. While they were benefiting from the prosperity generated by the entrepreneurial skill and maritime activities of the traders in the country's ports, they looked down upon the commercial community, regarding only themselves as the aristocrats of the land and as such the keepers of Oman's traditional ways of living. It was an attitude of mind that, in itself, brought about division. However, it was a divide which was to bring its very own bitter harvest to the agrarian land-owners for with their self-imposed isolation continuing, their links with the merchants in Muscat and other ports deteriorated, leading to a corresponding reduction in revenue. The inevitable result was that agriculture became unprofitable and over the years was reduced to subsistence level.

In 1792 Sayyid Hamad bin Said died of smallpox and was succeeded by Sayyid Sultan bin Ahmad, his uncle and one of the conspiring sons of Imam Ahmad. As Imam Said was still alive and living in Rostaq no election took place and the choice of Sultan was apparently based on his strength of character, which promised a continuance of Sayyid Hamad's firm, unflinching rule. The fact that it was this very quality that had led him to conspire against his own father was on this occasion overlooked, an indulgence in respect of an otherwise unpardonable transgression which highlighted the pragmatic nature of the Omani people. But even given the strength of Sayyid Sultan's rule, his time in power saw a turn of events which not only ushered in a development of great national significance but also revealed the country's principal, structural weakness; the nature of its very acceptance relegated the country to a long period of foreign dependency and indeed, to a sustained intrusive influence in the affairs of the Omani state.

The first recorded formal links between Oman and Britain date from 1645, during the rule of Imam Nasr. A talisman of the Ya'Arabi dynasty was, as we have seen, a style of pragmatism that sought to contain and confront, to a national advantage, both internal and external pressures and influences. One such external influence which Oman knew it would ignore to its cost was the rising power in the Gulf of the British East India Company, whose London-based 'Most Honourable Court of Directors' enjoyed powers which exceeded that of many sovereign governments. With their ships making regular passage through the waters of the Arabian Sea and the Gulf, en route to either India or England, the Court of Directors sought trading rights in the ports of Oman. As their presence in the region was endorsed by a well-equipped British Navy, it was a request Imam Nasr, with his usual good sense, thought prudent to accommodate by granting the Company a trading station in the Port of Sohar, north of Muscat. The Company was not slow in expanding upon such a concession. In February of 1646 Philip Wylde signed a Treaty which guaranteed Britain a monopoly on trade with Oman, followed by a further Treaty in 1659 which emphasised the point. The wary respect engendered among Oman's establishment figures for such a vigorous and exclusive relationship can be easily gauged by learning that in 1650, when the British ship *Fellowship* sailed grandly into Muscat harbour, its captain had 'the best house in town' placed at his disposal.

Not that this new arrangement with a forceful foreign power, based on the shifting sands of trade, was all to the Company's exclusive advantage; there were definite gains to be had by the Omanis as well. In 1668 when Omani seafarers were establishing the basis of their country's own empire on the east African seaboard and consequently the sea-lanes into Muscat harbour were becoming ever busier, the English captain John Klempthorne conducted a survey of both the harbour and its approaches. The subsequent navigation charts were of considerable use and value to Oman's crucially important maritime community. During the early 1700s the country began placing orders for ships in the dockyards of British India, which gave Omani sailors very considerable advantage in their increasingly longer voyages, given the superior design of British-built vessels. By 1798 the relationship gave the impression of one based on mutual interest, with the East India Company's agent at Muscat issuing a comforting proclamation, one with the air of mutuality: 'The enemies of one will be the enemies of the other'.

It was, of course, a shrewd and well-timed move by the Company, which viewed the recent victory of Napoleonic France in Egypt with mounting alarm, accompanied as it was by a foray of diplomatic initiatives in the region designed to give France a permanent place in the scheme of things. The French had to be kept well away at all costs from the Company's greatest prize, India. It was decreed by its Most Honourable Court of Directors sitting in London that in such a strategy, Oman had a vital role to play.

So it was that an essential provision of the Treaty of 1798 was Oman's explicit undertaking not to permit either French or Dutch vessels entry into any of its ports, or allow them to establish trading or manufacturing establishments of any kind in the country. The fact that Sayyid Sultan bin Ahmad put his hand to a Treaty containing such intrusive conditions, which trespassed in very real and immediate terms on Oman's sovereignty and national integrity, is indicative of his pragmatic nature. In fact, Sayyid Sultan appears to have been very much a realist, accepting that he was in no real position to resist British demands which, in any event, did leave him in control of the domestic rule of his state. But facts are indeed stubborn things and the fact remains inescapable; by the conditions of the 1798 Treaty, Sayyid Sultan surrendered significant aspects of his country's independence to a foreign power. They were to be but the first intrusions on Oman's sovereignty by Great Britain. But there were more, many more, yet to come.

Within two years of the 1798 Treaty, the Directors of the East India Company had lobbied the Government in London to take further measures. The Government was itself considerably exercised by the threat to British interests in the region posed by a Napoleonic France and her allies. So a further treaty was prepared and presented to Sayyid Sultan for signature, one which made provision for the permanent presence in Oman of a Resident British Political Agent, who would, across the generations, keep a more than avuncular eye on the interests of his country in this far-flung corner of remote Arabia. On the morning of 18 January 1800, Sayyid Sultan signed this agreement which bound his realm ever closer to the imperial breast of far-off Britannia, with Captain John Malcolm signing for Britain. Its language was rich and heavy with the promise of mutual and eternal fidelity, declaring that, 'The friendship of the two states may remain unshook to the end of time, till the sun and moon have finished their revolving career.'

It was with an eye on the past and the varying interpretations of its events, such as the period in the early eighteenth century when Omani seamen had on occasions attacked vessels of the East India Company, that this latest Treaty demanded 'an English gentleman of respectability shall always reside at the Port of Muscat', in a bid to 'prevent future misunderstandings' (a masterful example of diplomatic understatement).

Within three months of signing the treaty Britain had taken steps to ensure that this provision was given physical expression. It established a British residency at a secluded cove on Muscat's shore, conveniently within the shadow of Sayyid Sultan's Palace. The very first time that the building opened its doors for business was on the morning of 16 April 1800. The British Political Agent, the 'gentleman of respectability', was able to report to London just three years later with considerable satisfaction, that the Treaty was indeed being upheld. The then ailing Sayyid Sultan had turned away Napoleon's envoy, who had arrived in Muscat seeking accreditation to the Omani Court.

Four years after the signing of the Treaty there came a pivotal event in Oman's history, when Sayyid Sultan bin Ahmad died. While his rule had been confronted between 1800 and 1803 by a tribal invasion of the desert-dwelling Wahaibis, bearing the evangelical message of their own fervent version of Islam, from what is today Saudi Arabia, his authority had gone unchallenged from within his own realm. Yet his passing prompted yet another outbreak of the petty intrigue, spite and bickering which has so often bedevilled Oman's ruling family, particularly when the question of succession arises. A cousin of Sayyid Sultan, Badr bin Saif bin Ahmad Al Busaid, contested that the leadership belonged to him, a claim the other principal male members of the family bitterly rejected. Following two years of family strife, enough eventually became enough for the late Sayyid Sultan's 17-year-old son Said. In 1806 he took matters into his own hands by assassinating the troublesome Badr and, in the process, obtained power via the expedient of murder. But the long and truly exceptional rule of the young Sayyid Said Sultan commenced at a challenging time, for the country was yet again facing the threat of alien invasion and domination.

The Wahaibi leaders in the deserts to the north-west of Oman had long smarted over their ignominious retreat of 1803, but they were biding their time, waiting for yet another of Oman's periodic bouts of internal unrest. Then the advantage could be seized, a further opportunity for invasion and subsequent forced conversion of the Omani people to the Wahaibi version of Islam. During the distractions caused by the two years of family squabbling over the succession, the state was thrown into virtual impotency so the Wahaibis had taken their opportunity to enter Oman and were now in control of much of the interior. Sayyid Said recognised that he had, as an imperative, to quickly consolidate his new-found power by driving the invaders back from where they had come. Demonstrating not just personal courage but that very special brand of political pragmatism displayed by Oman's former rulers, he turned towards the British and later, the country's former enemies, the Persians, for assistance in the task of national salvation. It was a strategy which, for the British alliance at least, gave credence to the words contained in the 1798 Treaty with the East India Company regarding common enemies. The young Said must be given credit for the political skill he demonstrated by insisting that such a lofty principle be honoured by that 'Most Honourable Court of Directors' in far-off London.

The battle to evict the invaders proved long and arduous and even with the very considerable military assistance afforded by the British and the Persians, it was not until 1820 that the will of Sayyid Said bin Sultan prevailed throughout the land. With the religious zealots driven back into the north-western deserts of the Arabian Peninsula, Said could at long last turn his attention and his abilities to restoring prosperity along with a sense of national direction to the people of which he was now undisputed leader. He quickly showed that he was equal to the task and using vessels built for him in the shipyards of British India, reinvigorated his Navy, which promptly imposed its not inconsiderable will on others in the waters of the Gulf. These were nations such as the Persians and the Bahrainis, who had the temerity to obstruct the new order represented by an Oman in ascendancy. At the soul of the vigorous new strategy was trade and under Sayyid Said's rule the Omanis' long-proven ability as merchants of sustained skill and enterprise was reborn. Muscat flourished again, as did its merchant class, with the result that a period of peace and prosperity was once more seen in Oman. And with the return of national self-confidence, Sayyid Said began a policy of extending his state's influence beyond the shores of his own country. Oman was about to bring a new dimension to its imperial inclinations which had initially surfaced in the mid-seventeenth century.

Said's policy was underwritten by the vastly increased capability of the fleet now at his command, evidence of which is immediately apparent by reference to the records of the East India Company. Between 1820 and 1835 when Sayyid Said bin Sultan was at the pinnacle of his power, with the return of peace following the expulsion of the Wahaibi invaders, the Bombay shipyards built vessels of significant tonnage and armament for his country's navy; ships which were paid for by the successful rebirth of Oman's mercantile activities. The largest of these was the 1,175 tonne, 74-gun *Liverpool*, believed to have been named in honour of the East India

Company vessel which had taken Said bin Sultan through the waters of the Arabian and Red Seas, on a pilgrimage to Islam's most Holy City Mecca, in 1824; 1833 saw the launching of *Sultanah*, equipped with 12 guns. The *Bombay Gazette* of 4 September 1833 reported:

> On Saturday last (August the 31st) was launched from Mazagon Dockyard a beautiful vessel of 312 tonnes, built for His Highness the Imaum of Muscat and immediately after clearing the dock was taken in tow by the Indus Steamer and tugged up to Bombay in beautiful style.

Later this vessel, of a speed and splendour previously unseen by Omanis, sailed to London for repairs at the Royal Navy Dockyard at Woolwich. In 1836 the Omani ruler sent the *Liverpool* to England as a present to King William IV, where it was renamed *Imaum* in honour of Oman's generous and accomplished ruler. The English monarch reciprocated by despatching one of his royal yachts, the *Prince Regent*, which sailed into Muscat harbour under the command of Captain Robert Cogan in 1837, the year which saw Queen Victoria's accession to the throne of England. It was a period of national consolidation, the scale of which Oman had not hitherto witnessed and Sayyid Said, while endorsing his power via the vastly-improved fleet of ships, had not ignored his state's territorial ambitions. In 1832 he turned his attention to measures that would confirm his grip on the settlements originally established by Omani sailors and traders some 180 years earlier.

Slavery was still the mainstay of these Omani settlers' economy, with Zanzibar being the place to which slaves were first taken from the African mainland prior to dispersal to ports on the Arabian Peninsula. But agriculture, in the verdant well-watered lands of the east African coast and on the islands of Zanzibar and Pemba, had long proved a lucrative and satisfying way in which to raise revenue and it was to this aspect of development that Sayyid Said turned his particular attention, intending to consolidate Omani colonial rule through farming.

Some years earlier his sailors had returned from a Far-Eastern voyage which had taken them into the ports of present-day Indonesia, where they had obtained cloves, a spice which at the time was unknown to them. Realising that it would flourish particularly well in the warm, humid climate of Zanzibar, on which Oman's ruler had established his headquarters, Said began a comprehensive programme of cultivation. It was an initiative that met with considerable success with a wide variety of crops eventually being grown in addition to the clove plantations that, in time, produced revenues which accounted for one third of the state's budget back home in Muscat. News of such a green bonanza was not slow to reach Oman, with its harsh, largely unyielding lands and within the space of a few short years increasing numbers of settlers had left home and native hearth to join their ruler. Sayyid Said was now spending longer periods on Zanzibar, from where his rule of the Omani settlements on the East African coast, such as Mombasa, could be more effectively exercised than Muscat.

Indeed, no other Omani ruler was so directly responsible for the spread of Arab and Islamic influence in East Africa, Zanzibar and Pemba. However his record of achievement was to bring conflict from which the country did not even begin to recover until it entered the era of oil in 1967.

Essentially the long-term, negative aspects of Said's involvement of Zanzibar were twofold. As his subjects prospered, both on the mainland of east Africa and on the two islands off its coast, the amounts of cash they repatriated home to Oman was considerable. But instead of investing such funds in, for example, improving the country's irrigation system, which would in turn have improved agricultural production, the recipients of such healthy sums embarked upon an ostentatious programme of palatial house-building and other manifestations of material consumption. As a direct result agriculture again went into national decline, with the inevitable result that the country fell into an ever-increasing state of torpor and poverty. The motherland which so many Omanis of vigour and enterprise had left for a better life in East Africa and its offshore islands, became very much the poor relation with sad and astonishing speed. It was a situation of national decline which, of course, was not at all helped by the now almost permanent absence from Muscat and Oman of Sayyid Said. Indeed, from the early 1830s until his death in 1856, the Omani ruler's visits home were but fleeting and even then took place with increasing infrequency. In 1853, he announced his decision to transfer his Court, and with it his capital, to Zanzibar. It was as if Queen Victoria had transferred the Court of St James to Jamaica. Britain, ever anxious to keep an eye on all things Omani, was not slow in appointing a Consul to the island and with such an appointment Britannia's apron strings were drawn ever tighter around Oman's midriff.

Throughout these prolonged periods of absenteeism from Oman, Said's relationship with Britain became even more entangled and prior to moving onto the second, most significant and fundamentally negative aspect of this relationship, it is of no small interest to consider some of the more colourful occasions which continued throughout what was to become a time of very considerable strain in relations between the two states. That such events took place at all is quite extraordinary, given that during the very same period of pomp and circumstance, Britain continued to bring its influence to bear on Oman in a manner which had adverse and far reaching consequences for its ruler, his state and his people. But take place they did and they were by all accounts really rather splendid.

By 1837 Sayyid Said had so well established his administration in his colonies, that he was able to announce the appointment of his first Ambassador to London, his Governor of the port of Mombasa, which had become prosperous under Omani rule. To mark the significance of the occasion Sayyid Said dispatched six fine Arab horses to London as a personal gift to the young Queen Victoria who, only a short while earlier, had celebrated her coronation at Westminster Abbey. The following year Ali bin Nasr sailed aboard *Sultanah* for London as Oman's very first Ambassador to the Court of St James, taking with him a veritable cornucopia of gifts for Queen Victoria: an array of jewels, fine carpets and silk shawls. The young Queen recorded his presentation at Buckingham Palace in the following terms:

> At a little before eight I went into the White Drawing Room where Lord Palmerston introduced this Envoy of the Sultan of Muscat, Shaikh Ali bin Nassor, accompanied by Captain Cogan, an intelligent man who is in the East India Company's service.

Of Said's envoy, the English Queen observed:

> He is a very striking looking person, age 67; he is not tall, a very dark mahogany colour, with fine intellectual black eyes, thick lips and very short, sort of black beard; he showed no hair, his dress was beautiful; he had a fine shawl turban on his head, one side of which hung down; a dark blue cloth dress which showed a scarlet vest, a shawl girdle through which was stuck a dirk and an oriental cimetar, slung over the left shoulder, completed the costume of this interesting man. The presents, which are very handsome, particularly ten beautiful shawls, were placed on a table in the room.

Four years later Ambassador Ali was back in London, arriving once more aboard *Sultanah*, which sailed into St Katherine's dock in June of 1842.

Following a meeting with the Prime Minister of the day, Lord Aberdeen, he went again to Buckingham Palace where he presented yet more Arab horses along with other gifts from Sayyid Said to Queen Victoria. As always, the Queen committed the occasion to her diary:

> We received the Envoy from the Imaum of Muscat, the same old man who was sent here in '38 and who I was glad to see again. He had a young and fine interpreter with him, also in the national dress. The Imaum has again sent me many presents and similar to those I received four years ago, including ten very fine shawls.

On this occasion Ali bin Nasr did not confine himself to the British capital and embarked upon an extensive journey through Queen Victoria's realm of England, visiting the industrial conurbations of Birmingham and Manchester where, in meetings with businessmen in both cities, he made a favourable impression. After a year of conducting a series of diplomatic initiatives at the Court of Queen Victoria with her Ministers of State in Whitehall and the country's captains of industry, Sayyid Said's envoy set sail for Zanzibar, accompanied by the increasingly ubiquitous Captain Cogan. But for all the pomp, geniality and expressions of mutual fidelity, things were not what such occasions of state suggested.

The world beyond Oman's shores and its African dominions was changing at a speed and in a manner that must have appeared quite incomprehensible to Sayyid Said bin Sultan and his Court. In 1802 the selling of slaves had been abolished in the West (although not the actual practice of slavery) and the all-powerful British Navy was now committed to preventing, wherever and whenever it could, the capture and trafficking of humans. The outside world was about to intrude into one of Oman's most profitable and well-established practices, with the British using their now-consolidated influence in Oman's affairs to quite literally force the pace of change. It was a storm of external influence which was to severely buffet the Omani state and directly lead it to a prolonged age of dependency and national decay from which only the discovery of that black gold, oil, was to rescue it 130 years later. Britain at the start of the nineteenth century, its very own century of global imperial power, was now most definitely on the side of the angels and for its client state, Muscat and Oman, nothing would ever be quite the same again.

The well-practised Omani art of pragmatism would without doubt have led them to consider that while the advantages to their state and country in its ever closer association with Great Britain were many and immediate, there could well be very real disadvantages in an alliance in which Oman was without question the weaker partner. Although they were now able to call upon British naval and military power to protect them, should the established order of things change then there were no circumstances in existence whereby the Omani state could mount a challenge to the British and prevail. Indeed, as skilful a political leader as Sayyid Said had proved to be, he had known full well that when he signed the 1798 Treaty, with its implicit demands upon Oman not to enter into bilateral relations with either the French or the Dutch, he was in no real position to resist these British conditions.

As it had been then, so it was in 1822 when the British, via the offices of the East India Company, obliged Oman to sign a treaty which imposed restrictions on its role as a major slave-trading nation. The restrictions, with their promise, all too soon realised in Omani eyes, of hitting at the heart of the hugely profitable slave trade, were bitterly resented by the country's merchant class; not least by Sayyid Said who was himself involved in the business in which the British had themselves so recently taken enthusiastic part, but which they now sought to end. In 1839 yet a further treaty was presented by the British for signature by Oman's ruler, emphasising and increasing the range of restrictions contained in the treaty of 17 years earlier. On this occasion, the agreement differed not only by being cloaked in grandiose terminology but also by affording Oman alternative ways to trade.

Titled *The Convention of Commerce*, it was signed by Sayyid Said on 31 May 1839, with the ever-present Captain Robert Cogan, who signed for the British Crown, at his side. One of its provisions was a quid pro quo of sorts, which afforded Oman 'Most Favoured Nation' status in its trade with Britain and, indeed, throughout the lands of the mighty British Empire. The belief has long persisted in both Omani and British academic circles that in addition to such a 'sweetener', the British would almost certainly have provided Sayyid Said bin Sultan with personal financial inducements, as a form of coercion to sign the treaties, but no tangible documentary evidence has ever come to light to substantiate such a belief.

Captain Cogan had sailed to Oman from England to sign the 1839 Treaty and recorded the visit in his diary, an entry in which he illustrated an aspect of the dominant position Britain now had in the country: 'Muscatis are to have most favoured nation status throughout British possessions. The

British may buy houses, which may not be searched until the Consul is present.' Despite the body blows to the Omani economy delivered by the treaties' restrictions on its slave trading, restrictions the British Navy were now policing, happier exchanges with Britain did continue, such as Ali bin Nasr's visit to London.

In 1840 the Raj, the British Imperial Government in India, appointed a Captain Hammerton as British Political Agent in Muscat. He was at great pains to assure Sayyid Said that despite Britain's insistence that Oman desist from trading in slaves, the greatest possible importance was placed by London on its close relations with Muscat. Declared Hammerton upon arriving in the Omani capital, 'This Prince has ever evinced the most friendly dispositions to the British and the Governor General deems it so essential at the present moment to cultivate the most intimate relations with him.'

It was also in 1840 that Oman achieved a very special first for itself by dispatching an envoy to the United States of America, in a ship specially designed for the purpose, becoming in the process the very first Arab state to establish diplomatic relations with Washington. It was proof that although under pressure and with a rapidly declining economy brought about by British demands, Sayyid Said bin Sultan still continued to exercise his very own flair at political skill and diplomatic innovation.

But British pressure on Oman continued and in 1845 Sayyid Said was obliged to sign yet a further treaty, the provisions of which were so restrictive that while there was yet one more treaty to come, it spelt the end for the country's role as a principal trader in slaves from the African Continent. British provisions for enforcing the end of this lucrative trade by Omanis did not however end with the 1845 Treaty, or the one which was to follow in 1873. A sovereign rule was made that any slave who could reach the flagpole in the courtyard of the British Residency in Muscat, and clasp his or her arms around it, would be granted a manumission certificate by the Consul, guaranteeing the slave freedom, which the Omani authorities were obliged to honour. This relic of the past remained for many years and when the flagpole succumbed to old age its former significance was marked by a brass plaque set in the floor of the Embassy courtyard. This in turn was only cast into oblivion in 1993 when the British Embassy was relocated to the seaside suburb of Shatti Al Qurum in Muscat. Shortly after the British departed their beloved Embassy, the beautiful and historic building, in the words of a former Ambassador 'this dear old house', which had been witness to so much history between Oman and Britain, was unceremoniously bulldozed to oblivion on the express orders of Sultan Qaboos, to the dismay of many Omanis and Britons alike.

The end of slave trading days was an economic blow delivered to the state that was not slow in falling, with the inevitable consequences being felt throughout the entire country. It was a situation that quickly assumed a momentum all of its very own. The economic decline in the nation's fortunes prompted the departure of yet more Omanis from the motherland to the greener pastures of Zanzibar where their leader, Sayyid Said, was now for all practical purposes permanently based. As greater numbers left, amongst them some of the country's most talented and enterprising, so did the economic situation in Oman correspondingly decline. Then in 1856 Sayyid Said, one of Oman's most remarkable rulers, died. At the time of his death he was visiting the British Crown Colony of the Seychelles in the Indian Ocean, aboard his frigate *Victoria*, named in honour of the British monarch he had so admired throughout his momentous rule, but whose government had brought a terrible change and dependency to his state that came to haunt and isolate it from the political mainstream for a century and more.

Before his death, Said, in a measure designed to prevent an outbreak of the family bickering and intrigue to which it was so prone (and which in the past had caused so much bitter division and consequent national damage) had ordered that upon his death a system of joint rule be established between two of his chosen sons. Thuwainy was to be given the rule of Oman while Majid was to be allotted the rule of his African possessions, centred on Zanzibar. Oman's skilful and experienced ruler had good cause to adopt measures designed to prevent yet further family division. In 1844 he had disinherited his eldest son, Hilal, on the grounds of his eccentric and anti-social behaviour, not the least of which were his addiction to alcohol and trespass into his father's harem. Sayyid Said, in an act that serves as yet further proof as to how dominant Britain had now become both in the governance of Oman and the domestic arrangements of its ruling family, wrote to Lord Aberdeen (at the time Britain's Foreign Secretary), disinheriting his first-born son.

In September of 1845 Hilal, in great secrecy, sailed to London where he petitioned the Government to intercede in his favour and in effect, persuade his father to reinstate him as the natural successor which, he argued, was his birthright. Lord Aberdeen obliged, writing to Said on his son's behalf, but to no avail. In a spirited reply, Sayyid Said wrote, 'You say he is my eldest son, yet amongst the Arabs being the eldest son is of no consequence, but the ornament and dignity of a man in his conduct.' Enraged by Hilal's direct appeal to the British, his family banished him from Zanzibar forever. He died in the British Crown Colony of Aden in 1851.

Said's strategy of the division of rule over the two component parts of the Omani state, far from achieving the unity within the ruling house it was designed to promote, led directly to a sustained period of family feuding and intrigue which only the intervention of the British brought to an end. When matters between the two brothers had reached such a fractious state that Thuwainy was preparing to seize Zanzibar from Majid by force, the British Government in India, acting on the instructions of London, dispatched the Raj's Governor General, Lord Canning, to arbitrate.

On 2 April 1861 Lord Canning delivered his verdict. From that time onwards Oman and Zanzibar would operate, and be regarded by London and its dominions, as two quite separate states. The ruler of each would have the Islamic Ottoman title of 'Sultan', which meant that Oman and Zanzibar would now be Sultanates in their own right. The Canning Award, as it became known, also stipulated that the independent Government of Zanzibar would make an annual payment to Muscat of 40,000 Maria Teresa silver dollars (a not inconsiderable sum for the time), as a form of compensation to Oman for its loss of revenue. It was a classic Victorian example of 'divide and rule', although the fact is inescapable that it had been brought about, in this instance at least, by the propensity of Oman's ruling family for intrigue. Nonetheless, this further intrusion into the quality of their sovereignty appears not to have been immediately apparent to either Thuwainy or Majid; neither did the future implications for the independence of their now separate states appear to have been a matter for concern.

Following the announcement of the decision, Thuwainy wrote to the noble Lord Canning, 'We heartily accept and thank God for your efforts on our behalf, praying also that your goodwill may be rewarded and that you may never cease to be our support.' Majid, in his letter, was no less effusive. 'I feel very much obliged to the British Government for all its kindness and favour and having averted from my dominions disorders and hostilities. During my lifetime I shall never forget the kindness it has shown me.'

Ironically, Sayyid Thuwainy's expression of gratitude to the British for their support, which he hoped would 'never cease', was all too soon given a particular relevance. The ink may indeed have been dry on the Canning Award, but the enmity between the two brothers was far from over, for the payment of the silver dollar coins fell almost immediately into serious arrears. The only course open to London was both clear and immediate.

Acknowledging that it was their intervention which had prevented Thuwainy from seizing Zanzibar from Majid by force, the Government took the decision in 1871 to pay the levy itself via its administration in British India. Following India's independence in 1947 payment of the silver coins to Muscat became the responsibility of the Foreign Office in London, a payment it maintained until 1956 when, with the agreement of the Sultan Said bin Taimour, it ceased. The levy was regarded by both sides as an antique arrangement from the two countries' past, one that was no longer appropriate in the middle of a rapidly changing twentieth century.

Today the large round silver coins, bearing the unmistakable matronly features of Maria Teresa of the old Austrian-Hungarian Empire, can be purchased in the ancient and winding lanes of Muttrah Souq in Muscat, often having been incorporated into pieces of jewellery by Oman's celebrated silversmiths. But however quaint the payment may now appear, the implications for the sovereignty of Oman would be difficult to over-emphasise, given that it represented for over four generations the only consistently reliable form of state revenue available to the Sultans.

While Zanzibar was obliged following 1861 to become a British protectorate with a resident British Governor, Oman and Muscat retained nominal independence. The Union Jack never flew over Muscat to signify the country's status as an outpost of the British Empire, although Britain continued to play a dominant role well into the second half of the twentieth century. But the indelible fact remains that via Sayyid Said bin Sultan's letter to Lord Aberdeen in 1844, in which he disinherited Hilal, Britain was given a green light to play a principal role in the succession process. The government was given, in a very real sense, the power to make and indeed, unmake, Omani Sultans on both the island of Zanzibar and in Oman proper, a fact of history which echoed resoundingly on 23 July 1970.

The plea of Said led directly to the Canning Award, which eventually gave Britain an economic grip on Muscat which had many consequences during the closing years of the nineteenth century and for much of the twentieth. Indeed, the subsequent development of the Omani state can only be realistically understood in the light of this political reality.

When taking nineteenth-century conditions into account, there could arguably be a case made for Britain's dominant role in the succession process: that it represented a better influence on the stability of Oman and its good governance, better, that is, than the constant tribal conflict and family intrigue that would once more have thrown the nation into chaos. But the Omani people entertained a fierce pride about their national independence and there were many at the time who bitterly resented Britain's overweening influence in their affairs of state, a sentiment which still held sway in the late twentieth century. Ironically it was a Briton, Bartle Frere, a Governor of Bombay, who in passing judgement on the Canning Award in 1870, wrote that Britain had brought about 'the ruin of a flourishing country and Kingdom'.

Seven years after the Canning Award it was an Omani leader who inspired a spirited attempt to arrest the decline of the country into a state of foreign dependency. The death of Sultan Thuwainy in 1868 had launched Oman into a further episode of family feuding and tribal conflict, the ferocity of which was without equal. This period of national disorder was only brought to a temporary end by the emergence of one of Thuwainy's cousins, Azzan bin Qais. Azzan assumed for himself not just the leadership of Oman but reverted to the title of Imam. He had the endorsement of a sufficient number of tribes in Oman's interior and while he was not the beneficiary of the standard election and customary public acclamation, his call for the country to reassert its independence and make a sustained national effort to dilute the ever-encroaching influence of the British won him adequate support to take over the reins of power. While Azzan bin Qais failed in his aims, his activities between 1868 and 1871 are noteworthy. They demonstrate, in the most eloquent of terms, his keen awareness that as long as the ruling family continued with its catalogue of wholesale intrigue, so would the tribes of the interior continue to believe that they could act and operate as independent entities with no obligations to the Omani state. He also realised that as long as such national division went unchecked the greater was the opportunity for the country to fall prey to foreign interference and domination.

Azzan bin Qais believed that only by achieving a strong central government would the state flourish and, what is more, be able to reassert its independence, in the process repelling unwanted alien influences upon it. It was a policy the British viewed with express distaste, realising only too well that if a strong Omani state emerged it would represent a very real threat to the established order of things. This could, given the strategic location of Oman, threaten Britain's sea-lanes to India, the very same situation that they sought to avoid in 1798 when they had gained their first, significant influence in Oman's affairs.

A report from the British Political Agent, Colonel Lewis Pelly, to the Political Secretary in Bombay serves as an illustration of just how frustrated the British were at the spirited policies of Imam Azzan:

> I asked the agent (of Azzan bin Qais) how it happened that while the Sultans of the old dynasty permitted the tribes on the frontier to remain in quasi independence and refrained from intruding on them with force, the present Government pursued an opposite policy. He explained that under the old dynasty the Sultans were not in sufficient strength to subjugate the border tribes. But that the policy of Azzan's Government had from the first been to subjugate all the tribes of Oman to the central authority and that the Government were determined to adhere to this line of action, as they considered that the Oman territories could never be at peace, or possess a strong Government, as long as the tribal chiefs considered themselves independent.

All of this was simply too much for the British Government to stomach and in an act of political expediency which went straight to the heart of Oman's administration, it promptly stopped payment of the Canning Award and withdrew recognition of Azzan. But it went further still, giving both encouragement and financial aid to a rival claimant to the Omani leadership, Sayyid Turki bin Said, another of Sayyid Said's sons. Emboldened not just by the finances of the British, but by their active encouragement to overthrow his cousin, Sayyid Turki bin Said mounted an armed rising against Imam Azzan. The subsequent fighting in the streets of Muscat was short, sharp and brutal and during January 1871 Azzan bin Qais met his end in a pitched battle at the Muscat portside suburb of Muttrah. Sayyid Turki immediately installed himself as Sultan and the British duly obliged him with immediate recognition and a resumption of payments. But his rule ushered in a time of political indolence, with the limited writ of Oman's latest Sultan being characterised by indecision, the total absence of any sense of national direction and a lack of control outside the country's capital and its ports. As a direct result the tribes in the country's hinterland were completely out of control, with Muscat being apparently unwilling or unable to assert its authority. The situation rapidly deteriorated until it became desperate, prompting a further round of mass emigration by Omanis to the greener pastures of Zanzibar. According to at least one contemporary report this left whole areas of Oman depopulated. Then, just two years into his reign, the British delivered an economic bodyblow to the rule of their protégé.

In 1873 a further Treaty of Commerce was presented for signature, one which, on this occasion, was transparent in its intentions. Oman would henceforth accept the British demand for 'the effective suppression of the slave trade'. Oman's role as a slave trading nation was now at an end and while the economic implications were disastrous, Sultan Turki knew only too well that he was quite unable to mount any effective opposition to the British Navy. The tribes of the interior watched the impotence of Muscat and were not long in mounting a whole series of armed uprisings against the rule of Sultan Turki bin Said. In one such attack in January 1874, the powerful Al Harthy tribe (the descendants of which yield significant social and economic clout in today's Oman), the capital itself almost fell, with the armed men of the tribe besieging the walled city of Muscat from nearby Muttrah, which they briefly occupied. Sultan Turki, embattled in his palace by the sea, enacted a time-honoured Omani tradition by sending out cash to dissuade the enemy. It worked but the tribe returned in June 1877, again occupying Muttrah, only repelled on this occasion by the British man-o'-war HMS *Teazer*, which made its presence most effectively felt by discharging cannon fire over the heads of the rebels.

Faced with cannon fire from the British Navy, the Al Harthy tribal leaders suddenly saw Sultan Turki's point of view and ended their occupation of Muttrah, returning to their stronghold in the interior desert region. What the naval guns of the British could not disperse was the rapid decline in the country's financial fortunes. The 1873 treaty had triggered an economic downturn which had a fearful and debilitating momentum all of its own. With the slave trade most definitely at an end, there were insufficient funds for investment in agriculture, as a result of which the industry slipped ever faster into subsistence production. And, as had happened 30 years earlier, this provoked yet further wholesale emigration to Zanzibar.

In 1883 Sultan Turki bin Said died, his state's finances close to ruin, with his rule during the closing years of his life having been confined to Muscat and the Batinah coastal corridor. By the year of the Sultan's death, the tribes of the interior, which still made periodic raids on the capital, were themselves divided by bitter, petty squabbles. The sadness and despair of Sultan Turki's reign was exacerbated by the fact that his eldest son had been born mentally retarded and was, therefore, disqualified from inheriting the throne. With the hereditary process still very much in place, his second son, Faisal, became Sultan of Oman. His inheritance was bleak but with the tribes in disarray no immediate challenge was mounted against his rule. However, with Oman's economy now in free fall and the Sultan's writ extinguished in the interior, it was a situation of calm that could not last.

Just two years after ascending the throne, Muscat faced its strongest armed attack yet from the men of Oman's vast hinterland. Indeed, by 1885 the national situation was so manifestly bad that even the fractious, quarrelsome tribes had agreed to put aside their attitudes of mutual antipathy and join forces in an attempt to end Oman's rule by Sultans. As before, the campaign was led by the proud, fierce Al Harthy tribe and on 13 February 1885 they attacked Muscat at several points. On this occasion the British, knowing a well-planned and well-equipped assault when they saw it, failed to intervene on the Sultan's behalf despite a desperate appeal from him to do so. Thrown back on his own resources, Sultan Faisal took the only course known open to him. He embarked upon a frantic round of fund-raising amongst the merchants of Muscat which enabled him to buy off the tribal leaders, but not before they had occupied his capital. But the expedient of paying one's enemies to go away prevailed and on 10 March the Sultan's rule was again restored in Muscat. The Sultan may have escaped overthrow but his state was now heavily in debt. With revenues from slave trading at a complete end and agriculture providing virtually no cash at all, his administration's only source of revenue remained the annual payment by Britain, as stipulated in the Canning Award. Such a situation was not slow in making itself felt in the funding of the State's institutions; during the closing years of the nineteenth century they fell into decay and decrepitude until, for all practical purposes, they ceased to function at all. No small wonder then that Sultan Faisal, who bitterly resented Britain's failure to come to his aid in 1885, began to cultivate a relationship with the French, whom he believed would be more relaxed about the trade in slaves. They were also facilitating the supply of arms to the rebellious tribesmen at the north-west frontier in British India, a trade that would be made much less problematic if they could be trans-shipped at Oman ports. The acrimonious ambitions of France and Britain in the region were based on a rising colonial rivalry and given his own dire financial circumstances, Sultan Faisal can only be given full credit for attempting to play one side off against the other, all the time hoping it would be to his eventual advantage.

The British were ever anxious and preoccupied with maintaining their grip on India, the jewel in the crown of the British Empire, so immediately acted to eliminate the need for Sultan Faisal to consort with the French. They were swift to respond and in the very same year, 1895, the beleaguered Sultan was afforded a loan of 60,000 Maria Teresa silver dollar coins which was followed in 1897 by a further identical payment, both of which had to be repaid from the Canning Award in monthly instalments.

While such loans were not sufficient to clear the State's debts, their payment put Oman even deeper into Britain's pocket, a harsh fact which did not escape the increasingly desperate Sultan.

Relations were not helped by his personal relationship with the current 'Englishman of Respectability' at the British Residency. In the late nineteenth century Colonel Miles was one of the longest-serving British Political Agents at Muscat. He may well have been an officer, but in fact was anything but a gentleman in his dealings with Sultan Faisal whom he constantly bullied. When not engaged in such anti-social behaviour he was by all contemporary accounts insufferably patronising. It has to be recorded that Colonel Miles had his suspicions, not just that Sultan Faisal was double-dealing Britain in his overtures to the French, but that he had diverted a good proportion of the two loans into his own personal treasury, as opposed to using them to meet the commitments of the State. While the money loaned by the British bought Sultan Faisal time, his resentment towards them was now, understandably enough, set in stone. Consequently, he again began to deal secretly with the French, receiving an envoy from Paris whom he accorded the status of Political Agent. But he went further, granting them port and bunkering facilities at Bandar Jissah on a small but well-sheltered inlet just five miles from Muscat. The British regarded this alignment with the French not just as a betrayal but an Omani repudiation of the Treaty of 1798 and reacted with predictable fury. In an act of high imperial drama, they summoned a now hapless Sultan Faisal to the deck of a British man-o'-war anchored in the harbour, beneath the ramparts of his castle, and obliged him to publicly repudiate his agreement with France. So that he was to be left in no possible doubt as to Britain's demand, British warships, on the orders of Lord Curzon, the recently appointed Viceroy of India, were moved into position in Muscat harbour with orders to open fire on the town in the event of the Sultan's refusal. Of course, such a spectacle was one of public humiliation for the Sultan, one that served as a particularly painful reminder that Oman, while not a part of Britain's Empire, had become a client state and that the best course open to him was to quietly comply with London's demands. While the whole episode constituted a 'diplomatic' triumph for the British, they did act to soften the blow to such a spirited attempt by Sultan Faisal to re-establish his State's sovereignty, by removing Colonel Miles and replacing him in October 1899 with the gentler Major Percy Cox, a man with an avuncular air that was more suited to the hour. A man with an appetite for travelling into the interior, where few British Political Agents had hitherto ventured (with a consequent result that they knew little of the tribes that lived there), the presence of Cox ushered in a more gentlemanly atmosphere between Britain's representatives and the Omani ruler.

On one of Cox's expeditions to Abu Dhabi by sea, followed by an overland return to Muscat, he was accompanied by the Sultan for the voyage. Cox recorded in his diary:

> When the Sultan heard of my lively ambition to make an expedition from Abu Dhabi to Muscat, he entered heartily into the proposal and said he would be glad to seize the opportunity as coming as far as Abu Dhabi . . . I was, of course, only too willing and we proceeded there in company; he and his retainers in his steam yacht the *Nur Al Bahr* and I in HMS *Redbreast*, one of the small gunboats of the East India Squadron.

This air of geniality was given fresh impetus in January 1903 when Sultan Faisal's heir apparent, the young Sayyid Taimour, was taken by Percy Cox to Delhi, to witness the Coronation durbar of Britain's King-Emperor, Edward VII. It was an occasion of such pomp and power, enacted by a country at the pinnacle of its imperial might, that it cannot but have impressed and overawed the young Taimour, who was later to become Sultan. The sight of Indian Maharajahs and Princes kneeling in homage before the King beneath the burnished canopy of state, must have been breathtaking. Of course this was the intention; such overt displays of might and power were a cornerstone of cementing both direct colonial rule and underwriting influence in those parts of the world, such as Oman, which had not actually become a part of Britain's great imperial family.

Just ten months after Sayyid Taimour's attendance at the Delhi durbar another ostentatious display of Britain's power took place in Muscat itself, with the arrival on 18 November 1903 of that icon of empire, Lord George Nathaniel Curzon of Kedleston. As a fascinating cameo in Oman's history and an expression of imperial power it does warrant attention. A contemporary report records Curzon's vessel, the *Hardinge*, dressed with masthead flags, entering Muscat harbour escorted by the flagship *Hyacinth* and the cruisers *Fox*, *Argonaut* and *Pomone*. Awaiting the Viceroy's grand arrival at the mouth of the harbour were two more cruisers, the *Lawrence* and the *Lapwing*. As this flotilla entered the harbour the *Hyacinth* discharged its cannons with a 21-gun salute which was answered by the Sultan's batteries from the Portuguese-built Fort Mirani on the rocks opposite Faisal's Palace, which then as now, stands guard over the approaches. As the flotilla dropped anchor the Sultan's batteries again roared into life, discharging a further 21-gun salute as a personal welcome to Curzon. Sultan Faisal's heir, Taimour, led the delegation of welcome, accompanied by his uncle Sayyid Mohammad, boarding the *Hardinge* to greet this great proconsul of Empire and to issue, in his father's name, a personal welcome to Oman. Shortly after the delegation had returned ashore to yet more salutes of gunfire, Sultan Faisal, together with Major Cox, took to his official launch, and following an inspection of the impressive display of British naval power boarded the *Hardinge* to meet with Curzon. The meeting took place on the quarterdeck, which had been hung with luxuriant tapestries and covered with gold-threaded carpets for the occasion. When the Sultan returned to his palace at the water's edge it was the turn of *Fox* to fire its guns in salute. Onshore flags fluttered in the breeze and in an act of symbolism, a line of gaily coloured bunting ran from the ramparts of the Sultan's palace to the walls of the British Residency next door (against which, Percy Cox once laconically wrote, the crashing waves caused 'a continual thud'). The next day, 19 November, Muscat was the scene of a durbar all of its very own. With the guns yet again roaring out salutes, Lord Curzon, the Viceroy of British India and Sultan Faisal bin Turki of Muscat and Oman, sat side by side on the deck of HMS *Argonaut* as representatives of Oman's military and civil elite arrived for presentation. One hundred British Marines formed a guard of honour as the guests were piped aboard. The band of the Royal Marines played on while members of Oman's Royal Family and its establishment mingled with such British luminaries as the Secretary of the Foreign Department in the Government of India, Sir Louis Dane, and the British Minister at Tehran. In an address cloaked in the obtuse double-speak of high diplomacy, Curzon praised Sultan Faisal's 'enlightened Government', presumably for having seen the British point of view when publicly humiliated on the deck of the British man-o'-war only five years earlier. As a grand finale to the day's events Curzon invested Oman's ruler with the Grand Cross of the Order of the Indian Empire. In a final gesture of goodwill, the Sultan was told that to mark the occasion, his state's debts were to be written off by London.

As impressive as all of this most definitely was, it meant little to the tribes in the country's vast interior, where unrest and disaffection with Sultan Faisal's rule continued to fester. They had been particularly incensed by his diplomatic defeat and consequent public humiliation aboard the British warship. The show of naval strength by the British, so prominently displayed at the time of the visit by Lord Curzon, only served to heighten their resentment at what they saw as evidence of the loss of the country's independence. All of this they blamed on Sultan Faisal, somewhat unjustly in that he had inherited a banquet of consequences born of Oman's former domestic divisions, which had made the country such easy prey for the British. But the warrior tribes showed a scant regard for history. All that mattered to them was the all too apparent impotence of their state and they pined and then plotted anew, for the return of the Imamate system of rule with its fair but austere regime, which had in the past produced a quality of national strength.

It was a particuarly delicate and sensitive time for Sultan Faisal. The British, never having really understood the tenacity of the men of the interior, made a demand that was to ignite a comprehensively-supported armed rebellion against his rule. Ever anxious that the free trade of guns and ammunition in Muscat could become a threat, the British demanded a ban on the export of guns and the establishment of a bonded warehouse for the safe storage and control of those arms required by the Sultan's soldiers. Not only was the trade in guns profitable to many tribes, but this latest foreign influence was seen as one that would ultimately deprive the men of the interior of their right to bear arms, the sign of manhood since time immemorial. For these proud men of the interior it was a step too far. Galvanised by yet further interference in the affairs of their country and the fact that it was led by a ruler who appeared unable to halt the continuing slide into dependency on a foreign power, they met together in assembly in order to decide what course of action to take. On this occasion it was not the Al Harthy who took the initiative, but a leader of the Al Ghafri clan from the increasingly influential Bani Riyam tribe, who called tribal leaders to an assembly. The meeting took place at Tanuf in May 1913, not far from the former Imamate capital of Nizwa, and stating that rule by Sultans no longer commanded the respect and allegiance of the general population, the tribes declared a re-establishment of elective government. Raising the white flag of Imamate rule they elected Salim bin Rashid Al Kharusi as Imam and resolved to mount an armed attack on Muscat and bring an end to the Al Busaid dynasty.

But before such an attack could be organised and launched Sultan Faisal bin Turki died, in the October of 1913. Sayyid Taimour became Sultan, but as with his father before him, his inheritance was bleak, with the country still in debt and the tribes of the interior in open revolt. For the first 18 months of his reign he attempted with increasing desperation to reach an accommodation with the rebels, but such initiatives were to no avail. Then in early 1915 a decisive development occurred which brought together, as never before, the coalition of tribes planning and equipping themselves for an assault on Muscat: the Al Harthy tribal leaders had joined the ranks of the rebels, bringing with them not just a reputation of having been tested in battle, but a new sense of urgency and direction. Led by Sheikh Issa bin Saleh Al Harthy the attack was launched with such skill and ferocity that had it been fought on an Omani to Omani basis, it would have undoubtedly succeeded. But on this fateful occasion the British did not stand idly by as they had done before in 1885. The point of attack was the barracks of the Sultan's small standing army at Bait Al Falaj, just three miles from his palace. However, the British had long known of the planned attack and had shipped into Muscat a battalion of Baluchi soldiers, who had a well-founded reputation for discipline and valour second only to the Gurkhas. Faced with troops under British command and with an outrageous technical superiority, the tribes were repulsed, although it is a matter for British record that they fought – and died – hard.

With the rebels' return to their desert strongholds, a peace of sorts descended on Muscat, although the structural problems of state remained. Sultan Taimour's administration lurched from one financial crisis to another, his dependency on the British remained for all to see and the interior of his country operated as a separate, independent entity. Never before in the long history of the country had the term 'Muscat and Oman' appeared more appropriate. Sultan Taimour may well have ruled in Muscat but greater Oman, the truly vast hinterland, remained way beyond his reach. There Imam Salim's rule held sway. The Sultan appealed on more than one occasion to the Political Agent for the loan of a British-led battalion that would march off into the interior and put down the rebels once and for all, but he always declined, preferring to keep what was now a permanent military presence in Muscat under British command. Such a refusal was, of course, resented by the Sultan. He knew perfectly well that while the forces of Imam Salim had been driven back at Bait Al Falaj, their intentions remained what they had always been: his overthrow and with it the end of the Al Busaid dynasty and the re-establishment of Imamate rule. After the battle of Bait Al Falaj it was now all too evident to the tribes of the far interior that the Sultan was being kept in power only by the British presence, a fact which generated a boisterous loathing of Britain but about which its representatives in Muscat, at least for a while, appeared mainly ignorant.

The British had other matters on their mind. The outbreak of war in Europe in August 1914 understandably became their principal preoccupation for the next four years. When the conflict quickly spread to the Middle East, it directly led to a repeat performance in Muscat, albeit in miniature, of the visit by Lord Curzon 12 years earlier. On 11 February 1915, the Viceroy of India, Lord Hardinge of Penshurst, steamed regally into Muscat harbour in convoy, aboard the *Lawrence*. He was returning to India from visits to Kuwait and Basrah, where British troops were in battle with the Ottoman Turks, allies of Kaiser Wilhelm's Germany. Once more the sound of cannon fire echoed round the barren, stark hills encircling Muscat. As Sultan Taimour sailed out from his Palace to greet Hardinge, HMS *Odin* fired a salute. Later Hardinge went to the Palace where the beleaguered Sultan addressed this latest proconsul of the British Empire to visit his realm in terms both plaintive and sycophantic:

> In the name of God, the best of names! Not only with my lips but with all my heart I beg to express my gratitude to the British Government for the friendship which she has shown me and for the goodwill existing between me and her . . . I am honoured by this visit within so short a period after assuming the reins of Government, whereas my late father did not attain such an honour for many years after his succession to the throne.

It was as close a public acknowledgment as any national leader could give that his rule now depended on an alien power, while still retaining some crumbs of credibility within the shores of his own realm. But Sultan Taimour bin Faisal managed on this occasion at least to retain for himself the somewhat austere consolation of integrity, speaking as he did in front of his own Court and establishment to Lord Hardinge.

When that terrible and awesome struggle known as the Great War came to an end in November 1918, the British once more turned their attention to seeking a truce between Sultan Taimour and the people of the interior, instructing their Political Agent in Muscat, Orde Wingate (who was on secondment from the Indian Civil Service), to work towards such an end. A man of acute sensitivity and political skill, Wingate had an instinctive feel both for the imperatives of the Sultan and the tribes in Oman's hinterland. He was determined to end this long-running dispute which had so bedevilled Oman's governance. The negotiations were long and laborious, naturally enough, continuing throughout 1920, a year which demonstrated yet again the fragility of Arab tribal alliances. For that same year saw the assassination of Imam Salim bin Rashid Al Kharusi, as a direct result of which Wingate concluded the negotiations with Sheikh Issa bin Saleh Al Harthy. The Al Harthy were once again in the ascendancy, a fact given particular emphasis when Sheikh Issa's nominee for Imam, Mohammed bin Abd Allah Al Khalili, was elected. The treaty of 1921 was signed at an assembly of tribal leaders led by Sheikh Issa at Seeb, just beyond the site of today's international airport of the same name. It ushered into existence a highly unusual, if not unique, system of government, the very nature of which must have seemed a complete contradiction of their long-held beliefs to some of those who signed it. It gave lawful authority for British influence and involvement in the governance of Oman, against which they had for so long railed.

Given that it was to remain in force for almost half a century its details are of no small interest. The Treaty of Seeb had as its preamble the following:

> In the name of God, the Compassionate the Merciful, this is the Peace agreed upon between the Government of the Sultan, Taimour bin Faisal, and the Sheikh, Issa bin Salih bin Ali, on behalf of the people of Oman whose names are signed hereto, through the mediation of Mr. Wingate, I.C.S. Political Agent and Consul for Great Britain in Muscat, who is empowered by his Government in this respect and to be an intermediary between them. Of the conditions set forth below, four pertain to the Government of the Sultan and four pertain to the people of Oman.

'Four pertain to the Government of the Sultan and four pertain to the people of Oman'; there could be nothing more explicit, more tangible than these sixteen words on the division of the country, a separation of power that must have been anathema to Sultan Taimour and which gave a new, damning definition of the term 'Muscat and Oman', first introduced in the late eighteenth century by his ruling ancestor, Sayyid Hamad bin Said. The Treaty established quite precisely the powers and limitations of both sides and gave a clear dimension to the term 'Muscat and Oman'. For example Sultan Taimour was bound by the Treaty to renounce all authority in the interior and jurisdiction over the tribes, although they could enter Muscat and other port towns to conduct business. In return the tribes were now obligated not to attack Muscat and other coastal areas where the Sultan's rule held sway, and they were now bound by the Treaty of Seeb not to challenge the authority of Sultan Taimour bin Faisal in any way.

By putting his hand to the Treaty, Sultan Taimour not only signed away his right to govern vast areas of his own realm, he also sanctified yet further British influence in the day-to-day running of his own administration. The agreement also opened the way for the appointment and secondment of British executive administrators who were to exercise authority in the Sultan's name over the next 50 years. Obviously sensitive to the demeaning aspects of the Treaty for Sultan Taimour, the British included a measure to enhance the 'fresh start' it offered, granting a loan from its colonial administration in India to the Omani ruler. On this occasion, the loan was adequate enough for him to pay off all his Government's debts to the merchants of Muscat, in whose grip he had for so long laboured. However, the Sultan had to repay the British within two years. An express condition of the loan was that he accept a financial adviser, seconded in the first instance from the Government in British India. As the Treaty of Seeb had made provision for such an element of British guidance there was little the Sultan could do but to accept the adviser's arrival in Muscat, although the first civil servant from Bombay to be appointed to the job did not stay long, finding it impossible to impose any accounting or other financial discipline on the Omani ruler. Consequently, within three years of the Treaty, the finances of the Omani State were once more chaotic, with debt piling up on yet more debt in the absence of financial prudence and control.

The British made another effort in 1925, this time seconding a keen young official from its administration in Palestine. He was, in effect, the Sultan's Financial Secretary. Bertram Thomas had come to be regarded as one of Britain's most notable Arabists through his 1930 crossing of the Rub Al-Khali, the barren and forbidding Empty Quarter. Unfortunately, his interest in desert travel successfully challenged that of instituting financial control onto the Sultan's affairs, although it should be recorded that during his five-year term he did make some progress in establishing accountancy procedures at the Palace. But as a means of achieving long-term fiscal probity these were, alas, none too successful. When his tour of duty came to an end he left the State's finances in a greater mess than he had found them.

Sadly, the words used to describe the rule of Sultan Taimour bin Faisal are 'none too sucessful'. As the 1920s drew to a close he must have looked back at his years at the centre of Omani power with an enduring sense of melancholy. While excitement and promise for the future had been generated by personally witnessing the pomp and circumstance of Edward VII's 1903 Delhi Coronation durbar, such youthful confidence would have been harshly diluted ten years later when upon the death of his father, he inherited a realm that was going from rack to ruin at a pace of knots. His major challenge of debt was exceeded only by the constant threat from armed tribesmen during the first seven years of his reign, who nominally owed allegiance to him. As a man who was obliged by history to attempt to contain the ills of the past with few tools of his own to do the job, Sultan Taimour is a leader who rightly deserves sympathetic understanding rather than recrimination. The fact that he was only saved from being overthrown by British intervention at the battle of Bait Al Falaj must have been the bitterest of medicines for the Sultan to swallow. It demonstrated most abundantly to all his people, whether in Muscat or Oman, that he did indeed owe his continued presence on the throne to foreign elements.

Just as his youthful experience of being at the centre of real power had begun in India, so did his final contact with it take place outside of Oman. In 1928 he went to London, the capital of his political masters, and in the process became the very first Sultan of Oman to have first-hand experience of the land which had exercised such influence over his own for exactly 130 years. The world he would have witnessed was one of unprecedented technological change and innovation. Even before leaving Oman, he would have seen the flying boats of Imperial Airways (the precursor to today's British Airways) sitting grandly on the waters beneath his Palace in Muscat. In the face of such technical progress his antique land, with its ancient institutions, must have appeared even more fragile and vulnerable to the rapidly encroaching world beyond Oman's shores. He was photographed aboard a Royal Naval vessel in London looking sadly and reproachfully into the camera's lens. Four years after his return from London he abdicated under pressure from Britain which now considered him ill-suited to rule. In any event he was by now exhausted and dispirited by his attempts to govern Muscat and Oman. But his abdication was peaceful and he left Oman's stage with the British promise that they would take good care of and give guidance to his son and heir, Said bin Taimour.

On 11 February 1932, Said ascended the throne of Oman, a 21-year-old young man of sound, classical education, having attended Mayo College, the 'Eton' of British India, school to Maharajahs and their sons for generations. While his inheritance was also characterised by crippling debt he was of an iron determination to rid his country of its chains and, in the process, relieve it of the foreign domination which had for so long bedevilled and belittled Oman's institutions. But as his father had good cause to know, the bonds that bind a state to its past are not cut with either ease or impunity and the imperatives of the coming new age were set to make Said's mission doubly difficult. In the melancholy event, however, it was not an absence of cash but an abundance of it that would, with pivotal British involvement, come to sweep Sultan Said bin Taimour off his throne and into the sands of time.

# CHAPTER FOUR

# A Little Loving

'And in the afternoon there was usually a little loving.'
– His late Highness Sultan Said bin Taimour of Muscat and Oman, on life at his Salalah Palace.

Britain and much of the world beyond Brittania's shores surrendered itself to previously unseen expressions of public grief on the morning of Saturday, 6 September 1997. As the funeral cortege of Diana, Princess of Wales, made its mournful way from St James's Palace to Westminster Abbey, the attention of the international media was, naturally enough, focused on London. For the previous six days people had assembled in front of her residence, Kensington Palace, to lay flowers in tribute to an icon of the modern age.

Smaller but significant numbers had gone with floral tributes to Harrods, the London department store owned by Mohammed Al Fayed, father of Dodi Al Fayed, whose son had died alongside the Princess in a Paris underpass during the early hours of the previous Sunday. Still smaller numbers still had gone with bouquets to Woking, in Surrey, the site of the first Mosque to be built in Britain (during the reign of Queen Victoria) and with it Brookwood, the first Islamic cemetery to be established in the British Isles. Earlier that week, in accordance with Islamic law governing the burial of the dead, Dodi Al Fayed had been laid to rest there. After his funeral the numbers grew to such an extent that on the orders of Mohammed Al Fayed, Harrods sent refreshments for the public who had travelled to Woking, some for hundreds of miles, to pay their respects to the very last consort of the Princess.

Yet what few knew was that just yards from the grave of the man who had made such a precarious journey into the affections of the British public, lay an Arab monarch who just 25 years earlier had been laid to rest without state tribute or public acknowledgment of any kind. For the 38 years of his reign he had been Britain's staunchest ally in the Arab world, both in war and peace. At home he had painstakingly, and with precious few resources, rescued his country from the stranglehold of debt, an achievement which had so long eluded his royal ancestors. As such, he should have been the subject of British approbation, beneficiary of abiding British patience and support, the recipient of those self-proclaimed British virtues, honour and loyalty. Although he received such treatment from both the British Crown and individual Britons who loyally served him, just when he needed London's support most it was withdrawn in a manner that was covert and quite devoid of either honour or integrity. His sad journey from his palace by the sea in far-off Arabia to the cemetery in a dormitory town in southern England, close to where trains rattle by each morning loaded with commuters bound for the British capital, is in essence a cautionary tale without equal. It is also a witness to the shifting sands of high diplomatic intrigue, the evasion which always accompanies it, state treachery and human greed.

Sultan Said bin Taimour set about his work of national salvation with an iron will. His cardinal aim of breaking his state's sad, humiliating cycle of debt and foreign dependence was not seen as an end in itself but a means to an end. Once state solvency had been achieved, his secondary and no less ardently pursued goal was to keep it that way. In the early years of his reign, the policy was not helped by the Great Depression. The adverse effects on world trade had arrived on Oman's shores during the closing years of his father's rule. The internationally-felt slump generated by the recession led directly to a significant reduction in Oman of custom revenues, the principal source of state income. In taking radical measures to counter this new pressure on the available cash flow necessary to finance his state, Sultan Said did not spare himself, instituting within days of coming to the throne a halving of his own Privy Purse. Public expenditure was also greatly reduced. The Sultan's Treasury, as he was about to confirm, was completely empty and Oman was once again in debt to the merchants of Muscat. Yet despite a seemingly impossible task he had paid off the loan through a strict application of financial prudence by the end of 1933. In his own words, other dues were also 'liquidated'. It was an astonishing achievement.

What he could not liquidate was the continuing animosity to his rule by the tribes in the interior. As we have seen, the 1921 Treaty of Seeb had sanctified a division of power in the land unique in the annals of state. While it was a lawful humiliation for any Omani ruler not to be complete master in his own house, there was little that Sultan Said could do about it, unless of course the Imam, who held authority in the deserts and mountain settlements of the interior, took a course of action that violated the Treaty. So for the first 24 years of his reign the Sultan sat in Muscat and governed the coastal region to the north of his capital and the southern province of Dhofar, while Imam Mohammed bin Abd Allah Al Khalili sat in Nizwa from where he ruled the rest of the country.

Sultan Said was a monarch cast very much in the classic mode: dignified in his bearing; possessed of considerable social grace; fluent in three languages in addition to his own; a man of considerable personal courage. But as monarchs so often were at that time, he was remote from the people he reigned over. A man who exercised a healthy contempt for ostentation, he lived simply, almost frugally, and was very conscientious regarding the allotment of state revenues between his own Privy Purse and the National Treasury. Had his royal ancestors exercised such a distinction, it is quite possible that the persistent financial chaos over which they presided may not have been so severe. One of the very real benefits of the Treaty of Seeb, in fact the only one from the Sultan's point of view, was that it relieved him from paying constant bribes to tribal leaders of the interior as an inducement not to attack Muscat and the other ports under his royal jurisdiction. This in itself was considerably beneficial in reducing state expenditure.

But from the very moment he ascended the throne, Sultan Said's frugality was to take on a new dimension. An ever-prevailing aspect of life in the Arab world is the constant line of supplicants seeking handouts from those in power, or those believed by the public to be considerably wealthy. Oman's 13th hereditary Sultan exercised an abiding indifference to such a social practice, reducing public expenditure still further. It was a mental attitude born of financial expediency, strengthened by the Sultan's childhood, during which he had little contact with his own people. His early schooling had taken place in the Iraqi capital Baghdad, from whence he had gone to India, and it bred within him a remoteness that did little to endear Said to those who did readily pay him allegiance. A domestic arrangement which only served to emphasise his remoteness was his habit of spending more time in his palace at Salalah, capital of the southern province of Dhofar, over 1,000 kilometres from Muscat. Much was to be made of this later by the British officers who betrayed him.

= A LITTLE LOVING =

The Treaty of Seeb had paved the way for British officers, both civil and military, to serve the Sultan in a personal capacity. The cost of their employment was to be met by national revenues. The Sultan's small standing army, commanded by British officers and mainly comprised of Baluchi tribesmen recruited from Gwadar, Oman's colonial toehold in today's Pakistan, was the single biggest item of state expenditure. The Muscat Levies, as they were known, were an ineffectual deterrent to any determined external threat. But as a force that existed to principally protect the Sultan from dissident elements within Oman itself, they most certainly justified the expenditure they incurred. With very few other departments of state, it was a minimalist government with a vengeance, and while Sultan Said's remoteness may have been a source of irritation, it did at least leave people alone to conduct their lives along traditional lines. In this respect his rule differed very little from other regimes on the Arabian Peninsula prior to the age of oil, which was to bring in its wake such dramatic economic and social change.

The Sultan's Civil List was small, consisting of payments to a number of Walis, the Sultan-appointed state representatives in the regions, together with their minimal administrative establishment, customs staff and those employed at the central Government offices. These included an innovation of his own: a Ministry of the Interior, which was to act as a liaison between him and his regional governors. Justice was administered either by the Walis in the regions, or by the Qadhis, who presided over courts that dispensed justice according to Islamic law. The latter's salaries, together with the maintenance costs of the country's many Mosques, were raised from a tax on production, the Zakat.

The quality of justice dispensed in Sultan Said's time was considerably more merciful than that meted out in the other states of the Arabian Peninsula; a reflection of the fact that he was without doubt the most educated Sultan to come to the throne of Oman; a man of a civilised and cultured manner, a not insignificant fact given that his name and character was later to be officially and systematically blackened to support his forced removal. Public beheadings and the amputation of hands, while practised with mediaeval enthusiasm in neighbouring Saudi Arabia, were expressly forbidden in Oman. And the appalling cruelties practised by Imamate rule in North Yemen were also mercifully absent. Neither did his rule differ greatly from that of Imam Khalili, who reigned from the country's Imamate capital of Nizwa. By the standards of government at the time on the Arabian Peninsula, not only was there little distinction between the quality of administration practised in the respective states, for all practical purposes there was virtually no difference between that of Sultan Said and Imam Khalili. It is a matter for record that when, in 1980, an American academic asked an elderly soldier if the Imam's administration had actually constituted a government in the universally accepted sense, he is said to have thoughtfully responded, 'It killed, it taxed, it imprisoned. Yes, it was a government.'

It is with regard to the relationship between Sultan Said and the Imam that the Sultan's skill at statecraft becomes apparent. From the very moment of his accession he set about developing a cordial relationship with the Imam, Said's clear aim being the achieving of a reconciliation and eventual reunification of the country. Sultan Said was a man of great courtesy and upon the occasion of a Muslim festival the Imam always received the personal greetings of the ruler of Muscat. The Sultan also observed the conditions set out in the Treaty of Seeb in both spirit and letter. For example, the clause in the Treaty that obliged the Sultan's Government to return criminals who had fled from the interior to Muscat or other coastal areas was scrupulously observed. While he exercised the greatest respect in all his exchanges with the Imam, Said did refrain from addressing him as such. He remarked to his Minister of the Interior that to do so would signify that he, the Sultan, owed the Imam allegiance which, of course, he most certainly did not. However the Imam for his part did eventually come to address Said bin Taimour as 'Sultan' in all his correspondence.

During the second half of the 1930s the Sultan initiated a practice of considerable boldness and innovation, one which would be regarded today as a public relations initiative of some brilliance: he began to offer posts in his Muscat administration to qualified candidates living in the Imamate. The very first of such appointments were the Qadhis, who served at various centres under the Sultan's jurisdiction for many years. Imam Khalili readily gave permission for his 'people' to become part of Sultan Said's administration, placing no restrictions whatsoever on their return home to inner Oman for leave or retirement. According to contemporary reports, such a climate between the two men did breed a mutual respect although inevitably they remained wary of each other's motives. The Imam and his officials most certainly continued to believe that the Sultan was a creature of the British, regarding London's long-standing influence in the affairs of the country with fierce resentment, an attitude which had prevailed a long time. But by offering employment to judges who practised the cardinal ethic of Imamate rule, Islamic law, Sultan Said not only gained a wider acceptance for himself in the interior than might otherwise have been the case, but in a very practical manner also laid the foundations for the eventual reunification of the country.

The economy remained the Sultan's principal concern. Having so swiftly and successfully rescued it from the stranglehold of debt within two years of coming to power, he actively sought measures to increase state revenues that would keep the National Treasury in funds and out of the predatory grip of Oman's merchants. In order to attain such an end, he turned to the possibility of locating that much sought-after prize, oil, in his realm. It demonstrated how forward-looking he could be, despite the later allegations regarding his arch-conservatism by 'popular' 1970s demagogues. He knew only too well that in such a quest he would have a very real problem with the Imam, who would fiercely resist the presence in the regions under his control of any oil-exploration teams.

With the outbreak of war in 1939, Britain had used its treaties of friendship with the Sultan to harness the country into service for the monumental struggle with Germany and Japan. Ships of the British Fleet were granted automatic access to all Omani ports, together with unrestricted landing rights for planes of the Royal Air Force. London made due payment for use of such vital facilities on the route to India and the Far East, which had a most beneficial effect on the National Treasury. Some of the new funds were used by Sultan Said to establish and then strengthen links with tribal leaders in the interior, the Sheiks, many of whom visited Muscat fairly frequently through the right of passage provided for in the Treaty of Seeb.

It was a policy which promptly brought its own rewards. In 1945 the Muscat-based British Consul was able to report to London that the Sultan had become the arbitrator in a dispute between of the interior's most powerful tribes, the Ghafiri and the Hinawi. In return for his arbitration the respective tribal leaders had promised the Sultan not to participate in any election for a new Imam. The report to London also confirmed that the Sultan had received a letter from the Imam advising of the imminent arrival in Muscat of an envoy 'to discuss important questions'. This contact led to an initiative between Sultan Said and Imam Khalili, the establishment of a joint area of administration in a region long fought over by rival tribal factions, the Province of Sharqiya. It was an important step in the Sultan's long-term strategy of bringing about the reunification of the country, an aim which he knew only too well could not even begin to be achieved without establishing his own, legitimate claim to rule in some areas of the interior. The success achieved by the Sultan in pursuing his policy of détente with the people of the hinterland can be gauged by what happened when the Imam became seriously ill in 1948. Possibly fearful of the vacuum that would exist between the anticipated death of the Imam and the election of a replacement, some of the Sheiks suggested to Muscat that Said assume the title of Imam, in addition to that of Sultan. Realising his current limitations on power, Said is reported to have dismissed the idea as 'nonsense'. In any event, Imam Khalili recovered and with the Sultan having rejected the proposal of assuming the additional title, a moment in history passed which could have led to his goal of reunification.

But time was running out for Sultan Said and his gradual approach to achieving the country's unity. With the end of the Second World War came a whole series of initiatives by Western companies designed to identify new oil fields on the Arabian Peninsula. In Muscat and Oman the Sultan's keenness to welcome exploration teams continued to be hampered by the Imam's stiff opposition to permitting foreigners entry into the interior, where it was most likely that potentially profitable oil fields would be found. The very first licence for oil exploration in Oman had been granted by Sultan Taimour bin Faisal in 1924 to the D'Arcy Exploration Company, but it was not until 1948 that a representative of one of D'Arcy's successors, the Iraq Petroleum Company, attempted to implement the concession by entering Oman with a survey team.

Richard Bird, through his enterprise and perseverance, has a very special place in the history of Oman as an oil-producing state. He entered the country without the permission of Sultan Said, who protested to Bird's employers, the Iraq Petroleum Company, being sensitive to the politics of intrigue and treachery always present when great riches are in the offing. Not that Bird's personal courage and derring-do in entering Oman's interior did him or his company much good, despite his attempts to meet the Imam in Nizwa, and efforts to actually make several agreements with tribal leaders. Ever hostile to the presence of foreigners in the territory under his control, the Imam had Bird unceremoniously ejected back from where he had come into what was then the Trucial States, today's United Arab Emirates. While the source of the Imam's objections was xenophobia, the Sultan feared that if the Iraq Petroleum Company entered into agreements with various petty tribal leaders, it would not be long before Britain would accord them separate recognition, leading to yet further dismemberment of his realm. Sultan Said was endowed with a keen sense of history and had most certainly not forgotten the bitter lesson of Britain's imposition of the Canning Award some 87 years earlier along with the consequent geopolitical effects on his country. It was not an experience he wanted his people to go through again. His fears were not without foundation. In 1949 a prominent tribal leader on the Jebal Akhdar, or Green Mountain (which was to later become the scene of an armed uprising against the Sultan), told the British desert explorer, Wilfred Thesiger, that he wished to be recognised by Britain as an independent ruler. In the event there was a reconciliation between Sultan Said and Richard Bird who, under the protection of the Omani ruler, did make an exploration of the northern area of the country during the early part of 1949. Bird met with opposition from tribal leaders on this occasion too. They fired on his survey team, which promptly decamped, recognising the superiority of discretion over valour.

But it was violence of a very different kind which took place just three years later, when Oman faced armed occupation by one of its neighbours, encouraged by an oil company ever-anxious to increase the area in which it could operate, hoping to increase its profits in the process and improve its access to routes over which oil could be exported.

Saudi Arabia, to the west of Oman, had entered the Oil Age before the Second World War. With the rapid ascendancy of the American imperium in the Middle East, Saudi Arabia had joined forces with Uncle Sam to establish the Arabian-American Oil Company, Aramco, whose activities very quickly became inextricably linked with many aspects of that Kingdom's foreign policy. One of the objects of the Kingdom's and Aramco's desire was the Buraimi Oasis which, in 1949, was under the joint administration of the rulers of Oman and the Sheikhdom of Abu Dhabi. The Oasis lies at a point where the borders of Oman, Abu Dhabi (now capital of the United Emirates) and the Kingdom of Saudi Arabia meet and had long been the object of largely peaceful dispute.

At the time the dispute turned into one of armed occupation by Saudi Arabia, Britain was attempting to achieve a lasting settlement. Indeed, Britain had commenced the process of arbitration at the request of Sultan Said and the Paramount Sheikh of Abu Dhabi. But on 31 August 1952, the Saudis, not just exasperated that the process was taking so long, but fearful that the British would arbitrate in favour of Oman, dispatched an armed force to occupy the Oasis with Aramco's considerable logistical help. No sooner had they taken occupation than the Saudi Government launched a campaign designed to gain acceptance of their rule of Buraimi within the Imamate of Oman, going so far as sending a message to the Imam in Nizwa urging him to recognise the occupation and join Saudi Arabia in expelling alien influences from Oman. But the unexpected happened. The Imam rejected such blandishments, which as an inducement also included a very considerable amount of cash. Following discussion with his advisers, the Imam sent a message to Sultan Said offering his cooperation in any attempt to expel the invaders. The Sultan was not slow to respond, sending the Imam money, camels, rifles and ammunition with which to aid in ending the Saudi occupation. Upon receiving news of the occupation of Buraimi, the Sultan had also taken immediate action, proving that he was equal to such an hour of crisis. He set about establishing an expedition force of some 8,000 tribesmen, which assembled on camels at Sohar on the Batinah coastal corridor, from where they planned to ride on the Oasis, about 100 kilometres distant. For once the merchants of Muscat abandoned their well-practised art of opportunism and enlightened self-interest, donating supplies of food and ammunition free of charge. The crisis had the extremely beneficial effect of uniting Sultan and Imam, the people of the coast and the interior. On 7 October they were ready to set out to evict the Saudis from the Buraimi Oasis. But neither man had taken into account the British, or at least the ability of the American Government to have an overbearing influence on London in all things foreign. Not surprisingly the Saudis had been appalled at the rejection by the Imam of their overtures and were seriously upset when word reached them of Sultan Said's 8,000-strong force, knowing only too well that their occupation force would be quickly routed in the face of such determination by the Omanis to defend their territorial integrity. To stave off the humiliation of retreat or defeat, the Saudis pleaded with the American presence in the Kingdom to coerce the British into putting Sultan Said under pressure to disband his tribesmen and return to the table of arbitration.

In due course the British Consul, a Major Chauncey, made a journey of high panic from Muscat to Sohar with Britain's latest demands. He was doing Washington's bidding via the Foreign Office in London. So on 18 October Sultan Said ordered his greatly disillusioned and dispirited tribesmen to stand down. The very best the Sultan could do as a means of salvaging his Government's reputation was to have the British Consul confirm publicly in front of the assembled force that Britain was in favour of finding a peaceful solution through a continuation of the arbitration process. The strategy was designed to put responsibility for the stand-down on Britain's shoulders, as opposed to the Sultan's. The dispersal of the tribesmen was a disaster for Sultan Said, demonstrating in the eyes of his own people that he remained subject to British influence in the governance of the land and that, put to the test of asserting his own authority, he had utterly failed. Had the force marched on Buraimi and evicted the Saudis (which it would most certainly have done) the opposite effect would have been achieved. It was a great loss as Sultan Said's reputation of being his own man in his own realm could have paid enormous dividends for him and the country. It is no exaggeration to suggest that if the Buraimi operation had gone ahead, the unity it could have generated would almost certainly have averted the civil war into which the country was plunged just three years later.

Yet again Britain's intervention had changed the course of Oman's history and, given the nature of the intervention, things could never be quite the same between the Sultan and the people he governed, as indeed it had not been for so many of his ruling ancestors following an intrusion into the affairs of the country by British representatives. Just three years later, the British recommended military action to both Sultan Said and the Paramount Sheikh of Abu Dhabi, realising that any agreement which left even a nominal Saudi presence in Buraimi would be totally unacceptable to the people of the oasis. The indignation of the tribesmen at this British *volte face* can be easily imagined, having been so imperiously dispersed at Sohar. The Saudi occupation of Buraimi was brought to an end on 26 October 1955, by the British-led Trucial Oman Scouts (whose headquarters were in the Sheikhdom of Abu Dhabi), and a detachment of the Sultan's Armed Forces. But by that time the political landscape of Oman had changed yet again, a new configuration that was to bring another armed conflict, but on this occasion one much closer to home.

Imam Khalili, with whom Sultan Said had worked closely in the interests of all the people of Muscat and Oman, had died in May 1954. Following the Imamate pattern of elected rule he was replaced by Ghalib bin Ali Al Hinai, a man known for his austere views and, more ominously for Sultan Said, his attachment to Saudi Arabia. On his deathbed, Imam Khalili had withdrawn his earlier support for Ghalib as his successor following an appeal to do so from a prominent leader of the powerful Al Harthy tribe. They feared that rule by Ghalib would quickly lead to widespread conflict. Sultan Said knew of Ghalib's instincts and sympathies only too well and had attempted to prevent his election but to no avail. While Said had attempted to forestall Ghalib's bid for power through contact with tribal leaders in the interior, he had been unable to neutralise the tactical measures taken by Ghalib's brother, Talib, who was the Regional Governor of Rostaq and as such in a good position to influence people in his brother's favour.

Imam Ghalib was a man in a hurry, not just to consolidate his power but to extend it, a strategy supported by his Saudi sympathisers with guns, cash and the promise of recognition if the new Imam declared the Imamate independent of Muscat. At the back of the Imam's haste was the possibility that major discoveries of oil would be found in the interior, particularly at Ibri, where the Iraq Petroleum Company was prospecting at the time. The company, preferring to operate in areas under the Sultan's jurisdiction and thus be recipients of his protection, appealed to Muscat to act. In October 1954, a detachment of the Sultan's armed forces marched into Ibri, driving out the representatives of the Imam and, in taking possession of the town, cutting his lines of communication with his Saudi backers to the north of Ibri in Buraimi. Ghalib reacted with predictable fury, unilaterally declaring the Imamate independent of Muscat. His self-styled State of Oman, backed by Saudi money, opened an office in Cairo and applied for membership of the Arab League. But the fate of the Imamate was now written in the sand and with the Sultan emboldened by his force's successful operation, its days were truly numbered. Said's most cherished political goal was now in sight: the reunification of his country. All he had to do was to wait for an opportune moment to strike. In September of the following year a development took place which acted as the catalyst for what was to come, and with it, the time of waiting had well and truly passed.

A British Intelligence Officer in the service of the Sultan's armed forces, Colonel Malcolm Dennison, reported to Salalah where Sultan Said was in residence that an Egyptian intelligence operative had arrived in the Imamate capital of Nizwa via Saudi Arabia and the Buraimi Oasis. His express purpose was to liaise with those officials of Ghalib charged with establishing the Imamate as an independent sovereign state. Within a month of this, as we have already seen, the Saudi occupation of Buraimi had been brought to an end by the British-led combined force from Abu Dhabi and Oman. The Imamate was now cut in two, its final dismemberment was only a matter of time. Sultan Said acted decisively in December and with the British Trucial Oman Scouts in Buraimi Oasis, ordered his troops stationed at Sohar on the coast, to march into the fortified town of Rostaq in the interior and occupy it in his name. The choice of Rostaq had been carefully made, as a prelude to an attack on Nizwa. The attack on Rostaq was launched on 13 December and following four days of battle it fell to the forces of the Sultan, but not before Talib made good his escape westwards across the desert to the land of his backers, the Kingdom of Saudi Arabia. On 15 December a separate detachment of the Sultan's army, the Muscat and Oman Field Force, marched into Nizwa with virtually no resistance and occupied the town's imposing fort. Imam Ghalib had earlier distributed guns to local tribesmen with instructions to fight, but none of them did, so he fled to Saudi Arabia and exile as his brother had done just days before.

The Imamate was now finally at an end and Said crowned his achievement of unification with a symbolic gesture evocative of the new age that Oman was soon to enter, when the camel would give way to the Cadillac: he drove in a motor car from Salalah in the far south of his realm, through Oman's great central desert region, onto Nizwa and Ibri, finally arriving in the Buraimi Oasis. From there to Sohar he journeyed by camel in traditional style, but returned to the car for the final leg of his journey down the Batinah coastal corridor to Muscat. It was the very first time that many Omanis saw their Sultan and the first time, too, for them to see a motorised vehicle. When in Nizwa, on 24 December, Sultan Said had addressed local tribal leaders in the ancient long room of the town's great fort, while outside an estimated 5,000 assembled from far and wide to see the undisputed ruler of Muscat and Oman. It was an historic occasion and both the Sultan and the Omani people knew it well enough. In his address Sultan Said said that he had taken his course of action in the interests of national unity and to put an end to a situation in which Muslim was pitted against Muslim. Speaking in a place where, only hours before the last Imam of Oman had made declarations on the durability of the Imamate, the Sultan publicly offered amnesty to all those ready to work with him in establishing the unity of the country through a central administration. He also guaranteed continued employment for Imamate officials in such an administration. The success of his forces' occupation of Ibri, the eviction of the Saudis from the Buraimi Oasis, the capture of Rostaq and Nizwa, his unprecedented royal progress by car and camel, his declaration on the unity of the country, allied to his words of reconciliation in the former centre of Imamate rule, had a powerful impact on the people of Oman. They felt justified in their new-found confidence in the Sultan and, indeed, in the future of the country as a unified state.

No finer evidence of the public goodwill generated in the interior by this sequence of events can be given than by recalling the arrival at the gates of Muscat of some 500 tribesmen mounted on camels, a week after their Sultan had arrived there by car. The Sultan, greatly moved by such an unprecedented demonstration of fidelity, personally greeted each and every one of them.

Yet Sultan Said failed totally to capitalise on a political and social circumstance unique in the history of his country. It was one from which, had he not retreated so soon back within the walls of his Palace after his string of successes, he could have led his people into a completely new beginning; one made possible by the national unity he achieved and, most crucially, the coming revenues from Arabia's black, viscous gold: oil!

It is difficult to identify the reasons for his abrupt return to this solitary life, broken only by infrequent contact with his senior officials, usually by radio telephone, such as his Military Secretary and his Personal Adviser, both of whom were British. He was well cast in the mould of an absolute Arab ruler, which confirms that he was by nature conservative, one who knew only too well that Arab coalitions, such as the one between the people of the coast and the interior he now ruled, are notoriously fragile; it only had to be thought that favour or familiarity was being extended or exercised in either direction to prompt a rapid return to the hostilities and consequent divisions of the past. Sultan Said also knew that any frequent contact with the people would inevitably lead to an endless chorus of appeals for cash and gifts which he simply did not have the resources required to respond to, quite apart from his frugal nature. In short, the Sultan was playing safe in his deliberate policy of remaining remote and inaccessible except to the very-favoured few (usually his British expatriate advisers), and continuing with a policy of minimalist government at least until a development programme could be paid for once oil had been discovered in commercially viable quantities. All he wanted was time, but in the event this was the one commodity not to be made available to him. Way before the commercial production of oil first commenced in 1964, a remnant of Oman's past re-emerged to ambush the present.

As we have already seen, with the fall of Rostaq and Nizwa, Imam Ghalib and his brother Talib had fled to Saudi Arabia. Talib, always one with an excess of revolutionary zeal, had not taken the defeat and humiliation of the Imamate with equanimity. From Dammam, on Saudi Arabia's eastern shore, he had organised Omani exiles in the Kingdom and other states in the Gulf into the 'Oman Revolutionary Movement'. He then trained them and plotted for an opportune moment to return home and raise once more the flag of Imamate rule. In April 1957, he began a campaign of secret infiltration of Oman, landing groups of well-armed and well-equipped men under the cover of darkness, at several points on the country's coast. On 24 April seven of his men were captured well inland and on 5 May an estimated 150 were reported by tribal leaders to be moving inland, through the Sharqiya desert region in eastern Oman. The Sultan was sent messages advising him of such rebel infiltration, not just by loyal tribal leaders in the interior but by his own brother, Sayyid Tarik bin Taimour. The latter message alerted Said on 17 May that more armed rebels were expected to arrive on Oman's eastern shores on 14 June. Within a few days Tarik received a radio message from the Sultan's Military Secretary, Brigadier Waterfield ordering that no action be taken against the rebels and that the Sultan's Batinah Force, based at Sohar, should remain in barracks. A former Major in the British Army who had been seconded to Oman, he had resigned in order to become a contract officer in the service of the Sultan, who promoted him to the rank of Brigadier. Remarkably still no action was ordered, when on 14 June the anticipated rebels landed at the exact place on the coast given in Tarik's message to the Sultan. It would appear that, together with Brigadier Waterfield, the Sultan just did not believe that an armed attack of any consequence was about to be launched. Such an assumption was ill-founded indeed, for within days the rebels mounted spectacularly successful assaults on the fortified towns of Bahla and Nizwa, capturing and occupying both centres. The country was yet again in a state of civil war. The Sultan's Oman Regiment, formerly known as the Muscat and Oman Field Force, was severely mauled, becoming so demoralised after suffering such human loss and defeat that it never recovered and had to be disbanded. The situation deteriorated so rapidly that, with the victorious Talib raising in his brother's name the white flag of the Imam over Nizwa, Sultan Said had but one course left open to him. He appealed to the British for swift military assistance. Such an appeal served fresh notice to the people of the interior that the Sultan, despite his recent success, still relied upon the British to maintain his grip on power. This pivotal factor remained a long-held resentment of many in Oman and fed their disenchantment with Al Busaid rule. Naturally enough, Talib used the plea as a means of powerful, public propaganda against Sultan Said and rekindled by design old hatreds. In the immediate wake of the success of Talib's rebel groups, the Sultan ordered tribal leaders who had remained loyal to him to institute a systematic programme of reprisals against those in the interior who had cooperated in the return of the armed envoys of the Imamate. Date orchards, irrigation systems and homes were destroyed. This policy of swift retribution was not one that had universal support. The Sultan's own army recommended military action to dislodge rebel strongholds, as opposed to punitive measures against civilians, while some tribal leaders petitioned for amnesty as the best means of preventing further bloodshed. Most significant was the recommendation of his own brother, Tarik, that the only way to resolve this latest conflict without leaving in its wake a residual bitterness against the throne was a twin policy of firm, but fair, rule, to run parallel with a programme of reconstruction in the interior.

Lamentably, Sultan Said rejected such alternatives, with spasmodic acts of reprisal continuing, not just during the conflict but long after it had been resolved by the defeat of the rebels. But achieving that victory was far from easy and even the initial attempts by the British were frustrated. The appeal by the Sultan to London for military support was promptly answered and the fight-back began following the arrival in the country of a detachment of the Cameronians, supported by the Trucial Oman Scouts, who had so successfully ejected the Saudis from the Buraimi Oasis. The troops on the ground, which included the Sultan's Northern Frontier and Muscat Regiments, had support in the skies above from the British Royal Air Force (RAF), and the combined assault quickly brought about initial success. By the end of August both Bahla and Nizwa had been retaken and the rebels driven into the towering heights of the Jabal Akhdar, Oman's celebrated Green Mountain. From this mountain fastness with its many places of concealment, the rebels continued to harry the Sultan's Armed Forces and indeed the British with arms covertly supplied by their Saudi backers. A casualty of one such skirmish was the British Arabist and Intelligence Officer, Malcolm Dennison, then a Captain in the Sultan's Army, who sustained an injury which was to cause him pain and partial disability for the remainder of his days.

The many Omani-British attempts to dislodge the rebels from their strongholds on the Green Mountain were a complete failure. Having inflicted as much damage as they could achieve, the British withdrew in the autumn of 1957 fearful of becoming involved in a long drawn-out domestic war in a far-flung foreign field. In 1957 Britain was still smarting under its ignominious defeat at Suez a year earlier and London was particularly sensitive to becoming embroiled in foreign adventures east of the canal zone, never mind accusations of conducting neo-colonial, military campaigns by the councils of the world.

In a highly unlikely marriage of diplomatic convenience, those Arab states enamoured of Pan-Arabism and inspired by Egyptian President Gamel Abdel Nasser's success in the Suez Canal Affair, joined forces with the arch-conservative reactionary Saudi Arabia to publicly discredit Britain's involvement in what became known as the 'Green Mountain War'. Meanwhile in Oman itself, with the Cameronians, Trucial Oman Scouts and the RAF gone, the rebels stepped up their guerrilla style 'hit and run' tactics: mining roads; mounting sniper attacks; ambushing patrols of the Sultan's Armed Forces. Despite many spirited attempts, without significant tactical British military support the Omanis were quite unable to defeat the rebels. As 1957 drew to an end, they were reduced to defending Nizwa against attack, keeping open channels of communication to Muscat and occasionally blockading rebel routes of supply through the Green Mountain's many passes. The situation could not continue and London decided that the best possible course was to attempt a knockout offensive (even if that meant a temporary British involvement), as opposed to seeing the conflict turn into another long-running guerrilla war, with the attendant danger that it would escalate into something much worse. Britain dispatched its Undersecretary of State for War, Julian Amery, to Muscat in January 1958.

Following a round of meetings with Sultan Said, Amery returned to London, but not before inviting Sultan Said to pay a reciprocal visit to the British capital. In July the Sultan duly arrived, where he held talks with the Secretary of State for Foreign Affairs, Selwyn Lloyd. In return for granting an extension to an earlier undertaking that gave the RAF landing rights and accompanying service facilities in Muscat, Salalah and on the off-shore island of Masirah, Britain entered into a new agreement with Sultan Said (confirmed by an exchange of letters) which gave London a greatly enhanced role in the support and development of Oman's Armed Forces. Because such a role subsequently became so pivotal to the armed insurrection still some seven years distant and served to involve Britain still further in Oman's affairs, including its ability to 'make' and 'unmake' Sultans, the relevant paragraphs of Selwyn Lloyd's letter to Sultan Said of 25 July 1958, are of no small interest:

In pursuance of the common interest of Your Highness and Her

Majesty's Government in furthering the progress of the Sultanate
of Muscat and Oman, Her Majesty's Government in the United
Kingdom has agreed to extend assistance towards the
strengthening of Your Highness's Armed Forces. Her Majesty's
Government will also, at Your Highness's request, make available
Regular Officers on secondment from the British Army, who will,
while serving in the Sultanate, form an integral part of Your
Highness's Armed Forces. The terms and conditions of service of
those seconded British Officers have been agreed with Your
Highness. Her Majesty's Government will also provide training
facilities for members of Your Highness's Armed Forces and will
make advice available on training and other matters as may be
required by Your Highness. Her Majesty's Government will also
assist Your Highness in the establishment of an Air Force as an
integral part of Your Highness's Armed Forces, and they will make
available personnel to this Air Force. Your Highness has approved
the conclusion of an agreement for the extension of the present
arrangements regarding civil aviation and the use by the Royal Air
Force of the airfields at Salalah and Masirah. We also discussed the
economic development problems of the Sultanate and Her
Majesty's Government agreed to assist Your Highness in carrying
out a civil development programme which will include the
improvement of roads, medical and educational facilities and an
agricultural programme.

The Sultan made swift reply, in which he confirmed that Lloyd's letter and
his response 'should be regarded as constituting an agreement between us
and your Government'. In its implication of British involvement in Oman's
affairs, at both the military and civil levels, this latest agreement between
Muscat and London went further than that implied by the Treaty of Seeb
some 37 years earlier. Together with the treaties that predated it, the
agreement gave Britain financial control through the payment of loans and
subsidies; a predominant military influence through the expedient of
having a battalion of British-led troops stationed in the country; direct
political control as represented by a resident Political Agent; the right to
forbid bilateral agreements with other states; and established for Britain
exclusive, extra-territorial rights.

It remains a catalogue of political footwork by London across a 160-year
period which cannot but be a source of astonishment today. Of course

there always were threads of convenience, which were of immediate benefit to whoever happened to be ruling Oman at the time, running through all the treaties and agreements between 1798 and 1958. This latest agreement between Muscat and London offered very real hope to a beleaguered Sultan Said that British military power would, once and for all, smash into history through the discharge of superior firepower not just the representatives of Imamate rule but the very idea of its re-establishment in Oman. What would almost certainly have been less palatable to the Sultan was the demand in Selwyn Lloyd's letter, the understanding that in addition to a greatly improved military contribution to resolve Oman's difficulties, Britain was also to send to the country pioneers in the art of turning guns into ploughshares: civil-development experts who would advise on the improvement of communications in a land where the camel and the donkey reigned supreme as a means of transportation, promoting the establishment of medical and educational institutions; introducing new concepts of agriculture that would improve levels of production.

It has often been said (and written) that Sultan Said loathed the idea of enabling the nature of social change which the development of a state's infrastructure inevitably introduces. In so many instances this has been a wilful misrepresentation of his true character by those with their own self-serving agenda; that of continually seeking to justify his overthrow. What Sultan Said feared most was change that could not be paid for out of Oman's resources, making frequent reference in private conversation to Oman's history of debt which had led to its loss of sovereignty.

The 1958 agreement was not made at a time when the oil prospectors were making encouraging noises, but although commercial production did not commence for a further six years, Sultan Said had justified confidence that in accepting this latest British demand, he should have some money in the national Treasury to pay for developments, by the time any recommendations for national plans were implemented. But first came the implementation of the 'carrot' side of the agreement: the men and materials with which to wage war on the rebels and win for Oman a lasting peace in the process. And won it was. During the second half of 1958 the British RAF pounded rebel strongholds on the Green Mountain – in military parlance 'the softening up process' – while on the ground the British Colonel, David Smilley, a professional soldier of exemplary skill and courage, not only reorganised the various elements of Sultan Said's army into a highly credible fighting force, but became its very first

Commander. In November two squadrons of Britain's celebrated Special Air Service (SAS) were called into action en-route to England from service in Malaya, subsequently leading commando raids against the rebels. The end was not long in coming. In January 1959 a combined attack of SAS commandos, supported by a detachment of the British Life Guards and soldiers of the retrained army, successfully stormed the last rebel position on the Green Mountain. The rebel leaders managed to escape to Saudi Arabia, where their cause was given financial support by the Kingdom's Government together with Arab nationalist states for some considerable time, enabing isolated 'hit and run' cross-border tactics, such as sniper attacks and the mining of roads, to continue right up to the summer of 1962, when they petered out. But the Imamate was now finally at an end and with its total destruction the tribal confederations in Oman's interior, upon which it had relied for its very existence, collapsed too. As a result Sultan Said became the first Omani ruler for almost 200 years to preside over a unified state, with its people from the far north to the far south owing allegiance to him. In effect, albeit through British military intervention, he had been given another chance to capitalise on his position as the country's undisputed leader, one whose writ ran throughout the land of Muscat and Oman.

But yet again he withdrew from the nation's eye, for a variety of reasons that are difficult to establish. They probably ranged from fears for his own security; the importance to him of his beloved Dhofar, or most likely, a growing apprehension about being on the receiving end of the interference promised by the imminent arrival of those British civil servants bent on foisting upon him a programme of national development. In any event, Sultan Said left Muscat for his palace by the sea in Salalah with the Green Mountain War behind him, where he remained a virtual recluse for the remaining eleven and a half years of his reign. He could have made a nationwide tour during which he would have met a broad cross-section of the population, learning at first hand of their difficulties and expectations; explaining the economic difficulties he had inherited and resolved, with the prospect of oil revenues a distinct possibility he could have declared the plans he had to improve the people's lot through better communications and the delivery of health and education services. Had he done so the fate that ultimately befell him may not have come to pass. Not only would such an initiative have greatly enhanced his standing among the people of Muscat and Oman, it would have been very much in sympathy with the time-honoured Arab tradition of giving the people, through informal meetings between the ruler and the ruled, a forum where the concerns of the individual and the community can be openly expressed. Neither is it fanciful to suggest that Sultan Said was giving careful thought as to how best the revenues from oil could be used in the national interest. As we shall see, in January 1968, just five months after the very first exports of oil commenced from Oman, he issued a detailed explanation of the chronic economic situation with which he had been faced when coming to the throne in 1932, the measures he had taken to rescue the country from debt and the plans he had to improve the nation's condition through a comprehensive programme of civil development paid for with oil revenues. But by then, it was too late by far. In fact his 1959 retreat into self-inflicted isolation was the turning point for the people of Muscat and Oman. From that time onwards, resentment and hostility grew towards him, which, all too soon led to renewed conflict and, in the event, an excuse to remove him from the throne.

It can now be recorded in mitigation that his express fears over the rapid implementation of a British-sponsored development programme were twofold. He was concerned it would raise expectations among the general population that would quickly outstrip revenues from oil before they were actually received; also that his creaking, antique administration, which was minimal in the extreme, would not be able to contain the demands a radical development programme would place upon it and that such a situation would inevitably lead to yet further British involvement in the domestic affairs of Oman. Sultan Said never, ever forgot the simple and abiding truth that a country's political direction is driven by the state of its finances. His inheritance of national debt and the loss of national sovereignty which had accompanied it was an object lesson in how a state's affairs should not be managed and it was this very same awareness that dictated all he did as ruler of Muscat and Oman. While the conservatism this represents led to his eventual overthrow, there are few today who would not find sympathy and understanding for the attitude struck by Oman's ruler.

But the deed had been done, the deal had been struck, and in return for having his enemies defeated and scattered to the winds, Sultan Said was now obliged to accept a further intrusion into the affairs of his state. The British were coming yet again, not the welcome boys in khaki and airforce blue, but the tropical-kitted equivalent of Whitehall's pinstriped brigade. In this particular instance, however, there is good cause to entertain some sympathy for London. Both the politicians and the

Foreign Office mandarins were becoming wary of empire and its problems, not the least being the constant braying in the global forums such as the United Nations, at what was tediously termed the country's 'neo-colonial' conduct in states like Oman where direct colonial rule by London had never been established. In what was most definitely the post-colonial era for the former empires of the major European powers, entanglements such as was evidently the case in Muscat and Oman became increasingly less attractive. Yet in what was regarded internationally as very much a British constituency, Oman still held very real benefits for Britain, witnessed by the paragraph in the Selwyn Lloyd letter confirming the extension of landing rights in the country for the RAF. Oman was regarded by London, quite rightly, as an important stepping stone on the way to the country's remaining colonial possessions in the Far East: Malaya, where a jungle war was being waged against Marxist-inspired guerrillas, and Hong Kong.

Ever mindful that trade does indeed follow the flag, the British were also anxious to be well prepared to reap the financial advantage that an oil-generating economy would bring. Development meant not only the opportunity to be seen as attempting to bring Oman from its mediaeval condition into the contemporary world, but commercial possibilities as well. As everyone knew, not least Sultan Said, development costs money and where money was to be spent Britain wanted to be on the receiving end of a healthy amount of it. So it naturally followed that London's policy makers wanted to be seen in the wider world as bringing its well-established influence to bear on the Sultan to accept change that would radically improve the lot of the Omani people, while at the same time not upsetting existing arrangements which were highly beneficial to Britain and which continued to give it a crucially important presence in a vital region of the world.

The arrival in the country of British agents of change was not the only pressure bearing down on Oman's ruler. Following a four-year catalogue of failure and disappointment to find oil in commercially viable quantities, the Iraq Petroleum Company and its associates, which included Royal Dutch Shell, took the decision in April 1960 to withdraw from the country. Shell remained, holding 85 per cent of the total concession area and together with two smaller oil companies holding the remaining 15 per cent formed under Royal Dutch Shell management, Petroleum Development Oman (PDO). Shell, with its well-earned reputation for skill in oil exploration and its legendary perseverance, began a new programme of drilling and became increasingly hopeful of making significant finds. All of this was relayed to Sultan Said in his Palace at Salalah, usually by radio telephone, the link he used to maintain contact with his British-led army. For a man who had been so marked by his royal inheritance of state debt and the consequent need to live a frugal existence, the prospect of imminent funds way beyond the dreams of avarice was every bit as much an intimidation as living with so little. Though not worldly in the sense that the term usually implies, Sultan Said knew only too well that with the prospect of previously undreamt of riches would come additional pressures on him. It was not just 'the 10 per cent' school of sharks that bask and cruise through the world's oil lakes waiting for an opportune moment to make a killing which concerned him, but also those who were keeping him on the throne. The British, via their political, military and civilian presence in the country, would step up pressure on him to institute a rapid development programme and his previous and well justified response to such pressure in the past, namely that the country's meagre finances were not sufficient to make any significant impact, would no longer be acceptable

Within months of the exchange of letters in July 1958, the British-appointed Development Secretary had arrived in Muscat. Colonel Hugh Boustead was a man well cast in the British military colonial role; a man used to not just seeing to it that the Empire was kept in good order through a force of arms, but a brilliant administrator too, with a particular appetite and aptitude for innovation. The British, knowing Sultan Said and his conservative approach to new men with new ideas, had prepared well, making sure that he had had time to meet Bousted on his way to London via the British Colony of Aden. For his part Bousted knew and liked Arabs, with whom he had worked in Aden and in the Hadrahmaut, east of the great port city. There he had worked well with the local Sultans in Makulla and Quaiti, establishing in the process significant civil improvements in communications, health and education.

The Development Department was allotted £250,000 a year by Britain, with which Boustead made modest progress on the construction of earth-surfaced roads, the establishment of clinics and dispensaries, opened a school in the Muscat port suburb of Muttrah and two agriculture institutes, one in Nizwa, the other at Sohar on the agriculturally rich Batinah coastal corridor. Colonel Boustead remained as Oman's Development Secretary for three years. In 1971, following his knighthood, his memoirs of a military colonial life, *The Winds of*

*Morning*, were published. They contained an illustrative impression of Muscat and Oman at the time of his arrival there in October, 1958:

> Muscat was in a deplorable condition. This could only in part be blamed on local unrest, which amounted to rebellion against the Sultan's rule. I had seen what could be done in the Hadrahmaut and in Quaiti state in particular, with a revenue about one half of what the Sultan of Muscat drew in customs duties; yet here there were no medical services in the whole country. I made a tour soon after my arrival with an economic expert and a representative from the Development Division at the British Embassy in Beirut. The latter told the Sultan after the tour that in 25 years of experience of most of the countries in the Middle East, he had never seen a people so poverty-stricken or so debilitated with disease capable of treatment and cure. This report led to the building of some 20 health centres and dispensaries throughout the Sultanate. Although the rebel forces had been driven into the Jabal Akhdar, a 10,000-foot mountain massif, irregular bands still penetrated the plain and shot up convoys. But their principal activity at the time was planting mines along the roads.The large, plastic mines caused many casualties. It was not the most auspicious moment to inaugurate a brand new Development Department, the more so since the Sultan was, I felt, very half-hearted about plans for health, education, agriculture and so on. My first job was a road, something the Sultan was really keen about, but before I could start on anything I had to organise the Department and find staff.

Boustead's use of the very British art of understatement in relation to the guerrilla attacks by Imamate rebels from their remaining strongholds on the Green Mountain is an appropriate reminder to record that following their final defeat three months later, in January 1959, Sultan Said ordered a fresh round of reprisals against village communities on the Mountain who had collaborated with Talib's attempt to re-establish Imamate rule. The nature of the reprisals were particularly harsh, involving a withdrawal of the right to travel to neighbouring towns, such as Nizwa, to sell produce and a denial of passports with which to travel to other Gulf states to seek work. The British did raise their objections to such measures, as did the Sultan's younger brother, Sayyid Tarik, who was promptly banished from Oman for his pains. But on this one issue, where it would have been beneficial in the long term for the Sultan to have yielded to the British, he proved to be very much his own man. Such acts of reprisal only served to increase the resentment among the general population towards Sultan Said. But his appetite for firm rule, always an article of faith for the arch-conservative even when it can only be counter-productive, prevailed with the Sultan. Seeking justification for the reprisals, he pointed out to his critics the sporadic cross-border attacks by the rump of Imamate forces in Saudi Arabia which continued up to the summer of 1962 before finally petering out.

As admirable as Boustead's efforts were in attempting to improve social conditions for Omanis during his time as Development Secretary, they proved to be too little too late for many in the country, particularly the young men, with the almost inevitable result that the pace of illegal immigration increased to other Gulf states and beyond. By the early 1960s it was estimated that some 70,000 Omani men were living and working in Saudi Arabia to the west and in other Gulf states to the north, a considerable proportion of a total population then put at approximately 400,000 souls. Many found work in the oil industry, others worked in offices, hotels or in domestic capacities (in Kuwait for example, Omani immigrants were insultingly referred to as 'wet workers'). Others enlisted in armed units, such as the Abu Dhabi Defence Force and the British-led Trucial Oman Scouts, where they were well-regarded for their discipline and instinctive military skills. With their innate sense of political awareness heightened by the greater public airing that Arab nationalism was given outside Oman, some made their ways to those states which were at the time beacons of Pan-Arabism, such as Syria, Iraq and Egypt. From there many went on to places of study in China, the Soviet Union and the Stalinist states of Eastern Europe. As we shall see, this development had a particularly significant bearing on events in Oman during the latter half of the 1960s and the early part of the 1970s, a decade which from its very beginning ushered in dramatic change which swept all before it, relegating the Oman of old to the history books.

Colonel Hugh Boustead's frustrated departure from Oman in October 1961 was followed by the appointment of two other Britons to the post of Development Secretary, both of whom presided over a modest and cautious programme of civil development. They liaised with the Sultan in his Salalah Palace, often with considerable difficulty and only by radio telephone. To add insult to injury this was usually through a third party.

But then in 1964, in a development which was to ignite dramatic, social, economic and political change, PDO announced that oil had at long last been found in commercially viable quantities in the country's interior. From that moment on things would never be the same again, indeed could not be the same ever again in Arabia's most extraordinary land. While it took time for PDO to develop the necessary, highly technical arrangements for the oil to be piped from the interior to a coastal terminal for export, it was soon confirmed that all would be in place for exports to commence in 1967 and with it an influx of previously undreamt of revenues.

The British, ever anxious to relieve themselves of the financial burden of supporting Oman, which in any case they now saw as quite unjustified, withdrew the annual subsidy which funded the Development Department in March 1967, even though the first exports of oil did not commence for another six months.

Sultan Said, sitting in his antique palace on the Salalah coast, with no executive administrative staff of any real consequence to support him, and maintaining infrequent contact with his capital over 1,000 kilometres to the north, cannot but have realised that with the country on the threshold of entering the oil era, the winds of change were now going to blow exceedingly strong, whether he liked it or not. It would be particularly insensitive not to entertain some sympathy for Oman's ruler who, for all his failings, was a man of considerable integrity and dignity, generous to those he trusted and who served him well, a monarch in the style of the sixteenth century destined by birth to face the challenges of the twentieth. Against all the odds, he had delivered his state from debt, yet had rarely been without internal challenge to his throne. If he was suspicious of sudden change it was because in the turbulent, fractious climate of Oman, he knew well enough that change does not always bring benefits to those that are promised them. When that occurs, it just generates further dissent. By holding his own, being his very own man, he did at the least prove a strength of character that would have received nothing but applause in different circumstances. The minimalist nature of his Government was no worse and, in some instances, considerably more humane than others existing on the Arabian Peninsula at the time.

The order he gave in January 1968 for the establishment of a Development Board is the most reliable evidence we have which demonstrates that while it may well have filled him with foreboding for the future, Sultan Said knew that the change oil would inevitably bring had to be catered for. It was one that greatly exceeded the remit of the British-sponsored Development Department which preceded it. With the Sultan's Government paying the bills, a Development Board Director and Secretary were appointed. They were both British: Mr Pelly and Mr Heber-Percy, the latter having links with the British counter-intelligence organisation MI6. An architect was commissioned to prepare a blueprint plan for the development of Muscat and the portside suburb of Muttrah and a Director of Public Works was recruited from India.

From August 1967, the oil flowed out and the revenues flowed in, with the most important man of the hour being PDO's Managing Director Mr Francis Hughes, another Briton who was a frequent and welcome visitor to Sultan Said's Salalah Palace. As the significance of the revenues quickly became ever more apparent, the Sultan appointed a Petroleum Affairs Secretary, a Major Hirst formerly of the British Army, but he proved so incompetent and generally ill-suited to the task he was expected to undertake that he fell by the wayside. Yet another Briton with access to the Sultan at virtually any time of his choosing, who was everything that Major Hirst was not, was Peter Mason, the General Manager of the British Bank of the Middle East. At the time exports of oil commenced, the company had enjoyed a monopoly in the country for almost 30 years. Peter Mason, for excellent reasons, quickly commanded the trust and confidence of Sultan Said and remained a close personal ally of the Omani ruler for his remaining time on the throne. From the expatriate clique of British Army and Intelligence Officers serving the Sultan, only civilians Francis Hughes and Peter Mason distinguished themselves by being truly equal to the demands of the hour; the change and new, national direction that it was generating had a civil dimension not suited to a continuing obsession with military matters.

Nonetheless the Sultan, ever conscious and anxious about his own personal security and that of the State, devoted some 50 per cent of the new revenues to his Armed Forces, the administration and day-to-day operations of which were still the responsibility of Brigadier Waterfield. In February 1970, Waterfield resigned at London's request, and was replaced by a Colonel Hugh Oldman, a man with a somewhat pompous air according to contemporary Omani reports, who was fond of including in his vocabulary words such as 'integrity, honour and loyalty'. Yet he was to blithely abdicate all three at the time of Sultan Said's forced removal from the throne of Oman. This apparent air of being of superior conduct, allied to a keen sense of his own importance, prompted Oldman to demand the title Defence Secretary, as opposed to that of Military Secretary. It was subsequently a source of wry amusement to the Sultan, given that Oldman did nothing to defend Oman's Head of State and, indeed, plotted against him with a Britannia which proved all too ready to waive the rules, in a country awash with previously unseen riches.

Sultan Said was planning change in the form of a programme of national development and knew only too well that during the years of state poverty, great deprivation had been visited on the Omani people. All this was apparent in a statement he himself wrote and had published in January 1968, five months after the first exports of oil commenced. It is a statement essentially explaining the financial situation he inherited; his effort and consequent success in resolving them and a clear unambiguous declaration of his intention to launch a whole new series of national development projects paid for by oil revenues. It is in a crucially important respect a statement of self-justification for the dire social conditions of the country over which he ruled. There is no real doubt that had his regime not fallen just two and a half years later in a British-engineered Palace coup, the actual pace of development would undoubtedly have been significantly slower than subsequently proved to be the case. As we shall see, however, there is now a growing body of opinion among economists and strategic state planners in Oman and elsewhere, that many of the social and economic difficulties which now trouble the Sultanate, have as their origins the dash for modernity that took place in the 1970s and 1980s. Such an awareness comes with the benefit of hindsight, yet it is a matter for record that there were those in the early 1970s who cautioned against a spending spree of such magnitude that the national coffers were all but bare by the middle of that decade. That situation was only saved by the Organisation of Petroleum Exporting Countries (OPEC), of which Oman is not a member, coincidentally, instigating massive price rises. They also warned that the recruitment of several hundred thousand labourers from the Indian subcontinent, required in order that the many and varied construction projects could proceed at the speed officially demanded of them, would lead to a failure of artisan skills being transferred in a measured and responsible manner to Omani nationals. This is another structural failure for which the country now pays dear.

However, the January 1968 statement by Sultan Said, known at the time of its publication as 'The Word of Sultan Said bin Taimour' (reproduced in full in the Appendix), is adequate proof that while the pace of development would have been more in keeping with the priorities of an arch-conservative such as the Sultan, the officially-generated line that he had turned his face irrevocably against using oil revenues for national development is a lie; a particularly disgraceful one at that, given that it has been maintained to the present day by those who never cease to remind the world of the high public morals they represent.

But that is the present and in 1968, with the oil revenues pouring in, covetous eyes were cast in Oman's direction. It suddenly began to be described in the Western press as the world's 'last feudal, mediaeval state on Earth'. The very thought of an absolute monarch ruling over less than half a million people, in a country that was ripe for 'development', concentrated minds most marvellously. For development meant that money would have to be spent, a process that could only mean profits of a particularly gratifying kind in such an unregulated land as Oman, with precious few educated, professional executives of its own to act as a check on rapacious, expatriate behaviour. In short, the scramble for Oman was now well and truly on. As 1968 progressed a new element was added to an already high-octane mix, a growing guerrilla war in the legendary Province of Dhofar which could, with a little judicious handling, lead to yet further avenues for making fast money through the sale of arms. The so-called 'Merchants of Death' raised their finely tuned nostrils to the prevailing wind and turning in Oman's direction, took a long, deep and wholly intoxicating inhalation of the air of far-off Arabia Felix.

The means by which the opening shots in the eleven-year-long Dhofar war were made came from the ability of the former Imam of Oman, Ghalib bin Ali, to raise funds from his hosts for those malcontents from the Sultanate. The official line has been that the father of the Dhofar civil war was Sultan Said bin Taimour, through his harsh rule and a prolonged unwillingness to take the people of Muscat and Oman into the twentieth century. But such an assertion, while neatly meeting the requirements of state propaganda, is a gross oversimplification. For the Dhofar war to be put into a realistic and accurate context, the revolutionary fervour of the Pan-Arabism of the 1960s and early 1970s has to be taken into account. There were several factors: the glowing embers of Arab resentment towards the West, and particularly towards Britain for its abdication in 1948 of its responsibility for Palestine; the humiliation of France, Britain and Israel at the hands of Egyptian President Nasser at the time of Suez in

1956; the triumph of nationalist forces over North Yemen's royal regime in 1962. All contributed to fuelling the concept of armed insurrection against Sultan Said by dissident Omanis. Many still regarded him as a willing tool of the British. The revolutionary litanies of Marx, Engels and Lenin made little impact as a rallying cry in the early days of the guerrilla movements formed to overthrow the Sultan. But such idealogical inspiration did come to gain influence and exercise consequent motivation, as the numbers of Omanis who became exposed to it increased as a result of undergoing military training in places like Iraq and later in neighbouring South Yemen. In the revolutionary jargon of the time, the aim of expelling 'the British imperialists and their neo-colonialist running dogs' from Muscat and Oman became as significant to those who had taken up arms as that of overthrowing an autocratic ruler they had come to despise. The role played by the Dhofar War is of such significance in the Oman story that it warrants the chapter devoted to it later in this book. But it is no small irony that at the very moment Sultan Said was ruling a united land and contemplating unprecedented state revenues that would enable him to alleviate the poverty and deprivation of his people, he was so buffeted by the winds of capitalist plenty and the opposing gusts of communism that he was swept ignominiously off his throne and into a subsequent catalogue of state-sponsored denigration from which he is only now slowly but surely emerging.

But while the winds of change grew to hurricane force, howling ever more ominously around the walls of his Salalah Palace, Sultan Said bin Taimour remained inside, virtually a recluse from the modern world which was demanding his full attention in ever more strident tones. For the last few years of his reign he ventured so infrequently out of the Palace that a great many Omanis believed him to be dead and thought that the British were declining to announce the fact for their own ends. As ever with Oman's rulers, personal security was an obsession with Sultan Said and an incident on 28 April 1966 served to justify his fears to some degree.

As he was inspecting a guard of honour made up of soldiers from his Dhofar force, several shots were fired at him by members of his own bodyguard at close range. They missed, though managed to wound their Commander, a Pakistani on contract to the Sultan's army. It was later proved that the would-be assassins were members of an organisation calling itself the Dhofar Liberation Front (of which we will see more later), who had infiltrated the Sultan's army with the express purpose of killing him. His reaction was predictable. Immediate punitive measures were ordered against the Jebal, where the assailants came from, a towering mountain range that overlooks the Salalah Plain and coast. A strictly-enforced economic blockade was mounted against the communities on the mountain and many Dhofari soldiers were dismissed who had no connection with those who fired the shots. Such reprisals had the inevitable effect of alienating still further the Sultan from his people and the punitive measures he had taken proved to be a particularly effective recruitment sergeant for those who not only opposed his rule, but who were to take up arms in an attempt to end it. The most negative aspect of this particular incident was that the Sultan remained within the walls of his Palace for the remainder of his Oman days, with even the occasional visit to London courtesy of the RAF coming to an end. But as the 1960s drew to a close life inside the Palace, with its retinue of servants principally of African origin, continued at a calm and measured pace. The Sultan's wife, Sayyida Mazon bint Ahmed Al Mashani, a kindly Dhofari lady of grace and charm, and mother of Sultan Qaboos, presided over the many and varied domestic arrangements. Visitors were few and then mainly British expatriates. Peter Mason came bearing news of the continuing rise in state revenues from the export of oil, while Francis Hughes would arrive with equally satisfying reports on PDO's production activities. Radio telephone contact continued with the Personal Adviser in Muscat, Major Chauncey, and following Brigadier Waterfield's departure in February 1970, Colonel Oldman would occasionally be invited down from the north to discuss his duties as Defence Secretary. Said being an excellent judge of character, ensured that Oldman was never to enjoy the confidence of the Sultan experienced by his predecessor. On the development front, Development Board Director Pelly, aided by Development Secretary Heber-Percy, pressed slowly but surely ahead with those plans approved by the Sultan, a water supply system in the capital area, the installation of electricity supplies, the development of the port at Muttrah and plans for the minting of a new national currency. So while all was most definitely not well with Oman's world, the Sultan was at least on the throne and ruling over a unified country that was taking its first cautious steps towards the age of modernity.

Inside the walls of the Palace, however, the vulgar and unseemly scramble to spend the oil revenues remained a secondary subject of domestic discussion, with the courtly life of an Arab monarch continuing very much as it always had done. In this context, the sour face of Sultan Said painted by those who, even today, continue to justify his overthrow, is not one faithful to the real picture. Away from the cares of office, Oman's Sultan of the day had in actual fact a very human face indeed. He had a great interest in natural history and its preservation, a quality, incidentally, inherited and maintained most admirably by his son. Sultan Said also had a happy family life, telling a visiting British political figure in a comment on Palace life, 'in the afternoon there is usually a little loving', a gentle indication as to the nature that an Arabian siesta can assume. The British Political Agents and Consuls General, who preceded the Ambassadors from the Court of St James to the Court of Sultan Said, were not salesmen in egalitarian suits as is so often the case in the twenty-first century, but men with the true concept of service in their souls. As the following 1960 letter to the Earl of Hume, then British Foreign Secretary, so adequately demonstrates, these were men with a well-developed and gentle sense of humour:

My Lord.

1. I have the honour to refer to Your Lordship's dispatch No. 8 of the 29th July, in which you requested me to ascertain, on behalf of the Lords Commissioners of the Admiralty, whether the Bb music, enclosed with your dispatch, was a correct and up-to-date rendering of the National Salute to the Sultan of Muscat and Oman.

2. I have encountered certain difficulties in fulfilling this request. The Sultanate has not, since about 1937, possessed a band. None of the Sultan's subjects, as far as I am aware, can read music, which the majority of them regard as sinful. The Manager of the British Bank of the Middle East, who can, does not possess a clarinet. Even if he did, the dignitary who in the absence of the Sultan is the recipient of ceremonial honours and who might be presumed to recognise the tune, is somewhat deaf.

3. Fortunately, I have been able to obtain, and now enclose, a gramaphone record which has on one side a rendering by a British military band of the 'Salutation and March to His Highness the Sultan of Muscat and Oman'. The first part of this tune, which was composed by the bandmaster of a British cruiser in about 1932, bears a close resemblance to a pianoforte rendering by the Bank Manager of the clarinet music enclosed with Your Lordship's dispatch. The only further testimony I can obtain of the correctness of this music is that it reminds a resident of long-standing of a tune, once played by a long defunct band of the now

disbanded Muscat Infantry, and known at the time to non-commissioned members of Her Majesty's Forces (and I quote the vernacular) 'Gawd strike the Sultan blind'.

4. I am informed by the Acting Minister of Foreign Affairs that there are now no occasions on which the 'Salutation' is officially played. The last occasion on which it was known to have been played at all was on a gramaphone at an evening reception given by the Military Secretary in honour of the Sultan, who inadvertently sat on the record afterwards and broke it. I consider, however, that an occasion might arise when the playing might be appropriate if, for example, the Sultan were to go aboard a cruiser which carried a band. I am proposing to call on His Highness shortly at Salalah on his return from London, and shall make further enquiries as to his wishes on the matter.

5. I am sending a copy of this dispatch, without enclosure, to His Excellency the Political Resident at Bahrain.

I have the honour to be, Sir,

J.F.S. Phillips.

Her Britannic Majesty's Consul General.

Muscat. August the 17th, 1960.

While it was not the habit for Sultans of Muscat and Oman to travel extensively outside the country, with the exception of India and from 1928, the occasional visit to England via Aden, it should always be remembered that the people of Oman are well-known for their interest in places beyond the shores of their own country and with such an attitude possess a particularly well-chronicled international outlook. If circumstances made it difficult for individual Sultans to travel as much as they may wish to have done, they always extended a most generous welcome to those who came to see them.

One such visitor who called upon Sultan Said's father in 1924, was Dr Shigetaka Shiga, a geographer from Imperial Japan. Upon his return home he wrote and published an account of a country and a Royal Arab Court that was at the time as remote as the moon from the contemporary world. His account makes fascinating reading:

I wore modern clothes and a hat to protect myself from the heat. Standing on a stone, I sang the Japanese national anthem. They all laughed at me. I had an ambition to meet the King, who had a history that ruled from beyond the Persian Gulf and its islands to Zanzibar in Eastern Africa, 100 years ago.

Doctor Shiga told local officials that he wanted an audience with Sultan Taimour so that he could discuss how the establishment of friendly relations between Japan and Oman could be achieved:

> As I entered, into the recess facing towards the direction of a balcony overlooking the sea, a great man who looked 40 was sitting on an imported sofa. The King said 'Thank you for coming here. Arabia is part of Asia, as is Japan. We leave Europe to the Europeans. We should build Asia as Asians, hand in hand. Therefore, why don't Japanese come to Arabia soon to do business and establish industry? This would prove friendship and help develop our Arabia. This would be a good way to prosper together.' I replied, 'As a Japanese, what Your Majesty has said is what I wanted to ask you and your people. I will convey Your Majesty's wish to my people.' Then I asked the King if he could give me his autograph as a souvenir.

Shiga was also an astute political thinker, writing:

> The Arabs want true independence and dislike the existence of Hejaz, Transjordan and Iraq, which were founded by the British who betrayed them at the end of the First World War. True independence means the achievement of an Arabia without British influence. This explains why the Arabs get angry at the Jews, who are going to construct their state in Palestine with British backing. Some 90 per cent of the population is occupied by Arabs. After the Jews had abandoned Palestine 2,000 years ago the Arabs came and established their homes. How can the Jews possibly return after 2,000 years absence and create a new state under British political support and the subscription of rich men living in Europe and America. Who can accept such an unreasonable proposal?

The ultimate consequence of Dr Shiga's visit to Sultan Taimour is of particular interest as a personal footnote to history. In 1932, after abdicating under British pressure, Sultan Taimour travelled to Japan, his initial interest in the country having been the Japanese geographer's visit to Muscat eight years earlier. Arriving in Kobe in 1936 he met and fell in love with a young Japanese lady, Kiyoko Ohyama, whom he eventually married. She bore him a daughter. But Sultan Taimour was no backsliding Captain Pinkerton of Madam Butterfly fame, and remained with his wife in Japan until the outbreak of the Second World War obliged him to leave, taking his little daughter with him as her mother by that time had died. Today, Sayyida Buthaina bin Taimour is one of Muscat's most loved and respected members of Oman's ruling family, one whose acts of personal kindness and generosity are legendary. In the autumn of 1978 she visited Japan for the first time. During her stay she went to the monument to her mother, constructed by her father, at the time of his wife's death. The Princess was close to her brother, Sultan Said, and as the years passed and she came to adulthood, she was one of the very few in whom he could confide with complete trust.

When Petroleum Development Oman commenced operations, it was the practice for senior company executives such as Francis Hughes, PDO's General Manager, to have male secretaries recruited from Britain. Female secretaries were not considered appropriate in an undeveloped Islamic state. Francis Hughes' secretary was Jim Maclean, a former British Naval Officer who had been Private Secretary to Lord Louis Mountbatten, the uncle of Queen Elizabeth II. In 1967, with the commencement of oil exports and a corresponding increase in the tempo of development nationwide, it was declared that female secretaries would now be permitted. Hughes was a frequent visitor to Salalah, in order to brief the Sultan on developments in the country's new industry, flying from Muscat in his own company plane. On one such visit in 1967 he suggested that 'Mac', as everyone knew Jim Maclean, should become Private Secretary at the Palace, a suggestion promptly accepted by Sultan Said. So it came to pass that Oman's ruler gained an efficient secretary and administrator, one who brought a high degree of order to the somewhat chaotic personal affairs of Oman's monarch. At the time of the Palace coup Maclean accompanied Sultan Said into exile at the Dorchester Hotel, on London's Park Lane, remaining with him up to the time of his death in 1972, following a heart attack on the staircase of a transatlantic liner. Maclean was later to tell close friends that the former Omani ruler died 'a sad old man'. While he was never permitted to return home, news of developments there were relayed to him by Maclean and a Personal Assistant, Joanna Burke. Through sustained acts of loyalty and personal kindness she justifiably won the trust and confidence of a now aging and increasingly infirm Sultan Said. Moments of light relief apparently came when news from home concerned the construction of such icons of modernity as 'offices for ministers which exceeded two storeys, roads which, in his view, went to obscure places and high-rise commercial buildings which were but monuments to the vanity of those in whose name they had been built'. Upon receiving such news, according to one who spent much time with him at the Dorchester Hotel, 'a broad, almost mischievous smile would spread across his face and the request would be made for the finer points or, in his view, the more ridiculous ones, to be repeated, following which a gale of deep throated, uncontrolled laughter would echo round the suite'. Other friends who saw much of the former Sultan during his two years in exile speak of his regret that development did not proceed as swiftly as it undoubtedly should have done between the summer of 1967, when revenues from oil would have adequately paid for it, and the summer of 1970 when he was overthrown. But he recognised that many who were urging such a policy upon him were doing so through self-interest and that they would have made considerable personal financial gain from the plans they proposed, through their commercial contacts. While such suspicions cannot have been warranted on all occasions, one only has to consider what subsequently came to pass during Oman's rapid development to understand that there was a considerable degree of truth in the fears and apprehension of a Sultan for whom time, quite literally, ran out.

The stories of his early, pre-oil revenue days and conservative approach to state-sponsored change are also legion. During the 1958 visit to Muscat by Julian Amery, the British Undersecretary of State for War, the question arose of the Sultan inaugurating a school-building programme. Amery was indignantly asked, 'And what will they do once educated? Apart from traditional pursuits such as farming and fishing there will be nothing, generally speaking, for them to do.' But Amery, a skilful politician and polished courtier, pressed on with his point of view. Then quite suddenly, it all became too much for this particular Arab monarch. 'Look here, Mr Amery,' said Sultan Said, 'don't you know your own country's history? You built schools for the masses in India! And then look what happened. Once educated, they threw you out!' It is, interestingly enough, a point of view and a matter of increasing concern exercising the minds of many of the Gulf's monarchs as men who have in full measure provided education for their people; they are now thinking in very melancholy terms indeed about the eventual consequences for their continued rule having done so.

Shortly afterwards, in an exchange of a similar nature with a British Army Commander who had the temerity to suggest that the building of more hospitals would be no bad thing, Sultan Said responded:

> We do not need hospitals here. This is a very poor country, which can only support a small population. At present many children die in infancy and so the population does not increase. If we build clinics many more will survive, but for what? To starve?

It was a curious kind of logic and some would assert exercises an indifference to the point of cruelty. But Sultan Said's attitudes cannot be compared with the imperatives that govern the conduct of Western industrialised societies. To do so would be as illogical as it would be disingenuous. Attitudes he struck also have to be seen in light of the poverty of the land he ruled, a point he was at pains to make with the visiting British politician, Julian Amery.

The state of national bankruptcy he inherited also made its own sad contribution to his unwillingness to spend money liberally, except of course on national and personal security, yet another contributing factor to his sustained conservative approach with regard to the running of state affairs. In the context of both state and personal security his abiding concern can be understood not only by remembering the many times in the country's past when Oman was occupied and the equal number of threats to the rule of his dynasty, but also as the 1960s drew to their turbulent close, the climate of armed revolution he saw all about him.

While it can be no real justification for his views on the provision of health and education services, it is an irony indeed that concerns about population growth and the consequent increasing unemployment of educated, professionally-trained Gulf nationals daily become the topics of urgency and official concern. In Oman, for example, with an annual population growth rate of 3.5 per cent (one of the highest in the world), official concern daily gains momentum regarding the demands such a situation is making, particularly on the state's delivery of health and education services. Unemployment among young Omanis is also a matter for mounting anxiety, particularly as the country approaches a period when revenues from oil will terminally decline. It is a coalition of concerns born not so much of the fact that Omanis are breeding like rabbits, but that they have stopped dying like flies, unlike in Sultan Said's day. Again, this is no real justification for his conservative views but, nonetheless, an irony in which he would have found an exquisite vindication for having expressed them well before it became fashionable to do so.

Even the nature of the attention he gave to national security was to be given as one of the reasons for his forced removal from the throne of Oman. At least it was one of the reasons given by those who sought to justify what they conspired to accomplish, namely that his conduct of the campaign against the forces of revolutionary change in Dhofar was unlikely to achieve victory. It was believed both in London and by the military in Oman, that the war was being lost.

While this is only one aspect of the story, the part that has been officially propagated for over 30 years, the fact remains that a conspiracy was arranged to remove a Head of State who had been a staunch friend of the British for almost 50 years, a conspiracy which had its origins every bit as much in Britain as it did in Oman, against which Sultan Said bin Taimour had no effective line of defence whatsoever. While his attention was increasingly directed against the visible enemy, the armed groups operating in Dhofar which sought his overthrow through the expedient of left-wing revolutionary fervour, the invisible enemy, a cabal of right-wing British military and intelligence personnel, were whispering insurrection into the ear of his son Qaboos. The latter, already disaffected by the domestic regime inflicted upon him by his father, was all too ready to listen and in the event, be persuaded that an act of treachery should be carried out in his name. It was a circumstance which gives yet further proof, if such were needed, of Britain's past ability to make and unmake Sultans of Oman.

Why Sultan Said, a suspicious man at the best of times, appears to have been unaware of such 'back door' machinations is a mystery which went with him to his grave, although the most likely reason is the one given above: that his energies were almost exclusively directed at defeating a foe which had the very same aim as the unseen enemy within his own Palace walls.

# CHAPTER FIVE

## Went the Day Well?

It is rare indeed in the annals of armed insurrection that a name can be put to the individual who actually ignited the flame of revolution, one who drew into his own hands the disparate elements of disaffection and gave them a sense of purpose and direction. In any realistic assessment of the origins of the Dhofar War, Britain's 'Secret War' as the press came to dub it, the credit for its initial moves to armed action must go to a one-time gardener at Sultan Said's Salalah Palace, Mussalim bin Nufl.

Following his dismissal in 1963, Nufl's sense of grievance against the Sultan festered in a particularly vengeful manner, a resentment which was considerably enhanced by the presence in his tribal territory of oil exploration teams. While small scale acts of sabotage were reported at the RAF base outside Salalah as early as 1962, the first recorded shots in the Dhofar War were not until April 1963, during an armed attack on oil company vehicles in the desert, inspired and led by Nufl. He then fled to Saudi Arabia with about 30 of his followers, where he made contact with Oman's former Imam, Ghalib bin Ali. Backed by Saudi money Nufl, together with another group of disaffected Dhofaris who had earlier crossed the desert into the Kingdom, travelled to Iraq which was then in the grip of Arab nationalist fervour. Following military training, with special emphasis on sabotage and guerrilla tactics at a camp outside Basrah, the group under Nufl's leadership returned to Dhofar in the summer of 1964. Saudi Arabia's government gave them promises of further financial aid, supplies of weaponry and vehicles with which to wage war against the Sultan. But money and equipment was not all that the Saudis together with their Arab allies (the Iraqis, Kuwaitis and the Egyptians), pressed upon those committed to fomenting dissent in Muscat and Oman.

They also urged a unification of the various Dhofari dissident groups which had over the years assembled in the states of the Gulf and the Levant. The aims of these rebels were many and varied. The Arab Nationalists Movement, for example, was a group of Omanis who were hostile to the very idea of the Imamate and saw themselves as agents of change that would sweep away the Al Busaid dynasty and in the process, rid the country of British imperialism. The Dhofar Benevolent Society was by contrast amenable towards the exiled Imam and ostensibly existed to alleviate the poverty of the people of Dhofar, with any revolutionary aims coming as a secondary consideration. A third group whose aims were less than clear was the Dhofar Soldiers Association, formed by ex-Omani servicemen, many from the armed services and police forces in the northern states of the Gulf. Following energetic prodding from their financial backers, principally the Saudis and Kuwaitis, the dissidents came together under the banner of the Dhofar Liberation Front (DLF).

As unlikely a marriage as the groups represented, they did not take long to act under Nufl's leadership. On 14 August 1964, an army jeep from the Sultan's Armed Forces ran over a land mine laid by the DLF, killing the driver and wounding a passenger. Other attacks quickly followed. RAF vehicles were sabotaged and an oil exploration team's camp came under machine-gun fire. Sultan Said acted with unprecedented fury and instead of winning hearts and minds, ordered the most savage reprisals including the imprisonment of those thought to be aiding the rebels and the destruction of wells in areas from where the rebels were thought to be operating, a particularly vengeful act in water-short Arabia. However, the attacks not only continued but increased in ferocity, so that by the autumn of 1964 the situation had deteriorated to such a degree that the decision was taken to station a contingent of the northern-based Sultan's Armed Forces in Dhofar Province for the very first time.

In the spring and early summer of 1965 the DLF suffered a series of setbacks when some 40 of its supporters were arrested in Muscat and Salalah, and Iranian coastguards boarded a dhow in the Gulf which was bound for the DLF, carrying arms from Saudi Arabia. This was a serious, structural blow to the organisation. Not only did the Iranians seize the arms destined for the rebels but they took into custody several key DLF activists who were carrying documents detailing the next, planned phase of the guerrilla war. Undeterred, the DLF held its first Congress on 1 June 1965 at Wadi Al Kabir in the Dhofar mountains. It lasted until 9 June when a ringing declaration was issued for a war of liberation to be waged in Dhofar, Muscat and Oman. Titled 'Declaration Issued on the Launching of the Armed Struggle', its general tone reflected a change; despite its disparate origins the movement's initial aim was the improving of the social conditions of the people of Dhofar and those of Oman's interior through the defeat of reactionary forces led by Sultan Said. Now, however, the language of the DLF was heavily laced with the excited hyperbole of Marx, Engels, Lenin and Chairman Mao's Little Red Book as a direct result of time spent by many of its cadres in Iraq, Syria and other hot spots of Arab Nationalism:

> Arab people of Dhofar! A revolutionary vanguard has emerged from among you and has taken upon itself the task of liberating this country from the rule of the despotic Al Busaid Sultan whose dynasty has been identified with the hordes of the British imperialist occupation. Brothers! This people has long and bitterly suffered from dispersion, unemployment, poverty, illiteracy and disease – these pernicious weapons introduced under the protection of the bayonets of British imperialism and used against the Dhofaris by the government of the Sultan of Muscat . . . The government of the stooge Said bin Taimour has enlisted the services of an army of mercenaries to frustrate the goals of Arab liberation in this country, but the DLF will be blazing fire against it in every part of the country. This same spiteful mercenary army has managed to obstruct the aims of the revolution in Oman. Brothers of Dhofar! Rally to the call of your Front which has shouldered the responsibility of achieving liberation in these crucial moments of our country's history . . . Sons of the cities, the mountains and the desert! Join the ranks of DLF, stand in line with it against imperialism and its agents, the treacherous Sultans, to achieve Freedom, Unity, Social Justice and Dignity. Brothers! The DLF call upon you in the name of the fatherland and Arabism to take up arms and engage in its struggle against imperialism and its mercenary troops!

It was all stirring stuff and inflamed by the revolutionary zeal of the occasion, the DLF struck again on the very day that the Congress ended, mowing down an oil company driver in a hail of machine-gun fire. The Dhofar War had begun in earnest, with small units of rebels making a whole series of hit and run attacks against government targets throughout

1965–7. In April 1966 the DLF came very close to assassinating Sultan Said, but by the spring of 1967 they were put under very considerable pressure by a 'search and destroy' campaign conducted by the Sultan's army. In addition the DLF were now experiencing problems of supply, caused by Saudi Arabia's King Faisal having belatedly realised the inherent threat to the Gulf's conservative, traditional monarchs posed by the revolutionary aims of the DLF. As a result he had given orders for his government's support of the rebels to cease. Supplies and safe havens afforded by the armed groups fighting colonial rule across the border in the neighbouring British Aden Colony and Protectorate were also in jeopardy, as British forces increased patrols and air surveillance on the Protectorate side of the border.

It was a situation which gave the Sultan a tactical advantage, a breathing space in which to pursue a policy of reconciliation, to implement social measures which would alleviate to at least some degree the dissent bred by poverty and disease, which had featured so prominently in the Declaration made at the DLF Congress. To their everlasting credit, both civil and military British advisers advised such a policy together with that of a general amnesty to Sultan Said but he resolutely turned his face against such politically innovative steps. Had he possessed at that particular hour the political courage and foresight to accept recommendations like that of one British Colonel, 'rebel movements have only been finally destroyed by leniency', the subsequent history of Oman may well have been very different from that which eventually came to pass. Some of the British officers in the Sultan's Armed Forces became convinced that the Omani ruler was not being advised of the real situation in the country by his officials (a widely held belief which, curiously, exists in Oman today) and that at least some of the directives delivered by the Palace did not originate from him. In any event, it is no exaggeration to comment that had a vigorous campaign been launched aimed at winning hearts and minds, containing measures that would have met the social grievances of the people during the first half of 1967, the Dhofar War could well have been won. But it wasn't and the opportunity of being able to act from a position of strength and military advantage passed. By the end of the year, history took a hand which not only prolonged the war for a further eight years but took it to new levels of ferocity.

As with Oman, it was the British East India Company, the surrogate envoys of British Imperial rule, which took what became Aden Colony and Protectorate into Britannia's embrace in January 1839. Captain Haines stormed ashore in a rocky cove, leading troops from British India and claiming the beach along with the land beyond for the Crown of England, by virtue of armed occupation. It was London's only directly ruled colony in Arabia, its toehold on the Arabian Peninsula, and over the years it was to send only its very best sons to govern it. What became the great port city of Aden, one of the most prosperous in the world, was the colonial part of the arrangement; the Arab principalities to the east of the city, Abyan, Lehej, Shabwa, Makulla, Quaiti and the legendary Hadrahmaut, constituted the Protectorate aspect of this hybrid system of colonial rule. It was this vast area of rolling dune, desert and towering mountain ranges that lent itself ideally to guerrilla warfare and to which the local armed insurgent groups took when the winds of change blew across the Arabian Peninsula in the 1960s. Fuelled by resentment at the presence of British colonial rule, the appeal of Gamal Abdel Nasser's fiery brand of Arab nationalism, and the overthrow of royal rule in North Yemen in 1960 by the forces of republicanism, a variety of armed groups mounted a particularly brutal and effective challenge to the continued presence of Britain.

They were pushing at an open door. By the early 1960s, the British had well and truly signalled the end of empire. From the islands in the Caribbean to its colonial empire in Africa and the Far East, it became only a matter of time before an orderly and honourable retreat could be put in place. But in Aden Colony and Protectorate the various revolutionary movements, ironically by virtue of a vastly superior system of education which had been established via British Colonial rule, were managed and motivated by intellectual elites. These revolutionary leaders had taken the apparent appeal of Marx, Engels and Lenin very much to their revolutionary breasts. Following a colonial war of particular brutality, Britain withdrew amid scenes of chaos and confusion in November 1967, abdicating power to what was at the time the dominant political group: the National Liberation Front (NLF), which took as its political rule of thumb *Das Kapital* and the spirit of Lenin's great October Revolution. The country was named the People's Republic of South Yemen, but the Communist 'brotherhood' was far from comradely. Following three years of bloody internal strife the Popular Front came to power, and in a particularly poignant example of Stalinist doublespeak, they promptly renamed the country the Peoples' Democratic Republic of South Yemen (the PDRY). The Popular Front (PF) was well to the left of the NLF, but continued its predecessors' policy of giving sustenance and sanctuary to the embattled Dhofar Liberation Front across the border. The PF had thrown the Omani rebels a badly-needed lifeline.

According to one prominent royal source in Oman, Sultan Said had been greatly saddened and disturbed by the collapse of British rule in India in 1947, so his reported dismay and alarm at Britain's withdrawal from neighbouring South Yemen 20 years later can be well imagined. It was the exact opposite of the fear of encirclement; suddenly the Omani ruler felt exposed and outflanked, increasingly alone in a world growing ever more hostile by the day. In the case of a Marxist-Leninist South Yemen his fears were not only well founded but quickly proven. If the NLF in Aden had been well disposed to the DLF, providing arms, money and medical facilities across a border notoriously difficult to police, the even more radical Popular Front Government increased its support tenfold. Forgetting the historical warning of Benito Mussolini to Adolf Hitler that 'fascism is not for export', the PF leaders began an energetic campaign of exporting the ideals of its very own home-grown revolution across the border into Muscat and Oman. It did not take long for such a campaign to have an effect. In September 1968, the DLF staged its second Congress, as a result of which the movement changed its name to the People's Front for the Liberation of the Occupied Arabian Gulf (PFLOAG), heralding the fact that it had now become fully politicised in the fashion of left-wing ideology. The change of name signalled a dramatic new direction for the armed insurrection being waged against Sultan Said bin Taimour. The forces of conservatism which are always present in nationalist movements had, in the renamed PFLOAG, given ground to the ideals of scientific socialism based on the works of Karl Marx and his allies in the doubtful art of left-wing revolution.

Having now 'joined the club', the PFLOAG had access to a whole new world of revolutionary inspiration and wasted no time in tapping these new sources of practical and ideological support. Within weeks of its Second Congress some 30 members of the organisation had arrived via Aden in Chairman Mao's China, where they embarked upon a crash course in the duties of guerrilla war commanders and political commissars. While the shift towards a more ideologically based movement introduced very real strains and divisions into the PFLOAG, the better trained and equipped force it quickly became brought its own reward. By the end of 1969 the guerrilla leaders and political commissars had returned from Peking's 'Anti-Imperialist School' and entered Dhofar in 15 well-trained, well-armed insurgent groups. In a series of excellently coordinated attacks, troops of the Sultan's Armed Forces came under mortar and machine-gun fire. They responded by stationing members of the Muscat Regiment on the Oman PDRY border in an attempt to prevent further infiltration by rebel groups.

Realising that the nature of the war had radically changed, with the protagonists now gripped by an alien and viciously applied creed (reports of acts of physical violence by PFLOAG members against villagers in Dhofar who declined to aid them became common throughout 1969), British military officers, many of whom had direct access to Sultan Said, appealed for an immediate increase in resources. They were particularly desperate for helicopters that would give his troops greater mobility in the face of what had now become a decidedly determined foe. But old habits died hard and the Sultan declined to release further significant funds which, properly applied, could have brought him victory even at that late stage of the conflict. According to at least one eminent military source:

> The Sultan gave the appearance of believing that the armed insurrection facing him was basically tribal in character and, like the Jebal Akhdar campaign of ten years earlier, it would eventually be defeated with the weaponry and troops then available to his British commanders. He could not have been more wrong.

It was a tactical blunder of terminal proportions. In the absence of adequate resources, the tide of war turned in favour of the latest armed apostles of Karl Marx and Vladimir Ilyich Lenin. So successful were the attacks by PFLOAG insurgents along the border that the Sultan's Armed Forces were obliged to withdraw from all their positions on the frontier in the spring of 1969, the very last presence in the border area being evacuated in May of that year. On 23 August the rebels entered the coastal town of Rakhyut, east of the Yemen border and took the town with little resistance, with heavy seasonal monsoon storms and mist (the fabled Khareef) effectively preventing government military assistance by either air or sea. True to the form of movements proclaiming 'the People' as their cardinal virtue, the Regional Governor faced a 'military tribunal' and having been 'convicted' of being a tool of British imperialism was summarily shot, together with most of the town's male inhabitants.

Seizing the advantage of cover given by the monsoon mists and the virtual absence of government forces in the border area, the emboldened rebels moved further into Dhofar, planting landmines on the road linking the inland settlement of Thumrayt to the provincial capital Salalah, and mounting a whole series of machine-gun and mortar attacks on army convoys. The PFLOAG struck again as the summer drew to an end, this time at the border settlement of Habrut where Sultan Said had ordered the construction of a fort just two years earlier and much to the chagrin of his British military commanders, who considered it a waste of time and scarce resources. In the attack the fort was virtually razed to the ground and the small, token force of the Sultan's Armed Forces who occupied it at the time were completely routed. It was a classic hit-and-run operation, with the PFLOAG insurgents quickly fleeing back across the border into the safe haven of the PDRY. The raid could not go unpunished, particularly as it represented a flagrant attack on one state from the territory of another. A gross violation of Muscat and Oman's territorial integrity had taken place. The Sultan's British commander of his small air force requested and promptly received permission to mount an airborne attack on the town of Hanuf, across the border in the PDRY. The subsequent air raid inflicted a satisfying amount of damage and of particular satisfaction was the virtual destruction in the town of the so-called 'Revolutionary Training School', where many PFLOAG members had gone for courses in guerrilla tactics and political indoctrination.

While the success of the attack on Hanuf considerably raised morale, there was no escaping the fact that the Sultan's Armed Forces were facing an increasingly desperate situation, for all their dedication to the difficult task at hand and the undoubted military skill of its British commanders. Contemporary estimates put the number of PFLOAG guerrilla fighters and irregular armed militia at 5,000, while the total strength of Omani government forces in 1969 never exceeded 1,000. In addition the commanders of the Sultan's army had to battle with the fact that they were seriously short of the necessary military tools to do the job expected of them. It was not a promising situation, prompting one senior British officer to comment, 'It is difficult to see us losing, but we might. It is difficult to see the enemy winning, but it might.' Then the Sultan at long last acted, releasing, in October 1969, expenditure for the purchase of helicopters and the raising of a fourth battalion. The arrival of such reinforcements coincided with the discovery of a new element in the Dhofar war, the Union of Soviet Socialist Republics.

Government intelligence sources had advised the Sultan's military commanders in the summer of 1969 that Moscow had made moves to involve itself in the conflict, via its heavily-staffed embassy in Aden, probably in a studied initiative designed to blunt the support being given to the PFLOAG by the People's Republic of China. In effect, the Russian Bear had woken up to the fact that it could not allow the Chinese Dragon to make the revolutionary running in such a strategically important region of the world. The active participation of the USSR not only gave the PFLOAG a valuable new source of weapons of greater sophistication, but introduced into the conflict a totally new geopolitical dimension, one that caught the attention of the policy makers in far-off London and Washington. As 1969 drew to an uneasy close it became apparent to an increasing number of people that the Dhofar War, described by a senior British Conservative politician as 'a sideshow of a sideshow', was suddenly of greater relevance than previously thought.

This is now the conventional wisdom regarding the change of attitude to the conflict when Britain's 'secret war' comes under discussion. Yet there was a less publicly discussed issue, one that was concentrating minds most marvellously in London as 1970 dawned, namely the question of what would happen to the revenues being generated by Oman's oil exports? In the words of at least one retired military intelligence officer:

'The question increasingly became that with an Omani Sultan showing considerable obduracy to British suggestions as to how he should spend his state's new-found wealth, what steps should be taken to make sure that a goodly portion of it came the chums' way?'

What steps indeed! Would the sudden concern about the outcome of the Dhofar War have been so strong in the West had the country been an exporter of prize cabbages instead of pumping oil? The answer to such a simple question is intriguing in the extreme, one which has long had an impenetrable veil of obsessive secrecy drawn most effectively over its discussion.

When the export of oil first commenced in 1967, Oman pumped just under 21 million barrels. The following year this had risen to 88 million barrels, rising to almost 120 million in 1969 and just over 121 million in 1970. These were minimal levels of production by comparison with the other oil-producing states in the Gulf. In 1970 Saudi Arabia pumped almost 1,387 million barrels, Kuwait 1,091 million, Iran 1,404 million and Iraq 572 million. Nonetheless it represented the creation of wealth far and

away beyond any previous expectation for poverty-stricken Muscat and
Oman. By the spring of 1970, Sultan Said's Treasury had received some 55
million pounds sterling as a result of the royalty tax on oil exports. For a
ruler who had reigned for so long with debt and its threat as constant
companions, the effect of such a bonanza on this man is not hard to
imagine. Neither was he unaware of the personal danger such easy wealth
represented. Speaking in the summer of 1996 a member of Oman's ruling
family commented:

> While he did not use the term 'carpetbagger', Sultan Said knew
> that they existed and that not all of them were foreign. I think he
> was excited and afraid of the future at the same time. He was also
> very tired of the British always telling him what to do with the
> money. He knew that he would eventually be required by them to
> bow down to their God – development – and by the time of the
> coup had started to go down that path but much too slowly for
> their liking. Yes, I think he really was afraid of the future, that
> living with great wealth was even more dangerous for Oman than
> living with poverty.

How right the Sultan was. As 1970 wore on and the revenues rose, so
correspondingly did the orchestrated campaign in the British
establishment press quite openly calling for his overthrow. The *Economist*
magazine of 4 April, wrote with its usual bluntness:

> The Sultan must be persuaded to allow his country to move out of
> the Middle Ages and provide the basic necessities of modern life
> for his people or he must be got rid of. The British Government
> alone has the means to do this.

Nine days later *The Times* obligingly took up what was now becoming a
clarion call and quoted the Shah of Iran, who was known as keen to
extend his influence to his country's old hunting ground, and as we shall
see, shortly did just that. *The Times* was predictably coy on a subject that
had been common currency in diplomatic circles for some considerable
time, quoting the Iranian leader as follows, 'Rulers who block reform will
simply have to be replaced . . . Medieval systems still surviving in the
area, particularly in Muscat and Oman, will have to go.' *The Times* sallied
forth again just three months later, calling in strident tones on 8 July for

Sultan Said to be got rid of. The fact that he had two-and-a-half years earlier published an apology for the hardships of the past, and his plans for the future in his 1968 declaration were of course conveniently ignored by this august publication.

Then within the space of seven days, history took a hand, in effect coming to the aid of those who had been plotting Sultan Said's overthrow for a considerable period of time, in Britain, Oman and elsewhere. While such developments were beyond the control of those secretly recommending overthrow to the Sultan's heir Qaboos bin Said, they did in themselves spell the end for one of Arabia's last genuinely aristocratic rulers of what is commonly known, and often fondly referred to, as 'the old school'. In short, sharp and brutal terms, Sultan Said bin Taimour's time was done. The fears he so wisely entertained regarding the craven and self-serving interests his country's new-found riches would attract, were about to be proven. The end was indeed upon him.

The first event was the move of the guerrilla war, suddenly and spectacularly, to northern Oman. On 12 June 1970 a new group with revolutionary aims, the National Democratic Front for the Liberation of the Occupied Arab Gulf (which had its origins in a group of Omani dissidents living in the Iraqi capital, Baghdad), attacked a military camp at Izki, south-west of Muscat. They then mined the road from there to Nizwa. While the attack was beaten off by the Sultan's army, it had a profound psychological effect on Oman's establishment proving that while the emergence of a new armed group indicated the splintering of the revolutionary movement, it still had the will and the means to take the war wherever it wished to in Muscat and Oman. Indeed, proof of plans for an attack in the capital were found after the Izki attack in the Muscat suburb of Muttrah. Several members of the NDFLOAG had been captured and following their interrogation, a raid on a house in Muttrah uncovered a significant cache of sophisticated arms. Following their defeat at Izki and the seizure of their arsenal in the capital area, the NDFLOAG dissolved itself and joined forces with the PFLOAG. But the threat of what they might achieve remained, both as an inhibition on the Sultan's British commanders and as a debilitating anxiety that the country faced a long, drawn-out guerrilla war of attrition, during which the recently-refunded coffers of Sultan Said's Government would be bled dry.

The second event took place thousands of miles away in Britain which went to the polls in a General Election on 18 June. The Labour

Government of Harold Wilson was roundly defeated by the Conservative party led by Edward Heath, against all expectations. While the Conservative party in government had a record of energetically and pragmatically working to dissolve the once mighty British Empire, it had long contained within its serried ranks individuals who pined for imperial times past with an almost exquisite agony. It also had supporters who, if not actually party members (an ill-assorted range, from Duke to dustman and back again), sought to breathe life into Imperial Britannia's long-dead corpse; to seek her second coming as a thrusting power that would straddle the globe once again. Principal among such desperadoes were members of the British Intelligence community (from whom, ironically, so many traitors have come), military men who had long regarded, with no small justification, twentieth-century life as constituting one long retreat; businessmen with an eye to opportunity; and principal among such a group, Britain's so-called 'merchants of death', the country's arms dealers. The latter have a tradition, and it is not necessarily an ignoble sport, of making common cause with those engaged in military intelligence work. The link between the two presumably being that both exist and operate best in a political vacuum.

The outgoing Government of Harold Wilson had announced Britain's withdrawal as a political military power from the Persian Gulf, a foreign policy that the new Government adopted and carried out in 1971, leaving in its wake the transformation of the former Trucial States into the highly successful Federation of United Arab Emirates. Despite this, the principal concern of both the Ministry of Defence and the Foreign Office in London was that of maintaining Britain's dominant position as a supplier of goods and services in a region which was a market for rich pickings, given the extraordinary wealth pouring into the individual states of the Gulf from oil revenues. Consequently, even allowing for the middle of the road consensus seeking, one-nation policies promised by the election of Edward Heath as Prime Minister, there was general rejoicing at the election of a Conservative Government in the halls of those individuals identified above. The Tories were still more likely than a Labour administration to sanction a little privately-sponsored derring-do in far-off Muscat and Oman (all but invisible to the British electorate). The forces of persuasion gathering at the foot of the dubious throne of plot and intrigue had one overriding advantage in having Edward Heath in No.10, Downing Street. For his horizon of ambition was Europe, having been a Conservative Member of Parliament at the time of Suez with its defeat and humiliation for Britain, he had no natural feeling of concern or instinct for the Arab world and no particular passion for what Britannia's children got up to there. On this area of foreign policy he was, in the words of a contemporary insider, 'very much inclined to accept advice put before him by functionaries and not to ask too many questions which he would have only found tedious and time-consuming'.

For those who had long seen the possibilities represented by a Middle Eastern monarch in receipt of rapidly rising oil revenues, in possession of a land crying out for development and already under pressure, the election of a pliable Premier to power was the last piece of the Muscat and Oman jigsaw falling neatly and conveniently into place. There were other considerations to bring into play in planning the overthrow of an Arab monarch with whom consecutive British governments had worked closely for 38 years and were bound to by Treaty, one that decreed that 'the friendship of the two states may remain unshook to the end of time, till the Sun and Moon have finished their revolving career': namely the Sultan's tendency of late to demonstrate a disturbing degree of personal initiative and independence from the long arm of British influence and interference. In very recent times, the unease in London generated by the Sultan demonstrating that he was his own man, had as its principal cause one little three-lettered word – oil!

At a meeting in the Chatsworth Hotel on Eastbourne's Grand Parade during the last week of August 1997, a former senior-ranking military Intelligence Officer who worked in the Gulf in the late 1960s and early 1970s remembered times past in far-off Arabia:

> It is almost too tempting when talking about the time running up to the coup of July 1970, which deposed the old Sultan, to conjure up the somewhat apt expression 'camels and straws', but that is exactly what happened. While there were many considerations bearing down on the military and intelligence boys, the threat, as they saw it, of a takeover of Oman by Marxist rebels, to give just one example, the straws that led to the breaking of the camel's back began, for a certain powerful and, I must say, opportunistic group among them, was news that the Sultan had granted oil exploration rights in Dhofar to an American corporation. The granting of these rights to the Americans, rather than to Shell or British Petroleum, raised howls of displeasure in London, particularly among those who were in the 'but what's in it for me?' game right up to their

armpits. Sure, the old Sultan knew that Albion was perfidious but also that some of her representatives were, particularly when the oil began to flow, personally greedy and therefore covetous and duplicitous and were men to be wary of. While the excitable bit, the possible Marxist takeover of Oman was furiously pedalled by some of our chaps to the politicos, particularly in those 34 crucial days between the return to power by the Tories and the day of the coup, the 'who gets what' game had been concentrating their tiny little minds for some time. But from the moment that Sultan Said granted concessions to the Americans he effectively sealed, in my opinion, his own fate. He had to go and the great campaign of denigration in London began. The Americans did actually find oil, but in quantities too small to be commercially viable. The irony is that they were drilling within 10,000 yards of what subsequently proved to be one of Oman's most productive fields. Now suppose, just for one moment, that their diamond bits had found what they and Sultan Said were seeking. Look at the Eastern Province of Saudi Arabia and the way the American oil companies involved reacted and behaved following the major finds there, in order to consolidate their interests as the extractors of the oil. My belief is that had oil flowed for the Americans in Sultan Said's time, they would have made damn sure that he not only became rock safe, but that Salalah and Dhofar generally would have been the great engine that drove Oman's future development. For sure, Said bin Taimour would not have ended up in Brookwood Cemetery in Woking, a reviled and execrated figure, heaved aside in favour of his son. And what then of the whole reeking gang of thieves, vagabonds and scoundrels we have all come to know so well and who have sucked Oman all but dry during the past 27 years? To use a further apt phrase, a conservative figure of the actual cost to the other country of their naked greed is reliably said to represent about two month's oil revenue out of every twelve. But what of them had the Americans probed the rock just 10,000 yards from their dryish wells? It is a tantalising thought, is it not? But of course, they didn't and with that the Americans, while not losing complete interest in Oman, just let the Brits get on with their own little games while Washington waited in the wings to see what transpired and then, what they might salvage for themselves. Because, to be sure, they did have strategic concerns. I know for a fact that, by the very late 1960s the CIA was warning Washington, correctly as it turned out, that the Ethiopian regime of Emperor Haile Selassie was facing imminent collapse and that a Marxist-inspired takeover was a distinct possibility. Such a possibility was of crucial importance to the Yanks because they had 'facilities' – a listening and over-the-horizon radar scanning post – at Massawa, the capital of the northern Ethiopian province, on the shores of the Red Sea. If the old Emperor fell and a Communist government came to power in Addis Ababa then, of course, the whole exercise would go down the tubes, which is what actually happened when, in 1973, the Emperor fell and the Communists came to power. Consequently, a new site, the CIA projected, would have to be identified. One such possibility which presented itself to the boys in long-term planning mode at Langley, Virginia, the CIA headquarters, as they bent double over their maps, was in the Limeys' old haunt of Oman. So, yes, while the failure of the Americans to strike oil in commercially viable quantities was a disappointment, the Americans most certainly did not take their eye off the ball. In effect, they just moved on to 'Plan B', confident that whatever the outcome in Oman might be they still had, as ever and always, an ability to oblige the British to do very much what they might eventually want to achieve. And that, yet again, is exactly what happened just five months after the coup. But as to the actual toppling of the old Sultan itself, well that was a very British coup indeed.

In the event it was almost too easy as coups go. It was not death in the afternoon but the deposing of a monarch by another, in that it was inspired and executed by the subjects and servants of Her Britannic Majesty Queen Elizabeth II. The fact that neither ruler was consulted nor made privy to its detail, the fact that one ruled while the other merely reigned is but an academic point; one best left where it is, in the closed book of high diplomatic intrigue, evasion and that essential Whitehall practice, being economical with the truth. Later, in exile, on the top floor of the Dorchester Hotel, ex-Sultan Said's little private joke was that from 23 July 1970, Whitehall had become, in his book at least, Blackhall. It was indeed the black art of treachery planned in London's most private corridors which led to his downfall. We shall never know if on that particular humid afternoon there had been 'a little loving'; but we do know from the words of a member of Oman's royal family speaking in 1996 that, as the afternoon wore on, the Sultan had become uneasy. His personal servants, many of whom were the fiercely loyal Khaadhim (the descendants of African slaves and key members of the Palace staff), had finely-tuned political antenna and had in actual fact been behaving in a nervous manner for three or four days past. With good cause, for it is now known that the coup had been initially planned for 22 July but had been postponed due to a fierce attack of nerves among the conspirators, from Qaboos downwards. Many of the Sultan's closest and most trusted British advisers, such as Peter Mason, were on leave in England and Jim Maclean was out of the Palace too. This, of course, was an essential part of the plan. Those retainers of old, Britons of the finest honour and integrity, men who would never have abdicated their duty or their loyalty to Sultan Said, whatever the prize on offer, were all absent from either the country or Salalah Palace on that fateful afternoon. Those who arranged the coup had seen to that. Then, as now, high summer is the time for an expatriate exodus from Oman and the coup had been carefully timed to coincide with the absence of those who would not have accepted it without putting up formidable resistance.

As we have already seen, the guerrilla attack at Izki on 12 June had an acute psychological effect on Oman's military establishment and had been the catalyst for increased pressure on the new Conservative Government to force change through a Palace coup. Britain's 'man in Oman', or at least one of them crucial to the success of the planned coup was the Sultan's Defence Secretary, Colonel Hugh Oldman, who took a pivotal role in Sultan Said's overthrow, supported by other British officers. But the decencies had to be observed and the man detailed by the British to make the actual, physical strike against the Omani ruler was another Omani, and a distinguished one at that.

Sheikh Braik bin Hamood bin Hamid Al Ghafri was the son of the Wali of Dhofar, the Governor of the Province. As such he was a man of considerable public standing. He had been well chosen, being known particularly as a man of considerable personal courage. In the late afternoon of Thursday, 23 July 1970, he arrived uninvited and unannounced at the gates of Salalah Palace, demanding to see the Sultan. Sultan Said, while expressing irritation and annoyance at such an unexpected intrusion, but believing that the matter which had brought the Sheikh to the Palace must be urgent, asked that the Sheikh be taken to his private apartments. Once in the Sultan's presence, Braik asked for the Omani ruler's abdication in sad but firm tones. Enraged, Sultan Said called upon his Khaadhim, who attempted to eject the Sheikh from the Sultan's presence. The precise sequence of events which then followed are far from clear, but it is no exaggeration to record that farce and tragedy were in equal attendance. What is beyond doubt is that the Sultan produced a handgun and fired at Sheikh Braik, hitting him in the stomach. It is known that at least some of the Khaadhim had guns and in the general panic which followed, one of the Sultan's servants fell to the ground, fatally wounded. In the mêlée which then erupted the Sultan was himself wounded in the stomach, sustaining a total of four shots, one of which was self-inflicted when he accidentally discharged his own gun into his right foot. To those waiting for news of the coup's success, it was now alarmingly clear that things were most certainly not going to plan. The decision was then quickly taken by British officers beyond the walls of the Palace that one of their number, the popular and fearless Major 'Spike' Powell who was known and liked by Sultan Said, should go into the Palace and appeal to the Omani ruler to capitulate. Once the decision had been taken Powell went immediately to the Palace. Scenes of wholesale chaos continued to reign inside. At the Sultan's request one of the Khaadhim sent an urgent message for help to Defence Secretary Oldman who, like his fellow British officers, did not respond. There was a specific instruction from London that British officers were not only to do 'a Nelson' (to turn a blind eye and most obviously, an ear) to any appeals for assistance Sultan Said may make at the appointed hour, but to obstruct any other members of the military, such as Baluchi or Pakistani men-at-arms, from going to his assistance. The cadre of British officers serving the Sultan, with Colonel Hugh Oldman technically their head, had all been well and truly briefed as to what was expected of them – inaction. As night fell the situation had still not resolved itself. It was approximately at this time that 'Spike' Powell arrived at the Palace. The Sultan immediately agreed to see him and came to the inevitable conclusion that with both himself and Sheikh Braik requiring medical treatment, he had little choice but to accept Powell's entreaties and capitulate. Thus did this British soldier, if hitherto virtually unknown, achieve for himself a particular role in the history of Oman. He later went on to serve in Rhodesia's armed services and met a particularly tragic end when he died in a Viscount airliner, shot down over Victoria Falls by the rebel movement Zanu PF.

But Oman's 13th ruler in the Al Busaid Dynasty had one final card to play, despite having realised the impossibility of his situation and accordingly bowed to the inevitable,. He sent word to those waiting beyond the Palace walls that he would only surrender to a British officer, a demand that demonstrated his particularly deft sense of history and political judgement. Sultan Said was determined that responsibility would be placed where it belonged for what had come to pass that day in Salalah. A member of Oman's ruling family commented in the spring of 1996:

> It is complete nonsense for the British to have presented to themselves that Sultan Said's demand came as a gesture of respect and affection for them. It is, in fact, a lie too far. The Sultan knew perfectly well that solemn undertakings of support, underwritten by Treaty, had been broken by London simply to serve British interests. By insisting that he would only surrender to a British Officer, he was acknowledging for history's sake as much as his own, that he knew perfectly well who had organised the coup against him and that by making such a demand future generations would know it too. He surrendered to those who had turned out to be the enemy. Which is what is done, isn't it? You surrender to whoever has defeated you. It was as simple as that.

Any doubt as to who exactly had arranged the Palace coup was resolved by the discovery of a document during the long period of research which preceded the writing of this book. It comes in the form of a 'secret' minute written by a Mr J.M. Edes of the Foreign Office's Arabian Department, which sets out in some considerable detail the arrangements which had been put in place for the reception of Sultan Said in Britain, 'following Sayyid Qabus's successful coup against his father, the former Sultan, last night'. It was, however, an exercise in forward planning laced with more than justified enthusiasm, for while it advises of the coup as having taken place 'last night', Mr Edes wrote (and clearly dated) the Minute 'July the 23rd', the day on which the coup actually took place. The document is further witness to the fact that the forced removal of Sultan Said was actually planned for the 22 July, a postponement of which the diligent Mr Edes was not advised. This document is so pivotal to the history of the coup, now regarded as Britain's last 'Last Hurrah' as a military and colonial power in the Arab world, that it is reproduced in full in the Appendix of this book.

The doubtful, if not dubious, honour of accepting the surrender of

Sultan Said fell to Lieutenant-Colonel Edward Turnill of the Sultan's Desert Regiment, who arrived at the Palace later that evening. It also fell to him to present two documents of Abdication, one in Arabic and the other in English, both of which had been well-prepared beforehand. The now ex-Sultan of Muscat and Oman, together with the wounded Sheikh Braik, were then taken the short distance by car to the British airbase outside Salalah town where they were put aboard an RAF Britannia. The aircraft prepared for departure to Bahrain where they were to receive medical attention at the RAF hospital at Muharraq. As they were waiting to depart the Sultan had what must have been a pleasant surprise after the drama and trauma of the past four hours. Jim Maclean, his Private Secretary, boarded the aircraft. Maclean, with his florid complexion and sense of irony, had come to accompany his royal master into exile. Whether he was made privy to the plot is unknown. Contemporaries of his claim that in later life, retired in his flat in Edinburgh with his boxer dogs beside him, he did confirm that he had been briefed on the coup but, powerless to prevent it, he could not bear the idea of the Sultan winging his way alone out of Oman into exile under cover of darkness. In a relevant footnote to this extraordinary time in the history of Oman, it is of no small significance to record that when Maclean died in the late 1980s the official demand was made that his private diaries be destroyed.

But the day was not yet done. Just before take-off, Sultan Said said that he had only signed the instrument of abdication in the English language, apparently with some degree of mischievous humour. The Arabic copy had remained unsigned when he left the Palace. As Maclean was to later comment, 'he should have remained silent'. A scene straight out of the *Keystone Cops* then ensued. A mad dash was made by road back to the Palace in order to find the Arabic version, return it to the RAF base and get it signed by the ex-Omani ruler, all before the scheduled take-off for Bahrain.

Following medical treatment, Sheikh Braik returned to Oman but ex-Sultan Said was flown on RAF Britannia Flight 6394 to Brize Norton in Oxfordshire. From there he was taken by road to the RAF hospital at Wroughton in Wiltshire. Upon his arrival at Brize Norton the ex-Sultan was met by a Foreign Office functionary by the name of Hayman who conveyed a short, oral message from the Secretary of State. Following his recovery he was taken to his place of exile, the Dorchester Hotel on London's Park Lane. Apart from short, carefully monitored visits with old friends in Britain, and a planned trip to the United States with a couple of 'minders' in tow (which was curtailed when, during the transatlantic voyage, an ultimately fatal heart attack took place on the staircase of the liner), Said bin Taimour remained in his suite of rooms at the Dorchester until his death on 19 October 1972. When the news of his death was relayed to Muscat, there was an embarrassing silence initially. It was only following a virtual ultimatum by London that unless specific instructions were received from Muscat as to the wishes for Said bin Taimour's burial, a unilateral decision would be taken. As we have already seen, he was laid to rest in Brookwood Islamic Cemetery at Woking in the county of Surrey. However, his resting place is unmarked, and while this is a common practice in the case of Muslim interment, there are many who believe that this is a clear indication that, even in death, Sultan Said bin Taimour Al Said is still considered too vital a witness to so much of Oman's recent past; particularly to its long entanglement with Britain. Consequently his place in history, including that of his burial, is best forgotten.

The Palace Coup of 23 July 1970 was unusual in that it did not come about as a result of a public-inspired uprising, with popular support in the streets. While the guerrillas of the Marxist-infected PFLOAG were in the deserts and mountains of Dhofar fighting their cause, it should be remembered that their aim entailed not only the overthrow of the Al Busaid dynasty, but the expulsion of the British from the land. Neither were Omanis principally involved in the planning and carrying out of the actual coup itself. There is no doubting the personal courage and conviction of Sheikh Braik bin Hamood bin Hamid Al Ghafri, who had the difficult and potentially life-threatening task of confronting Sultan Said in his private apartments in the Palace. But even he was chosen by the British for this task and primed by them to carry it out. The coup was unusual, too, in another relevant aspect. For almost three days no one in Oman knew anything about it, save those who had planned the coup. It was not until Sunday, 26 July, that the news of Sultan Said's 'Abdication' and departure from the country was announced. An air of absolute secrecy was strictly maintained between 23 and 26 July and according to at least one distinguished contemporary source, it was a time not of celebration but mounting tension. In the words of another prominent insider at the time, 'The main concern was, okay, but what actually happens now? The atmosphere is best described as one of uneasy calm. It was all very, very eerie.'

Sultan Said's son, Qaboos, who was now *de facto* Oman's 14th ruler from the Al Busaid dynasty, remained well within his quarters in the Palace compound at Salalah. But with the announcement of his father's 'Abdication' and his own accession to the throne of Oman, crowds did gather outside the Palace. On Monday, 29 July, the British Government announced its recognition of Qaboos as Sultan. On 30 July, Oman's new ruler flew from Salalah to Muscat, which he had not previously visited. Later that day he broadcast a message to the nation, from a hastily erected one kilowatt 'radio station' in the military camp at Bait Al Falaj. It was an address which offered liberation from the arch-conservative rule of his father, laced with an appeal to nationalist instincts, a conjuring-up of Oman's distinguished past and an expression of hope that the new era now being embarked upon would have God's blessing:

> I promise you to proceed forthwith in the process of creating a modern government. My first act will be the immediate abolition of all the unnecessary restrictions on your lives and activities. I will proceed as quickly as possible to transform your life into a prosperous one, with a bright future. Every one of you must play his part towards this goal. Our country in the past was famous and strong. If we work in unity and cooperation we will regenerate that glorious past and we will take a respectable place in the world. Yesterday it was complete darkness and with the help of God, tomorrow will be a new dawn on Muscat, Oman and its people. God bless us all and may he grant our efforts success.

Oman's new Sultan did well indeed to ask for divine intervention in the task facing him and the Omani people, for it was colossal. His inheritance was financially sound due to oil revenues and way beyond any previous Omani ruler's wildest dreams. Yet he faced a determined guerrilla foe in the south and, nationwide, a country that was bereft of any advantages of the second half of the twentieth century. Education and health services were minimal in the extreme, apart from facilities in Muscat and Salalah. Absent too was any manifestation of modern communications, such as a road network or a national telephone and broadcasting service. In terms of delivering on the promise of the creation of 'a modern government', the virtual absence of an administration was of even greater significance, a skilled civil service that could adequately and professionally contain the demands of such an ambitious programme of national development that was now proposed. Those British officers of Sultan Said's Government who were professional and had valuable knowledge regarding what little existed of the state's administration were asked to leave. Being of the highest possible integrity they had remained loyal to him and were no use to the new regime. A notable exception was of course Colonel Hugh Oldman, who had played a pivotal role in the planning of the Palace coup. But then he was Army and then as now, that was regarded as a quite separate entity from the other institutions of the state. Several senior Omanis were also dismissed, the Interior Minister and the Governor of Muscat, both of whom were considered unsound in the new scheme of things because they continued to express sentiments of loyalty to the deposed Sultan quite openly. Consequently, the immediate effect of the coup was a vacuum every bit as significant as the one that had existed before 23 July.

This is best represented by recording that the conspirators were so unsure of the state's financial situation, that Sultan Qaboos had to request Peter Mason to quickly return to Oman and advise him as to the exact amounts of money in his father's personal coffers and the amount in the national Treasury. Within two weeks of coming to power, Sultan Qaboos, having been assured of the healthy condition of his state's finances by Mason, announced a comprehensive series of measures designed to usher in the 'new dawn' for the country promised in his broadcast to the nation.

Basically these were: the establishment of a provisional administration, the Prime Minister of which would be Sayyid Tarik bin Taimour, uncle to Qaboos, who was invited to return home immediately from his exile in Germany; with immediate effect the dropping of the term Muscat and Oman as a contribution to the aim of achieving national unity, to be replaced by the title The Sultanate of Oman, a policy initiative that was to be accompanied by the design of a new national flag (a task undertaken by a British soldier in the Sultan's army); the immediate launch of an ambitious national development programme with the emphasis on health and education; the establishment of a nationwide infrastructure within which social and economic institutions could flourish. The announcement of the ambitious programme concluded with an appeal to all Omanis outside the country to return home forthwith, particularly those with professional skills that could be put to good use in the development process. The Sultan also confirmed his intention to take Oman onto the world's stage through a series of vigorous diplomatic initiatives that would, hopefully, lead to the state becoming an Arab League member and taking its seat at the United Nations.

Of greater, more immediate importance, with regard to the guerrilla war in the south, Sultan Qaboos announced a general amnesty for all PFLOAG members. This included the payment of cash grants to enable a return to a settled existence. He also confirmed his intention to improve the fighting capability of his Armed Forces, a move that would require considerable state expenditure, but a vital requirement if that new beginning for Oman was not to be suffocated in the embrace of scientific socialism. But in an often confused and rapidly changing situation, there was one certainty as the tide of war rose and fell. The departure from the country of Sultan Said, and with it the birth under his son's leadership of 'a new dawn', did not by any manner of means signal an end to the conflict. As we have already seen, a cardinal aim of the PFLOAG was not only to bring about the end of the Al Busaid dynasty, but to rid the country of British influence. And that was not all. The movement had moved away from one founded on resistance against the governing power to one of revolution, fuelled by the politics of Communist ideology. Consequently, the advent of Qaboos bin Said Al Said actually saw an intensification of what the PFLOAG had always referred to as 'The Armed Struggle'. More credit must then go to this young 29-year-old ruler who, from the very moment he ascended the throne of Oman, initiated a twin-track approach to solving the ills of his state and nation: a comprehensive development programme designed to alleviate the social deprivations so long experienced by the people of Oman; and measures that would greatly strengthen the fighting capability of his Armed Forces. In short, it was a classic example of leadership. If you want peace, prepare for war.

The offer of an amnesty fortuitously coincided with ideological strains appearing within the ruling ranks of the PFLOAG. These had their origins in the opinions of those represented by the various tribal leaders, the original source of resistance to the Government of Sultan Said, and those whose principal aim was to bring about a socialist revolution in Oman. Such a political divide led to numerous 'People's Tribunals', during which a considerable member of PFLOAG members found themselves accused of being counter-revolutionaries. Following the trials many were summarily executed as traitors to the cause. These acts of terrorism against their own members had the inevitable result of prompting many in the movement to take advantage of Sultan Qaboos's offer of amnesty, a development that quickly gained momentum when the number of summary executions dramatically rose. Captured PFLOAG documents put the number at being in excess of 300 in September 1970. Shortly after this particular period of internecine strife the Government's amnesty programme won a special prize, the voluntary surrender of the very man who had first taken up arms against the former regime, Mussalim bin Nufl. During his debriefing session he laid the blame for the damaging political divisions within the rebel movement to the existence at its core of those Omanis who had become devotees to the Maoist version of waging guerrilla war. Most of these rebels had gone on from the Arab states in the north to China for guerrilla warfare training and political indoctrination.

By the end of 1970 the number of defectors to the government had reached such proportions that the PFLOAG leadership adopted what amounted to panic measures. These ironically took the form of a further round of summary executions which, naturally enough, only led to another dramatic rise in the numbers of those surrendering to government forces under the terms of the amnesty. Many of those who came over to the government side, in many cases bringing their weapons with them, took advantage of the alternative offered to civilian resettlement; they joined the ranks of an irregular, tribal militia force, the Firqat. The establishment of the Firqat, composed of those who had surrendered, was as imaginative as it was innovative and it did not take long to prove its worth, particularly when its members carried out special operations against their former political commissars. The membership eventually rose to in excess of 1800. The importance attached to the Firqat by the government of Sultan Qaboos can be gauged by the request that was sent to London for assistance in their training for special operations. The request was promptly met with members of the renowned SAS arriving in Oman to take up their duties as training officers to this unique band of fighting men. But the memory of 1956 and the humiliation of the Suez debacle still haunted a Conservative Government, with all its disinclination to involve itself in foreign conflicts, particularly east of Suez. Allied to this was the ethos of the anti-Imperial age which had its very own long shadows to cast. So while London did not hesitate to dispatch the SAS to the Sultanate, it disguised its real fighting role by terming it the British Army Training Team (BATT) and as such its commitment to a foreign field of combat was never discussed in the House of Commons or willingly aired in the press. Nonetheless it is interesting to record almost 30 years after the event that senior British diplomats, including those on posting in the region, sent warnings to Whitehall of the possibility of British forces becoming bogged down in a guerrilla war that would be difficult to win. They worried that such an event might become the country's Vietnam, the 'horror in slow motion' which affected strategic policy makers, making its very own contribution to the doubt which surrounded the secret dispatch of the SAS contingent to Oman.

A retired British diplomat commented in the spring of 1998:

> One should not forget that the Dhofar rebel movement, for good or ill, did actually have for some considerable time the active support of the Arab League. For years Britain had taken 'stick' in the UN and elsewhere for its long involvement in Oman's affairs, criticism which rose ferociously when Britain became suspect of having engineered the coup against the old Sultan in 1970. Sir Anthony Parsons, a former British Ambassador to the UN, refers to this in his memoirs and he should know, given that he was a former Political Officer stationed in Bahrain, from where events in Oman before the coup were monitored. And he most certainly had major reservations about both the nature of Sultan Said's overthrow and indeed some of the figures involved in the struggle to get their hands on the potential loot. To sum up, the diplomats in Whitehall basically reduced Britain's role as one confined to protecting its commercial interests and that our continued political involvement after the coup should be reduced to a minimum. But the military, and particularly the military intelligence clique, won the argument. It really was as simple as that. And very well the select few have done out of it of course. But that, frankly, was the name of the game all along. It is also of no small interest to note that the fledgling government of Sultan Qaboos was obliged to pay Britain at the going, market rate for every kind and every item of military assistance provided during the Dhofar War. Consequently, the conflict was unique in Britain's post-colonial history. The very high charges levied by London is the principal reason why air cover was so often either entirely absent or distinctly thin at crucial times during the war. Sultan Qaboos couldn't always come up with the cash, particularly when London demanded advance payment for supplies. There are, I know for a fact, memorandums to this effect on the files at both that Foreign and Commonwealth Office and the Ministry of Defence in London.

A small, select group from the ranks of the SAS, those purveyors of tenacious courage, had actually arrived in Salalah within two days of the Palace Coup to act as personal bodyguards to Sultan Qaboos. But their brothers-at-arms were not long in following them. The first BATT detachments were posted to Taqa and the coastal town of Mirbat, 70 kilometres east of Salalah and the site of one of Oman's celebrated forts. They were not long in engaging the enemy. In March 1971 SAS troops took the fight to the rebels in their major stronghold, the fastness of the brooding mountain range that dominates Salalah's skyline. The Jebel is a mountain area of rolling green downland, wooded enclaves, caves, and particularly after the monsoonal rains in mid-year, thick impenetrable jungle. It was familiar terrain to the SAS, which had waged the victorious battle against the guerrilla forces of Communism in the jungles of Malaya in the 1950s. The experience gained there had been well-earned and most certainly not forgotten. Following a fierce battle they forced the Dhofari rebels to abandon an artillery emplacement which had been shelling Taqa. At the end of the year they scored another success, when in an airborne landing at Jibat they routed rebel forces. In their wake the SAS established a stronghold for the Sultan and themselves, on the Jebel, for so long a no-go area for government forces, holding it despite fierce and skilful rebel counterattacks. The tide was indeed beginning to turn. By the summer of 1972 rebel commanders knew that if morale was to hold and the increasing number of defections to the Sultan's forces was to be stemmed, a counter-victory had to be achieved and done so as a matter of some urgency. They vowed to strike fast, hard and deep.

It was decided that their target should be the small town of Mirbat and its fort. The offensive was carefully planned and designed to achieve the maximum effect. The moment of attack, with a well-armed assault force of almost 300 men, was to be the pre-dawn hours of 19 July 1972. It was at the height of the monsoon, the mists of which afforded cover so vital for the initial approach to the town and the fort. The town was garrisoned by an Omani platoon, a small group of Firqat and an eight-man SAS team led by Captain Michael Kealy, who were billeted within the shadow of Mirbat Fort at the house which served as the BATT quarters. The rebel plan was to overwhelm this small garrison with a massive assault of shells and mortar bombardment from a mountainside overlooking the town and the fort. The precise moment of attack came at the hour before sunrise. In darkness and through rolling mist the rebels made a stealthy approach, moving like fish through water. They crept silently towards the sleeping town and fort, closing in on their quarry from both the north and the east.

The first shots which rang out were aimed at the BATT house where the eight SAS were billeted. The Battle of Mirbat had begun. The rebels quickly reached the protective cordon of barbed wire which encircled the town and the fort and began to climb over it. Captain Kealy, quickly realising that a major assault was in progress, radioed for airborne support and a helicopter to evacuate those of his comrades who already lay wounded. Under heavy fire, he then sprinted to a gun emplacement where a 25-pounder was positioned beside the fort. Within seconds, two of those manning the gun lay dead, whilst it was being fired over open sights. Incidentally it was the last time that such a dated weapon was to be used in combat by British troops. As Kealy continued to discharge the gun at the enemy, aided by a fellow SAS member, the men inside the fort were subjected to relentless gun and mortar bombardment. The situation looked grim indeed but then came salvation from the sky above. Kealy's radio call for air support had been answered and three Strikemasters flew in low from across the sea, catching the rebels in the open and raking them with rocket and machine-gun fire. The tide of the battle turned in favour of the Sultan's army and the SAS. The assault on the town and its fort was repulsed. As the discordant sounds of war fell silent, the scene of carnage wrought by the indiscriminate detritus of battle was awful to behold. It was a scene that would not have been unfamiliar to those participating in another great battle, the siege of Rorke's Drift in 1879, when 100 British soldiers repulsed repeated attacks by 3,000 Zulu warriors in the uplands of South Africa. The area around the fort was littered with the dead and the badly wounded. Within the gun emplacement and the perimeter wire lay some 38 bodies. While there were many battles during the Dhofar War which witnessed acts of personal heroism, none draw such a graphic picture in the mind's eye as the Battle of Mirbat. The scene of battle, with the fort in the background and the 25-pounder gun blazing away was later to be commemorated by one of Britain's most distinguished artists, David Shepherd. As for the singularly brave conduct of Captain Michael Kealy, he was justifiably rewarded by his own sovereign with the Distinguished Service Order (the DSO), one of the British Army's most coveted decorations.

For the PFLOAG, their rout at Mirbat was a complete disaster, the adverse effect on morale being as damaging as the physical and material losses it sustained during the attack, with their fatalities exceeding 100 men. It was a turning point in the war, the beginning of the end for the rebels of Dhofar and while the road was still long and hard, few doubted from that moment on that victory would eventually be won. But the price was high, with the prosecution of the war costing Sultan Qaboos's government over 50 per cent of its oil revenues between 1970 and 1975. Its successful conclusion required considerably greater assistance than that purchased from the British. Under its last Shah, Iran was the superpower of the region, the Gulf's principal 'policeman' and it was not long before he expressed a willingness to aid his fellow monarch across the Hormuz Strait. In the autumn of 1972 the Shah dispatched a 200-strong Special Force unit and a squadron of helicopters to Dhofar. The Iranians took up strategic positions on what was known as the 'Hornbeam Line', a defensive barrier of barbed wire, mines and sensors stretching north of the coastal settlement of Mughsayl some 40 miles inland. The Line was a particularly imaginative example of military planning and engineering. Its basic purpose was that of creating a physical barrier between the fertile and heavily populated eastern part of the mountain range, the Jebal, and the more arid, sparsely populated western area. Given that the insurgents depended heavily for much of their support on the western area, the construction of Hornbeam, in which some 15,000 coils of barbed wire, 12,000 reels of razor wire, 12,000 pickets and 4,000 mines were used, proved to be a particularly effective weapon in the waging of the war. It isolated the rebels still further from their main area of operations and pushed them back towards the South Yemen border. And the valuable support given by the Iranians in manning the Line was not the only contribution to winning the conflict made by the monarch on the Peacock Throne.

Just a year later, in December 1973, three battalions of Iran's Special Forces arrived on active service in Dhofar, together with logistical support that included 30 Iroquois helicopters. It brought the total strength of the Shah's soldiers in the country to over 3,500 men. This had the effect of doubling the number of men-at-arms available to Sultan Qaboos and was a source of considerable encouragement to his own army, acting as a tremendous morale booster. 1973 was also significant in that another Islamic monarch committed a token force to the war, with King Hussein of Jordan sending men from his army to Oman's field of battle. Not that Oman's ruler rested on the laurels of such welcome support. From the moment of his assumption of power, he had concentrated considerable time, energy and money to building up the strength of his own armed forces and had seen to it that they became better equipped. It was an ambitious rearmament initiative which ran parallel with his Government's

Old Muscat, pre-coup and pre-oil.

The Palace and Customs House in old Muscat.

The British Consulate in old Muscat.

The former Embassy and
Consulate in Muscat.

The site in the British Embassy courtyard where the Manumission Pole used to stand.

The Kobe grave of the Japanese wife of Oman's former Sultan Taimour bin Faisal who was forced to abdicate by the British in 1932.

The new Sultan just 18 days after the Palace Coup of 23 July 1970.

The desert memorial to Lance-Corporal P. Reddy, 22 SAS, killed in
action on 22 December 1970 during Operation Breakfast.

Faccombe Manor on the Hampshire/Berkshire border,
one of Timothy Landon's many British properties.
(© Christopher Ling)

Sultan Qaboos meeting young Omanis at Salalah on the occasion of Eid, 1990.

civil development programme, which was beginning to deliver greatly-improved social conditions for the civilian population, proving its own reward by showing to even the most sceptical that a better tomorrow by far was on the horizon.

By the spring of 1975 the total strength of the Sultan's Armed Forces had risen from a total strength of 4,000 in 1970 (of which only 1,000 were of combat ability) to approximately 12,000, who were led by about 500 contract and seconded British officers. Throughout 1974 defections from the ranks of the PFLOAG had continued unabated, with the *New York Times* of 3 February 1975 quoting a British Major General as saying that the Dhofari rebels were now 'showing less zeal for combat'. The Oman Government put the number of defections at about the same time as having exceeded 1,000 men. The PFLOAG appears to have realised that the war was now being irretrievably lost, with the London-based *Spectator* magazine reporting on 7 February 1976 that captured rebel documents contained criticism that 'Soviet guerrilla training techniques are totally unsuited for an Arabian insurgency' and that recent reversals were due to 'poor communications and a lack of popular support'.

There was even more good news to come. The Shah of Iran guaranteed Oman's airspace protection from violation by enemy aircraft through his provision of ground-to-air missiles together with supporting air cover. Such a welcome act of support for Sultan Qaboos was followed in March 1975 with the dispatch by King Hussein of Jordan of 31 Hawker Hunter jet fighters, designed for ground-attack sorties. The end was now only a question of time. Indeed, the reality of the PFLOAG's bleak prospects of victory had long been recognised by its own commanders. Another captured document dated 7 April 1975, gave a harsh assessment of the situation, 'The present situation is in favour of the enemy from a military point of view. The enemy is superior to us in all areas.' And they were. Throughout the second half of 1975 the Sultan's Armed Forces pressed home their advantage, in a strategy designed to take the fight to the enemy, being particularly well-assisted in the vital task by a Special Forces battalion sent to the service of Sultan Qaboos by his fellow monarch, King Hussein of Jordan. The actual beginning of the end does have a date, 1 October 1975. With the monsoon well and truly over, the Sultan's Armed Forces launched an offensive in the western region of Dhofar, supported by their Iranian and Jordanian allies and led by a distinguished British soldier, Major-General Kenneth Perkins. Official British estimates put the number of rebels in the region at approximately 500, supported by about 350 South

Yemen Army personnel. In a series of successful operations over the following two weeks, the rebels' lines of supply from the coast were effectively cut, a strategy which left them largely impotent. On 18 October, fighter planes of the Sultan's air force, supported by Iranian Phantoms, bombed the town of Hauf, just over the border in South Yemen. It was the site of rebel headquarters and a direct 'hit' was made upon it. To augment the successful cutting of rebel lines of supply from the coast, British Army engineers built a new line of defence just three miles from the Yemen border which cut all routes of supply to the enemy from within their Marxist stronghold. By the first week of December, 130 rebels had fled to government lines and the 350 South Yemen soldiers had crossed back into their own country. The Sultan's armed forces then began a mopping-up operation of those rebels who had become trapped in the western region of Dhofar, taking into armed custody a further 90 men. The end of one of the most extraordinary guerrilla wars in a little-known region of the world was at hand. In the understated tones so beloved of the British Army an 'Order of the Day', dated 4 December 1975 recorded:

> At 1100 hours on the second day of December 1975, the Frontier Force made physical contact with the Muscat Regiment on the Darra ridge . . . It represents the end of organised resistance within Dhofar. His Majesty the Sultan was advised at 1200 hours on the same day that Dhofar was safe for civil development.

The same day, 2 December, was also the day upon which the last rebel-held settlement Dhalkut, on the coast close to the South Yemen border, fell to the Sultan. The day of battle in the deserts and mountains of Dhofar Province had indeed come to an end.

On 11 December 1975, the end of the war was officially declared by Sultan Qaboos in a broadcast to the nation, 'Oman's Armed Forces have secured the first total victory over international Communism by an Arab country.' The moment was indeed sweet and Oman's ruler had good and well justified cause to enjoy his hour of triumph. Principal to the victory had been the military strategy of attrition on the enemy's lines of supply, which was directly responsible for the high number of defections to government forces, as opposed to directing fire principally at rebel groups operating within Dhofar. Also of pivotal importance was the success of the sustained campaign to win the hearts and minds of the Dhofari people, which made a significant contribution to victory. Had Sultan Said, even as late as the 1960s, embarked upon a similar campaign then his subsequent downfall would not have been so easy for those who arranged it.

As wars go, in clinical terms, the cost in human lives was not that great. PFLOAG losses were officially put at 433, but the deaths of South Yemeni troops and their Communist bloc advisers have never been recorded. On the Sultanate side, the figure is believed to be between 55 and 75, plus an additional 18 British contract and seconded personnel. As a single national group, the Iranians sustained the heaviest losses, with over 100 dead and many being disabled.

As 1976 dawned Sultan Qaboos was the very first Omani ruler to preside over a country completely at peace with itself, with increasingly full coffers and having the enormous advantage of having successfully waged a military campaign. No previous Omani leader had experienced such a fortunate national climate in which to govern the country. The task, however, was one that was going to require more, much more, than military skill and the spending of huge amounts of cash to modernise an antique land, despite the unprecedented advantages available to him. He was going to have to demonstrate a coalition of human abilities virtually unique in the 'great game' of holding a nation together at a time of rapid change. And yet, as he proudly stood on the world stage, he was a man of whom the world beyond his shores knew precious little indeed.

# CHAPTER SIX

## The Prodigal Son

On 13 January 1964, John Duncan, her Britannic Majesty's Consul at Muscat, sat down to pen a report to the British Political Resident in the Persian Gulf, Sir William Luce, who monitored the fortunes of London's client states in the region, from the island of Bahrain.

While the letter was of a somewhat melancholy note, its purpose was that of giving Sir William a pen-portrait of a young man born to rule a country that had now assumed a particular significance for London with the discovery of oil in commercially viable quantities just a year before. While the mandarins at the Middle East desk in the Foreign Office had detailed knowledge of the young man in question, having had him closely monitored throughout his time in England and West Germany between 1958–64, as Muscat and Oman increased in significance there was good cause to ponder the future being mapped out for the country and the possible place in the scheme of things for the 24-year-old heir-apparent.

The young man was Sayyid Qaboos bin Said bin Taimour, son of the Sultan of Muscat and Oman, His Highness Sultan Said bin Taimour. In his confidential report, which is reproduced here in full (complete with its quaint, phonetic spelling), Consul Duncan got straight to the point:

> The British Consulate General,
> Muscat. January the 13th, 1965.
>
> Your Excellency,
> 1. I had a long talk with Qabus in his house at Salala on January the 10th.
> 2. I have only met him once before – at lunch in London. In Salala I found him friendly, agreeable and easy to talk with. He has the

natural dignity of his Father and, bearded and upstanding in Omani dress, he looks very much the young princeling. But I found him very difficult to place in terms of weight. His eyes are strangely dull and, I think, unhappy.

3. The set-up is odd indeed. There they sit, father and son in houses only 50 yards apart, and as far as I could make out they have only met on two or three occasions since his return at the beginning of December. I happened to ask Qabus if he had seen his father's renowned parrot. He said he had hardly seen his father, let alone the parrot. He studies the Koran and historical works from 9 a.m. to 12 noon every day under the tuition of Ibrahim as Saif – a senior Qadi from Muscat. And in the evenings he is frequently lectured by chosen wise men on Omani courtesy customs. Then he sits alone. We talked generally about the challenges which the impact of oil would bring but I did not try to draw him out at this first meeting.

4. Then I went across to the Palace for the usual morning meeting. I found the Sultan all agog in a jumpy way which I have not seen in him before. How had I found Qabus? Was he well? Did I think him of Sultanic timber? Was the house all right? I had a sudden and irrelevant vision of the 'When did you last see your father?' painting.

5. I said that I supposed Qabus would be considering getting married (knowing full well that the Sultan already has negotiations in train in the Sharqiya and Duru circuits). The Sultan said that Qabus does not speak with him about these things in the way he himself had spoken with his father, but he had heard indirectly that Qabus wanted to marry an Omani girl. He thought this would work out all right.

6. I then reminded him that he had spoken some time ago of his intention to send Qabus on a tour of the Sultanate. He said he had that in mind but the problem was to find a trustworthy companion. Perhaps he would send Chauncy with him. This was disconcerting and I said I thought it would surely be better for him to be accompanied by leaders from among his own people. The Sultan agreed, but he is clearly in a quandry about this.

7. He said that studies and indoctrination must continue for some months. It was really too early yet to decide what to do with him. He hoped to see more of him. I said I felt that Qabus would certainly like that.

8. Perhaps they will get closer together. The Sultan seems to be taking an inordinately long time to make the necessary move.

9. I am copying this letter to Frank Brenchley.

    J.S.R. Duncan.

The letter with its avuncular air of concern for the welfare of the young man born to rule and manifest worry regarding his isolation is nonetheless a classic example of the long-practised diplomatic art of exercising indirect power; as in a game of chess, the pawns are carefully placed on the board with the long-term aim of achieving the desired result. It is not known what 'moves' London had in mind for the young Qaboos in January 1965, although Duncan's obvious future intention to 'draw out' the son of Sultan Said on the question of his country entering the age of oil revenues is well illustrated in the third paragraph of his report. But in January 1965, there was still time to discuss the business of what to do with the money, as it was well known then that revenues that would bring Muscat and Oman into the league of the mega-rich would not actually take place for at least another 18 months. Still one had to make plans, if one was not to be caught with one's pinstriped (or khaki-coloured) pants down when the rush for the loot started. In the scheme of things to come it is also obvious that Qaboos's future bride was also a matter for official, if confidential, concern. For as Duncan confided to his immediate political master in Bahrain, while he had raised the matter of Qaboos's marriage, he knew full well that the Sultan already had negotiations in train about a possible betrothal. In actual fact, the Sultan had laid plans for marriage with a daughter of the much respected paramount leader of the Al Harthy tribe in the Sharqiya region.

As we have earlier seen, the Al Harthy were what they remain today in Oman, a respected group well known during the time of the Imamate to be fierce in battle and wise in civil counsel. An alliance between them and the ruling house of Al Busaid must have seemed like a particularly sound exercise in statecraft to the father of the young Qaboos. Consequently, during a courtesy visit made to the Sultan in Salalah by Sheikh Ahmad bin Mohammed Al Harthy, the former had proposed to the latter the betrothal of his only son to the Sheikh's eldest daughter. Agreement on such a marriage of high convenience was promptly made by the two men and an announcement of the engagement duly made. Before the happy day could take place the British-generated winds of change swept Sultan Said off his throne and the whole idea of marriage between the two young people lapsed. After the Palace coup, Sheikh Ahmad made one or two injudicious comments on the new scheme of things, true to the character of the independently-minded Al Harthy tribe, and was promptly placed under close house arrest for his pains by Sultan Qaboos, rendering an alliance between the two families ever more remote.

Qaboos himself was the consequence of his father's marriage to a young girl from the Jebali people, who principally occupy the mountain areas of Dhofar, particularly the brooding Jebal which dominates the Salalah skyline. Her home was at Taqa on the Dhofari coast, west of Salalah town. The Jebali are quite unique in Oman's lexicon of tribes, with their own language and culture, both quite distinct from that of the Arab population. Mazon bint Ahmad Al Mashani was greatly loved for her human warmth, generosity and wisdom, the latter being of singular value to her son after he assumed the burdens of state. While such human qualities greatly endeared her to a wide range of people, her intuitive sense, in the words of a former expatriate courtier, 'of what was best, right and what, therefore, had to be done' was feared by some of her son's ministers. They were, in the main, 'incompetent, greedy, devious and never hesitated to deliver her judgement to her son', who was (and remains) inclined to be too tolerant of human appetites which are often self-serving. It is his mother's generosity of spirit and capacity for acts of great personal kindness which he has demonstrably inherited from her; his own pattern of conduct in such a regard is legion. At his mother's death, on 12 August 1992, Sultan Qaboos lost more than a mother and Oman lost an untiring champion of its real interests.

A quiet cultured man, with considerable royal bearing and abiding dignity, Oman's 14th ruler from the Al Busaid dynasty is without doubt unique in the pantheon of Arab leaders and quite exceptional in almost every other way. His personal generosity and loyalty to those he believes have served him well is legendary, as are his broader concerns, for example for the natural order, not just at home but abroad. He gives an annual award via UNESCO for environmental enterprise. His love and knowledge of classical music, both Arabic and Western, also distinguishes him. This interest led him to establish Oman's very own Royal Symphony Orchestra. He is, according to the former courtier quoted earlier,

> A man with a remarkable knowledge of just how the world really works and what so often actually motivates people, from Ambassadors to private individuals, in their approach to him. He

loathes sycophancy and knows it when he sees it, although he is too sensitive, too kindly by far to discomfort the individual practising it by letting him know it then and there.

The Omani ruler is also keenly aware of history, not only of his own country but of the wider Arab world and familiar with the fragility of Arab coalitions. On occasion he is not averse to declaring that he is fully aware of the 'delicately balanced' nature of the relationships of those countries, including Britain, which so often proclaim themselves to be among the Sultanate's oldest and closest allies. A contemporary courtier comments, 'His Majesty knows only too well that the whole exercise is one of balance, maintaining that balance and keeping in play a whole series of checks on such relationships.'

Well, he should know, given his country's long and suffocatingly close relationship with Britain and particularly its mania for making and unmaking Omani rulers over the generations. It is a habit of which Oman's current ruler is not altogether sure that Britain has completely cured herself! But he only mentions this in the strictest of confidence, of course. The subject of the 'events' in his father's palace in Salalah on 23 July 1970 has long been off limits to those very few, carefully selected journalists who are granted a Sultanic audience. An American who some years ago asked of the possibility during his pre-audience briefing, was promptly told that under no circumstances must the subject be raised. However, as the subsequent royal interview drew to an end he did ask the Sultan about having in effect overthrown his own father, as a final, unscheduled question. A brief, oblique response was given, as the temperature dramatically dropped to that of South Pole proportions. Realising too late that he had overstepped the mark the hapless journalist attempted to make amends and apologised for having raised the matter, claiming that he simply hadn't been able to resist posing 'such a crucial question'. His Majesty the Sultan of Oman patted his robes and replied, 'Oh, that's all right. Don't worry about it. You see, in my job one meets all sorts of people.'

The reticence of Sultan Qaboos to discuss his childhood, his formative years or, indeed, the Palace Coup that was 'recommended' to him, is understandable enough when only the barest facts are known of his early life. He was born on 18 November 1940, at Salalah, the only son his father had. Consequently from the very moment of his birth he had the burden of hereditary Arab leadership placed upon him. Little has ever been known of his childhood, which was spent exclusively in Dhofar. While he was not allowed to mix with children of his own age from beyond the palace walls, he did venture out often with his Khadeem (personal servants). In the Dhofar countryside and on visits to the beach, he developed his love of natural history, the natural order of things which in the 1950s was considerably more abundant in southern Oman than it is today. He also learned to ride, doing so almost before he could walk, and remains a good horseman with a keen professional eye for a thoroughbred. But once back inside the palace his life was one of isolation and consequent loneliness. True, he had the affection of his mother and a companionship of sorts afforded by his personal servants, but it was far from being the social environment in which a young prince could prepare himself for the role history and circumstance would demand of him. His early education was entrusted by his father to an elderly Islamic scholar. Naturally enough he concentrated on giving his royal charge a thorough grounding in the spiritual imperatives of Islam and a comprehensive knowledge of Omani and Arab history.

However, it fell to the British to introduce the biggest single change in the life of the young Qaboos. Following repeated representation to his father by the British Consul, a frequent visitor to Salalah from Muscat, Sultan Said agreed in 1958 that his son should attend the Royal Military Academy at Sandhurst. Then, as now, this was something of a tradition for Arab princes from the Gulf. The British further recommended that before his entry to Sandhurst as an officer-cadet at the age of 19, Qaboos should spend at least a year, if not more, at a place of private tuition in England. During his time there, his academic capabilities could be broadened. What followed can only have been the most extraordinary change of atmosphere, both culturally and physically, for the 17-year-old Arab prince who hitherto had only known life within the walls of a palace in a remote region of Arabia. The experience could well have been a nightmare for the young Qaboos but turned out to be a time of unprecedented happiness.

Philip Roman and his wife Laura were the epitome of Middle England, living in the village of Felsham, ten miles east of Bury St Edmunds in the county of Suffolk. An academic who eventually entered the Church, Philip Roman provided pre-university tuition to private pupils; he was in actual fact a 'crammer'. It would have been a virtual impossibility for the British Government to have found a more suitable couple to chaperone and incubate the young, unworldly Arab prince. Their curious brand of suburban, right-of-centre, white Anglo-Saxon values and prejudices were typical of those so beloved by much of England's middle class, a large proportion of whom hold senior positions in such national departments of state as the Foreign and Commonwealth Office. In another sense, the Romans were an odd choice for an Islamic prince to be lodged with, but in the words of a former Foreign Office mandarin who had well-established links with the British Intelligence organisation MI6 in the 1950s and 1960s:

> It was all rather unusual but the Romans were absolutely ideal, a super choice for the very simple reason that they were such an unlikely couple for the job at hand. They did not go out of their way to draw attention to themselves. They were discreet. They made damn sure that Qaboos didn't go astray, was not exposed to the harsh mercies of the bright lights of metropolitan life, where he would have become exposed to undesirable, alien ideas. It was an ideal regime under which he could be fashioned for the future and, of course, well-prepared academically for Sandhurst.

Such a process was the principal duty of Philip Roman who accomplished the task with distinction, by all accounts. Life with the Romans was the young Omani's first experience of a regulated family environment and as a surrogate mother, Laura Roman, with cornflower-blue eyes and a firm manner, filled the role now expected of her with sympathy for the young Arab so far from home. She ran, in some senses, a spartan domestic regime; Calvinistic in a way which reflected many of the spiritual and social values espoused by the Islamic faith. There was no television set in the Romans' household, with both husband and wife frowning on the social excesses so frequently to be seen on the small screen; Qaboos took to going to a neighbour's house to watch theirs. It was a routine kind of hospitality, but one the young Arab gentleman never forgot. Soon after he became Sultan, the couple in question were astonished to receive a present from Arabia's newest ruler, a colour television of truly splendid proportions.

But the Royal military academy beckoned and in September 1960 Qaboos entered its hallowed gates. He was posted to Marne Company in New College. After the relative comfort and personal privacy of the Romans' household, the harsh utilitarian nature of Sandhurst came as a cruel shock. A fellow officer-cadet who was a contemporary of his recalls, 'Qaboos dealt with the harshness of life, its lack of privacy and its hectoring atmosphere by being rather aloof. This, of course, only made matters worse for him. He came in for a great deal of bullying.' On some occasions it must have seemed to Officer-Cadet Qaboos that he had left the confinement of his father's palace in Salalah for another 'hell on earth'.

It was at this particularly bleak time for Qaboos that he met a man who came to have an influence over him, one that not only catapulted him onto his father's throne before it was vacant, but led to him permitting an involvement in the subsequent affairs of his country. Cadet James Timothy Whittington Landon shared a study with Qaboos at Sandhurst. As an arrangement it was a fortuitous move on the diplomatic chessboard and a pivotal one in the end game that was to unfold a decade later. In fact, what is known in Oman and indeed elsewhere as 'The Landon Factor' is so extraordinary that it justifies a chapter in this book all of its very own. But in the meantime, it should be recorded that Landon did render valuable, noble service to Qaboos, one that is almost certainly the genesis of this unlikely relationship between two men of vastly different temperament: one, the young Arab prince, a kind, sensitive, spiritual man, an intellectual, with a love of nature and thanks to the guidance of the Romans, a considerable knowledge of European classical music; the other a typical representative of the British middle classes, 'a cold, cheerless individual', who in the words of a contemporary, was determined 'to get on and make out', particularly with England's ruling class to which he so ardently wished to belong. It was a journey made particularly difficult because of his Canadian birth and the 'colonial tag' which ludicrously, was still very much in existence at Sandhurst as late as the 1960s. While it took time for a friendship to evolve between the two men sharing the same study, it was given impetus by the protection afforded to Qaboos by Landon from the bullying to which the young Arab was being subjected. He was so unhappy at Sandhurst during his early time there that he used to go 'home' to the Romans every weekend rather than remain at the Academy. Once back in Felsham he was cocooned in the warmth of the Romans' care and in a reciprocal return of such affection, was not averse to helping out Philip Roman with the washing-up after dinner. They were to develop a particularly close relationship.

In August 1962, his Sandhurst ordeal came to an end with his graduation and attachment to the 1st Battalion of the Cameronians, who were then stationed at Minden with the British Army of the Rhine. The choice of the Cameronians had earlier been indicated to the British Government by Sultan Said back home in Salalah. He had a particular affection for this British regiment which had served him so admirably when he was experiencing his own difficulties in the 1950s, in Buraimi and later, during the Green Mountain conflict.

Following a year's tour of operational duty in West Germany, Qaboos, at the suggestion of the Foreign Office, went on to study local government through visits and short attachments to civic institutions in Warwick and Bedford. It is not known why the British were of the opinion that a knowledge of Middle England's domestic arrangements (the technicalities of dog control, the levying of rates and public hygiene) would have anything to offer an Arab prince, or indeed to what good use he could eventually put such experience once he had returned to his native land. But their idea as to how he should complete his sojourn abroad was most certainly more imaginative and of greater potential value.

It was proposed that he should embark upon the Foreign Office's version of the Victorian Grand Tour, a journey through several countries, during which he was closely chaperoned, as ever, by a 'minder' from the long but not so visible arm of the British establishment. His last port of call prior to arriving back home, courtesy of the RAF, was the British Crown Colony of Aden. There, in a demonstration of his aesthetic sense, he told the Governor of the day, 'If Muscat is half as beautiful as Aden in ten years' time, I shall be more than pleased.' As an historical aside, it is interesting to note that while it took a little longer than ten years, Muscat today is one of the cleanest and most attractive cities on the planet; Aden, once so prosperous, bustling and beautiful, has been reduced after 30 years of neglect and mismanagement, to the appearance of a city knocked back into the pre-industrial age.

Once Qaboos was back in Salalah, arriving there just as 1964 drew to a close, the former regime was reinstituted. Isolated from the world he had so recently been a part of and once more taught in the spiritual imperatives of the Holy Koran from an Omani religious scholar, he quickly began to pine for the world he had left behind, the only alleviation being visits from his mother, carrying the latest copies of *The Times* to arrive in the country. As a result of British pressure, Sultan Said did begin to allow his son visitors. Drawn from a small carefully selected group, acceptable to both the Sultan and the British, this somewhat narrowed the field. Most of them were from the British expatriate community.

One of them was a seconded officer on the staff of the Sultan's Armed Forces, where he worked as a desert intelligence officer. Following the young soldier's recall to London, and a crash course in intelligence work, he returned to Oman in 1967. The British proposed him to Sultan Said for the post of Senior Intelligence Officer in his army. From that time onwards his visits to the Palace to see Qaboos became frequent; visits which took place with the Sultan's prior knowledge and consent. Or at least, most of them did. Sultan Said most certainly had no knowledge of what the visitor eventually began to raise in conversation until it was too late. The visitor's name? Timothy Landon, Qaboos's former protector from the bullies at the Royal Military Academy at Sandhurst. In the back rooms of Whitehall, behind doors most firmly closed, plans were being carefully laid for the long-term future of that part of Arabia Felix.

# CHAPTER SEVEN

## Roll Out the Barrel

'The avarice of mankind is insatiable' – Aristotle

Oman's 'New Dawn' was not announced to the people of the country and the wider world until three days after the Palace coup. Until such time as Sultan Qaboos bin Said Al Said chooses to record for posterity his own personal experiences of being catapulted from obscurity into the role of Executive Head of State, only the established facts can be presented with which to draw a reasonably accurate picture of the hour that came immediately in the wake of his father's overthrow.

What can be most definitely recorded is that while his rich inheritance was unique among his royal ancestors, there was a virtual absence of any civil infrastructure (not even, for example, the rudimentary beginnings of a police force) around which he could build the 'modern government' he had so promptly promised an expectant nation. It is also known that when he entered those parts of his father's palace previously denied to him, the sight he met was chaotic. Government files and papers were found stored at random and not in any methodical order throughout the offices and private apartments. In the courtyard stood some 33 military lorries piled high with guns of varying makes, together with boxes of assorted ammunition. The new Sultan was not even aware of the state's financial situation, or indeed that of his father, until Peter Mason arrived back in Oman from England, from where he had been promptly summoned. In the absence of a civil service equal to the task, Oman's new ruler took the only means available to him to begin to administer the country. He appointed various members of his army to carry out a whole range of civil duties. Troops assumed routine, basic civilian duties such as making sure that motorists obeyed the new rule of driving on the right as opposed to the left, an initiative of the new regime which, according to an observer at the time, 'had elements of both farce and tragedy' as some took longer than others 'to get the hang of it'; providing medical care (an outbreak of cholera came soon after the coup); and, a short while into the 'new dawn', delivering the state's new coinage and banknotes to other country's remotest villages and settlements. But it fell to senior British officers to begin the actual process of governing the country and putting an administration together.

The first meeting of the Interim Advisory Council (IAC), which took place in a khaki-coloured military tent, had all the authority of a lawfully-constituted Cabinet. Principal within its ranks were the Chairman, Colonel Hugh Oldman, Brigadier Malcolm Dennison, the former Sultan's Political and Intelligence Officer who went on to become the new Government's Director of Intelligence and a member of the National Defence Council, and Major-General John Graham, who took the minutes of the IAC's very first meeting. In the absence of a suitable, Omani-staffed institution to assume the duties of governing in those early days of his reign, Sultan Qaboos had little choice but to sanction the placing of such authority in the hands of this small group of British Army officers. For a while at least they enjoyed immediate personal power not seen since the high days of the Imperial Raj.

But it was far from an ideal way in which to launch the new state. In the words of a senior British officer who was in Muscat at the time, too many of his fellow countrymen were prone to 'sycophancy in their dealings with the new Sultan of a quite appalling degree' and 'fawned around him and patronised him in the craven hope that they would make their mark with him and gain his favour'. In addition, many had agendas of their own which were not in Oman's best interests. There was, to give but one example, a signed contract for a road in Salalah that had been given to a German company; but the Sultan was persuaded to cancel it and award it to a British concern. This is not, however, to impugn the motives of the key players on the IAC. Men such as Graham and Dennison were of the highest integrity and while Oldman was in many eyes somewhat tainted goods for having planned and carried out the coup against the old Sultan, there was never any suggestion that he was not of the utmost financial probity in his new role as a member of the council. It was some of the other senior officers who actually carried out the orders and who on numerous occasions went to council members in order to push their own pet schemes. This practice is what gave rise to suspicion and resentment, particularly among Omanis. I do know that as early as 1971 Sultan Qaboos was aware of the bad blood between many senior British officers as they jostled for his attention intent on receiving favour and approval for their own proposals. The man so many of them loved to hate was Colonel Tim Landon, Equerry and the closest man of all to the Sultan. If any one of them held 'the keys to the kingdom', it was most definitely Landon. He was the source of great jealousy and because of his cold conduct made himself even more unpopular. It was all very much a heady brew. The situation was as unattractive as it was unproductive for the Sultan, but there seems very little he could have done about it in the early years of his coming to power. He knew full well, of course, that he owed his throne to many of them for either planning the overthrow of his father or standing down during the actual coup itself and refusing to aid the Sultan. The situation was not a pretty one at all. It was not long before Omani resentment at the all too apparent dominance by British officers over their new ruler began to surface. Yet the one initiative promised to the nation by the Sultan in his maiden broadcast, that could have done much to alleviate such local resentment, came to grief.

In that broadcast, Sultan Qaboos announced the imminent return of his uncle from exile, to take up the post of Prime Minister. Sayyid Tarik bin Taimour Al Said was by any standards a quite remarkable man. He had worked as a military liaison officer at the time of the Buraimi and Green Mountain conflicts and had vigorously opposed his brother's punitive measures against those involved in supporting the Imamate rebels, so much so that in 1958 he was banished by the Sultan from Oman. He had eventually made his way to West Germany where he married and worked as a roving representative for an international construction company. A linguist and a man of considerable personal charm, dignity and diplomacy, he had a knowledge and awareness of the world beyond Oman's shores that made him an ideal candidate to return home and aid Oman. Sultan Qaboos had appealed to all educated, professional Omanis to do just that in his broadcast. But in the case of Sayyid Tarik, Sultan Qaboos actually named him as the Prime Minister designate of the new Oman. Crucially, for it explains much of what later came to pass, Sayyid Tarik bin Taimour Al Said was of an independent turn of mind, intellectually agile with a thorough, down-to-earth understanding of how the world worked. He harboured no illusions about the true nature of the relationship between his country and Great Britain. He was forceful, fluent in debate and provocatively brave in expressing his opinions. He was considered a loose cannon, very much his own man and as such 'greatly feared', in the words of an Omani insider, by those who had so secretly and carefully planned the overthrow of his brother. Speaking in the spring of 1998 for the first time about Tarik's role as Prime Minister, a senior member of Oman's establishment recalled the extraordinary sequence of events that brought Tarik home, along with the tragedy which then unfolded for Oman's future:

Tarik had often written to Qaboos, his nephew, from Germany but we came to know that they were intercepted by Malcolm Dennison, the government's intelligence officer who, strangely enough, was the man used by the British to sound out Tarik as to whether or not he would return home if Said was overthrown. Just before the coup Dennison went to see Tarik, who was in Cyprus at the time. To speak honestly, Tarik didn't like Dennison that much. He certainly didn't trust him, but then he always was suspicious of the real intentions of the British in Oman. He always used to say that they, the British, were okay in their own country, but not in Oman! Anyway, Tarik put down certain conditions to Dennison, about eight I think, two of which were that there should be a written constitution and that Qaboos should become a constitutional monarch, with the Prime Minister having the powers of a chief executive. And a draft constitution was drawn up by a team of lawyers. Tarik was told by Dennison that Qaboos had agreed to such constitutional arrangements. When in the famous broadcast the appointment of Tarik as Prime Minister was announced, he returned home to Oman to take up his duties. Perhaps he should have sought clearer definition of exactly what his responsibilities would be. That he did not do so can now be seen clearly as a mistake. But he took both Sultan Qaboos and Dennison at their word and there was, after all, the evidence of the broadcast to convince him that what had been publicly said would actually take place. But even during his first visit to meet Qaboos, a whispering campaign against him was started by the British. It must have been difficult for Qaboos. Here were the men who had put him on the throne, telling him things they wanted him to believe yet he, the ruler of the country, obviously didn't have the experience of such office politics to put up forceful arguments against them. It is forgotten now, but he really was very inexperienced at the beginning. It really wasn't his fault. He simply hadn't been prepared for government and was a tool in the hands of the British officers. And they knew it and exploited this weakness at the top for all they were worth.

It is known that at their first meeting Sultan Qaboos told his Prime Minister that he wanted to keep under his control all financial matters, particularly policy relating to the oil industry, as well as both internal and external defence arrangements. While such a requirement would appear to have neutered to some considerable degree the powers and functions of an executive Prime Minister, Tarik would not have been that surprised, given his suspicions of so many of those whispering their own agendas into the ear of the man upon the throne. It had long been a practice for Oman's rulers to prevent Omanis from having any detailed knowledge of the country's finances, one most certainly carried out by his brother Sultan Said. Following his first brief visit to Oman since the coup, Tarik returned to his wife and family in Germany to consider his position. All the while the IAC continued its function of putting the beginnings of the new state together, presenting the Sultan with 'a positive avalanche' of proposals, mainly involving construction projects, the great majority of which he agreed to. Consequently when Tarik did eventually return to take up his duties, many fundamental decisions affecting the future of the country had already been taken. Naturally enough, he railed against what he regarded with no small justification as excessive and intrusive British expatriate influence in shaping his country's future, but to no avail. The mounting frustration now being experienced by Oman's Prime Minister was further exacerbated by the fact that he was not only not given information by British advisers on such crucial matters as policy directives and the state of the country's finances, but was not even furnished with a secretariat of his own which would have supported him in his work. Nonetheless, he did use the authority he could bring to bear and initiated several important development projects. These principally used the Development Board established by Sultan Said before his overthrow. Even given the inhibitions on his work, Prime Minister Tarik did manage to make considerable progress throughout 1971, being principally responsible for the establishment of several key ministries: Education, Labour, a Ministry of Economic Affairs and a Ministry of Health, crucial to a country that had such a crying need for a radical improvement in standards of public well-being.

But it was in establishing Oman on the world stage that Prime Minister

Tarik made an outstanding contribution, helping his nation take its rightful place in the community of nations. His linguistic ability (he spoke four languages fluently) and his considerable experience of operating in an international environment made him an ideal candidate to consolidate Oman's re-emergence as a nation state. During the course of the year he travelled extensively, seeking recognition for Oman and the subsequent foundation of diplomatic relations. He was so successful that by the end of 1971 diplomatic relations had been established with Morocco, Jordan, Japan, the United States of America and with Oman's neighbours in the region: the United Arab Emirates, Saudi Arabia and Iran. In October had come the big breakthrough: Premier Tarik took the Sultanate of Oman into the Arab League, against stiff opposition from many nationalist Arab states which regarded Sultan Qaboos as 'a British puppet'.

Membership of the League was quickly followed by membership of the United Nations. It was a truly remarkable achievement by Oman's Prime Minister, one which finally confirmed that the country had arrived in the world and put behind it its long night of isolation from the mainstream of international affairs. But, ironically, it was his long trips abroad which were used against Tarik by his enemies. The afore-mentioned senior member of the Omani establishment remembers the time well:

> Yes, it was all very unpleasant. As Tarik's stature grew in the eyes of the Sultan Qaboos, mainly for his achievements in the diplomatic field, so did the whispering campaign against him become ever louder. At the back of their minds, of course, was the fear that if Tarik became too successful, too powerful, he would reintroduce his original ideas, those he put to Dennison in Cyprus, that Qaboos become a constitutional monarch and that Tarik, as had been agreed in principle, would become an executive Prime Minister. Tarik told me himself, on more than one occasion, that the new Oman should make a complete break with the past and become, in time, a leader of modern, political, constitutional development in the region. Of course, this would have put a complete stop to the control of the country that a very small group around the Sultan effectively had and from which they still continue to profit. So the campaign against him became even stronger. Their aim? That Tarik had to go.

Faced with continuing obstruction from the Sultan's senior expatriate advisers, Prime Minister Tarik began to have serious doubts about the viability of his position as 1971 drew to a close. Fearing that he might force a showdown that would have damaging effects on Oman's so recently established international standing, the expatriate advisers suggested to the Sultan that Tarik be appointed the country's External Relations Officer in Geneva, where his international experience would be put to good use; and, of course, keep him out of Oman for much of the year. An office and a suitable residence were identified in the Swiss lakeside city but, suddenly, there were second thoughts. Given his reputation as a 'loose cannon', those senior British expatriates who had the Sultan's ear felt that the control of Tarik so far away would be next to impossible, so the whole idea was dropped.

For Prime Minister Tarik this sudden about-turn was the end. Quietly packing his bags just a few days before Christmas 1971, Tarik flew to Beirut with his young son Qais beside him. Before his departure he had written to his nephew resigning from the post of Prime Minister. The experiment in laying the foundations for constitutional government, the real 'new dawn' for Oman as proposed by the country's first, and to date, only Prime Minister, had failed. It had done so principally because of the self-serving manoeuvres of a tight little group of expatriates and senior Omanis, who knew perfectly well that the system the Prime Minister was working towards would have been a most effective check and inhibition on their private activities from which they were to enrich themselves. It was a lost opportunity, one which, had it been allowed to develop, would have laid valuable foundations for the eventual transition of Oman into the very first state on the Arabian Peninsula with a truly modern government. In the final analysis, that is exactly what Sultan Qaboos promised the Omani people in his premier broadcast to them over 31 years ago.

The extent to which Prime Minister Tarik's influence was feared can be gauged by the fact that following his resignation, those known to have been close to him in the Army and the Royal Oman Police were summarily dismissed from their posts. Sultan Qaboos did not announce the resignation to the Omani nation for six months. However there was a rapprochement between the Sultan and his former Prime Minister in 1975. Tarik returned to Oman to be appointed Chairman of the country's Central Bank, with his signature being carried on the Sultanate's banknotes until his death in 1980. In March 1976 the repaired relationship between uncle and nephew was given a new dimension by the marriage of Tarik's youngest daughter, Nawwal, to Sultan Qaboos. Upon marriage her name was changed to Kamile, at the Sultan's request. The marriage did not last however, and was subsequently dissolved.

The development of ministerial government continued, even in the absence of Prime Minister Tarik. A Court Office was established (known in Oman as the Diwan) and a Council of Ministers appointed, with the Sultan as Chairman. While the Dhofar War continued, it consumed just over half the revenues from oil. However a building boom did proceed, transforming the face of Muscat, and much of the country besides, at a truly astonishing speed. In a country that had so little, there was much to be done: not just ministries, schools, health centres and hospitals but roads, flyovers, commercial complexes (such as supermarkets and shopping malls), ports and harbours, airports, residential areas and luxury hotels. All appeared to sprout from the ground like grass after spring rains. A senior oil executive who was in Oman during 'the intoxicating years of the early 1970s', now in retirement in Britain, remembers this exciting time well:

> At one stage Muscat resembled one huge building site. Thousands, quite literally thousands, of manual workers from India, Pakistan and Bangladesh poured into the country, changing dramatically the social scene. Western expatriates, too, came to Oman to take up executive and supervisory roles, both in government and the private sector. The pace was fast and furious. In many respects it was, with the vast amounts of money slushing around, a little like Chicago in the 1920s but without the machine-guns. Still, it did not take long for the carpetbaggers to appear on the scene.

This jocular comparison with Chicago in the roaring '20s is more apt than it may first appear. In Oman, as in other parts of the Arab and developing world, it is a common and accepted practice for a Minister to use his position to enrich himself through the mixing of official duties with any commercial arrangements he can put into place. Many of Oman's nouveau riche, the so-called 'Muscat Mafia' that Omanis themselves love to hate, laid the foundations of their huge personal fortunes in the 1970s via the patronage of the state. As with the returns from slavery in the eighteenth and nineteenth centuries, the rich embarked upon an orgy of palace building, constructing houses of extreme cost and ostentation just like their merchant counterparts in centuries past. Their fortunes continued to grow through holding agencies for Western arms, automobile manufacturers, construction companies and franchises for consumer goods, and they consequently added yachts, private planes and residences in London, Paris and Marbella to their private fortunes. Most of this group began to appear on Oman's new roads in cars of the highest cost – Rolls-Royce, Mercedes Benz and BMWs – thus giving personal witness that the country had gone, for some at least, from the camel to the Cadillac in under a decade.

It must be established that the practice of enriching oneself through the expedient of holding high office did not have the air of censure during 'those intoxicating years of the country's "new dawn"', that would immediately descend upon the head of a minister guilty of similar conduct in the developed world. At the time even when Muscat's good and great cavorted with carpetbaggers, they were not breaking either the law of the land or customary, commercial tradition. What they failed to comprehend in their overweening arrogance and naked greed is that their conduct would, with the passage of time, recruit the resentment and hatred of their very own people. Neither was it taken into official account that the headlong stampede into all things modern would itself come to be seen by many Omanis as a remorseless march towards unacceptable levels of Westernisation of their society. Then, as now, the government information machine in Muscat was at constant pains to present the 'modern' face of Oman to visiting journalists. It conveyed the message that Oman was very much of the modern world which, as an interpretation, was open to question depending very much on what the term actually means in the eye of the beholder. If the term does indeed mean modern government, commercial and residential buildings and an abundance of American fast-food outlets, then such an official description can indeed be accepted. If, however, it means a country's domestic arrangements of governance, then one arrives at a completely different answer.

Even today the detailed causes of their disaffection are not precisely known (the series of events remains a closely guarded secret of state), but in 1972 the sound of distant thunder broke over the country with the arrest of a number of Omanis on charges of sedition. Some of those arrested were in senior positions, including men of the Sultan's army and the Royal Oman Police. Just what ignited their resentment has never been officially published, but it would appear to have been a combination of fierce anger at the ever-rising levels of condoned corruption by ministers, the very visible power enjoyed by a select group of expatriates close to the Sultan and a palpable fear that as the Westernisation of the country continued apace, the spiritual imperatives of Islam would suffer. In any event, following secret trials, many of those involved in the plot to overthrow Sultan Qaboos (and there was most definitely a plan to do so) were summarily executed.

Just a year later, on 23 July 1973, and the third anniversary of his accession to the throne of Oman, a further plot to assassinate Qaboos was uncovered. It was a sharp-eyed member of the Royal Oman Police who noticed that a light on a lorry driving into Muscat was malfunctioning. When he flagged the vehicle down, its occupants opened fire and killed him. After those in the lorry had been overcome by the police, it was established that they had been on their way to a Muscat stadium, where the Sultan was to be present, intending to assassinate him as he took the salute at a military parade. While this attempt was never officially confirmed, it did leak into the public domain, and coming so soon after the foiled attempt of the previous year, severely shook many, particularly those in high places. For while the war in the south was being won, the boom continued and the Sultan remained firmly on the throne, it was becoming increasingly apparent perhaps, that all was not as it seemed, that there were 'things' that were now going seriously wrong.

There was most certainly trouble in store at the state's Treasury. The huge amounts of money being spent on fighting the Dhofar war, re-equipping the army and the massive state-sponsored construction programmes, were now taking a severe toll on revenue. As we have already seen, by mid-1974 the country was heading towards debt, so much so that when Sultan Qaboos attempted to purchase Jaguar fighter aircraft and the Rapier guided missile system, he was told by his Treasury that it could not be done out of state resources; if the orders were to go ahead they could only be financed through loans. This had a salutary effect and in July the Sultan issued a Royal Decree which hoisted a storm-cone to his ministers: expenditure was to be curbed and, what is more, no further capital development projects were to be inaugurated for at least another 18 months.

But help was already on the way. In 1973, Westerners had come to recognise the features of the Saudi Arabian Oil Minister, the dapper, softly-spoken and skilful Sheikh Yamani. In his role as Chairman of the powerful Oil Producing Exporting Countries (OPEC), he delivered via their television screens and in the newspapers, a whole series of 'oil shocks' throughout the mid-1970s and into the first half of the '80s. In the words of the late Shah of Iran, 'This noble product has for far too long been sold cheaply to the rest of the world.' Under Sheikh Yamani's guidance this soon stopped. In the space of three short years the price of oil quadrupled, reaching the staggering price of 40 US dollars a barrel at its height. While Oman was not a member of the organisation it did, of course, benefit hugely from OPEC's efforts. Their actions ushered into this so recently impoverished land riches of such an extent that, in the words of the former oil company executive, 'it was quite remarkable that so many remained sane'.

As the 1970s drew to a close, the amounts of money being 'made' by Muscat's small, but dominant, merchant families (numbering no more than 12 in total), quite literally 'defied belief'. But as ever with money that has all too easily been 'made' rather than earned, it was a situation that brought its very own bitter, social divisions, the implications of which Oman lives with today; implications which increase in significance as austerity appears ever nearer on the national horizon. For as the public displays by the few of such wealth became ever more apparent and vulgar to the general public, Omanis regarded it with an increasing unease. Indeed they continue to do so, particularly as the country is being obliged to live in an era when oil prices are more moderate.

But it was not the dozen or so merchant families alone who 'were so earnestly taking a ride on Oman's gravy train', in the words of a British diplomat. No indeed. Muscat's oligarchy of businessmen-cum-ministers were joined on the diplomats' 'gravy train' by equally powerful expatriates; enthusiastic fellow passengers who were going along for considerably more than the ride.

# CHAPTER EIGHT

## The Wild Colonial Boy

On the evening of Monday, 9 February 1998, a middle-aged man described as short, stout and balding, entered the Tuscany Restaurant, situated in the Hyatt Regency Hotel of Muscat, to keep a dinner appointment. He looked warily around him as he walked towards his host's table, conveniently situated in the corner of the restaurant. The table meant he could keep an eye on the other diners and in an apparently well-set pattern of behaviour, see those he may want to see and take prompt steps to avoid meeting those he didn't. At the further end of the Tuscany, an ex-minister of the Omani Crown was dining with his family. Upon seeing the man enter the restaurant, he threw his napkin on the table and made an irritated, premature exit, his bewildered family trailing in his furious wake. Entering the hotel's grand, arabesque atrium lobby, he saw a former ministerial colleague. Muttering an Arabic oath he told him who he had seen and why he had made such a sudden departure from the restaurant. Speaking later the ex-minister said: 'My God, I know why he is here. It is because of "Hadaf". How much, in God's name, is enough? How much more does he want?'

'Hadaf', the Arabic for 'target', is the name given by the Royal Air Force of Oman to its plan for a new Air Defence Missile System currently stalled on grounds of cost. The award of this would bring huge financial return both to the company involved and the agents who had sold the chosen system to the Government of Oman on the company's behalf. While the veracity of the ex-minister's belief that the subject of his wrath had arrived from Britain in the hope of profiting from the arms deal has never been shown to be true, his supposition did gain currency in Muscat throughout the following week. What really is quite extraordinary on the face of it, however, is the former minister's deep, personal, irrational resentment and hostility to the individual in question. For if Oman's unofficial, that is unpublished, history is to be believed (and there is good reason to believe it), the man dining in the Tuscany Restaurant on that particular evening was the very same man who, at Britain's bidding, was principal in putting Sultan Qaboos on the throne of Oman, an act which released the country from its mediaeval existence. This being so, instead of the ambivalence and sometimes resentment directed towards him in Oman, surely the opposite should be the case?

James Timothy Whittington Landon, known widely by his honorific title 'the Brigadier', which was afforded him by Oman's ruler, and as 'Tim' to his friends, is very much a product of the British Empire. He was born on Vancouver Island, part of Canada's western seaboard, on 20 August 1942. His English father was in the Canadian Army, while his mother was Canadian. More to the point, he is unusual in today's crass, egalitarian climate in that he holds against all comers the attitudes (and indeed exercises the airs) that were the pillars of that same Empire, particularly in its former far-flung outposts, where the sun was never to set and where he continues to operate best. A friend who has in the past joined Landon at shooting parties at his Faccombe estate in Berkshire comments:

> The problem with Tim is that he behaves as if the sun has yet to set on the whole bloody arrangement and that those who don't share his increasingly desperate points of view are either weirdos, pinkos or layabouts. What amazes me, and so many who know him, is why he doesn't just enjoy his many properties in England, Scotland, Cyprus and Zimbabwe, fly around in his helicopter in ever-increasing circles and relax with his family and enjoy himself. Like most short men, he seems to have this terrible need not just to be powerful and important but to be seen by his associates as being so. He should just tell the rest of the world to go away and enjoy what he's got.

And far from having been strapped for cash as he was in the past, Timothy Landon has got really rather a lot.

Landon's education took place in England at Eastbourne College, in the Sussex coastal town of the same name, which his three older brothers also attended. Comments another associate, 'Not Eton you see, Eastbourne. Not quite the same thing at all, old boy.' For a young man of his allegedly right-wing views, the Army was the obvious choice and, as we have already seen, he gained entry into the Royal Military Academy at Sandhurst. It was there that his first meeting with the man born to rule Oman, Qaboos bin Said Al Said, took place. While they shared the same study, the bond between them, according to a member of Oman's ruling family, was not immediately struck: 'What really drew them close was Landon's protection of Qaboos from the bullying that went on at Sandhurst. That really was the beginning, as we have all come to believe, of the friendship between them.'

Following graduation from Sandhurst in August 1962, when he came 182nd out of 208 cadets, Landon obtained a short-term, three-year commission, as a Second Lieutenant in the 10th Hussars, entering the smart cavalry regiment on 8 August. In 1965, at the end of the commission in which according to an insider, 'he hardly excelled', he was given a further opportunity and was 'offered secondment to the Sultan of Muscat and Oman's Forces, where a small-scale guerrilla war had broken out in the south of the country. It was also a chance for him to clear his mess debts.'

The most important move on the chessboard had been made for Landon and while he would not at the time have known it, power and fortune was indeed heading his way. Once in Oman he showed an aptitude for military intelligence work and consequently was sent back to Britain in 1967 to attend a course that would better equip him for such duties. Back in Oman he came to the attention of Brigadier Malcolm Dennison, Sultan Said's Chief Intelligence Officer, who earmarked him for a rather special task. In 1996, a former desert intelligence officer of some considerable distinction spoke of 'Landon's new and rather special, very sensitive, very hush-hush' assignment:

> Basically what happened was that Dennison, or rather his political masters in London, sought to capitalise on Landon's Sandhurst association with Qaboos. There was one hell of a run on at the time. While it looked increasingly likely that the bloody Adoo (the local name for the Dhofar rebels) were going to give us a long, drawn out campaign, the oil money was most definitely soon going to gush and that really did concentrate minds. To make matters worse, old Sultan Said was beginning to behave more independently than he had ever done before. Things really were beginning to get out of hand. Obviously, contingency plans had to be laid and Landon fitted the bill admirably.

While Brigadier Malcolm Dennison was to often say that he played no part in the overthrow of Sultan Said, it was he who, in effect, made the first tentative moves to see what might be possible. A most senior member of Oman's establishment, speaking in 1996, said:

> Dennison not only knew at a very early time of Britain's growing frustration with Said that something may have to be done about it, but was heavily involved in attempting to see how Qaboos would respond to the idea of replacing his father by force. The choice for them was obvious. In fact, it was Dennison who got Said's permission for Landon to visit Qaboos, although the later meetings, those closer to the time of the coup, took place without his knowledge, they were secret. But the idea that Dennison didn't know about the plan is rubbish. It was he, as the Government's Chief Intelligence Officer, who fixed up the meetings between Qaboos and Landon! And he knew what they were for!

At these private tête-à-têtes in Qaboos's house within the grounds of Salalah Palace, the two Sandhurst contemporaries began to meet, but their conversation eventually strayed far from remembering old times together at the military academy. A prominent Omani businessman, and a former minister, comments:

> Landon was the man who convinced Qaboos over the months that if he didn't make a move against his father, the Dhofar War, and the money from the oil, would be lost. Qaboos himself would never have tried to overthrow his own father. He may well have been angry about not being given a job following his return from Britain, but he simply didn't have the confidence at the time to attempt such a thing. And even if he had thought of trying to do it, how would he have actually carried it out? It is widely known that even after the coup he lacked confidence and experience, which is why the British close to him were able to use their contacts to their own financial advantage. It was only later that he became stronger. But before the coup? Never. No Omani has ever seriously believed that in his heart.

With Landon metaphorically holding the hand of the young man so soon to be Sultan, the plan of overthrow was put into action. According to one British insider who was in Salalah on that fateful afternoon and evening of

23 July 1970, Landon was with Qaboos throughout those anxious hours, waiting for news of the coup's progress. Failure, apparently, 'was not in anyone's vocabulary', according to a British officer who was waiting for news at the nearby military camp at Umm Al Gwarif. As the shadows lengthened and darkness fell, word was received of its success with the former Sultan of 38 years' reign flying off into the night, out of Oman forever.

Around such historic events there is, inevitably, a forest of rumour, myth and speculation, particularly on the detail of the hour. This is a doubtful human activity from which Timothy Landon has most certainly not been immune. One account has him leading 'the assault on the Sultan Said's private apartments in the Palace and confronting him at the top of the stairs'. This colourful, *Boy's Own* tale lacks confirmation. He was not involved at all in the practicalities of removing Sultan Said from his throne; that was down to the courage of Sheikh Braik Al Ghafri and Major 'Spike' Powell. However, evidence that Sultan Said knew full well of Landon's direct involvement was given witness by a remark he made shortly before he died in London in 1972. Asked the nature of his greatest regret, this dignified old man of Arabia responded without hesitation, 'Not having had Landon shot.'

It did not take long for Landon to establish himself as a man with very considerable influence over Oman's new ruler, both in the affairs of state and beyond. There can be no doubt that having been pivotal in convincing his former study companion that a coup could successfully be carried out, he rendered him an essential service in the often anxious and difficult months which came in the coup's wake. For even given all the exaggeration and personal hostility that 'the Brigadier' generates, it is an indelible fact that the lifelong personal support given by him to the son of Sultan Said, beginning at Sandhurst, through his delivery, in effect, of Qaboos to the throne and including the months and years after the coup (when the monarch was by all accounts, 'terribly nervous, terribly unsure of himself') cannot but have established a bond. Given the legendary generosity of Sultan Qaboos, it also created a 'debt of honour' that he wanted to repay as Oman's Head of State. And repaid it has most certainly been, in the most abundant measure.

While Landon has a wide range of international business interests of his own energy and creation, the source and continuing basic supply of his personal fortune undeniably originates in the Sultanate of Oman. His annual appearance in the *Sunday Times Rich List* means that he does have rather a lot, with that prying and vulgar exercise not shrinking from what it obviously regards as its duty in the matter of who has got what and from where it originates. In the 2001 publication Landon's assets were put at three hundred million pounds, making him the 105th richest in the realm, on a par with the Queen, if you please! His entry carried the thumbnail comment:

> Landon has kept a low profile over the past year. A former army officer, he made his fortune from his close links to the Sultan of Oman, whom he befriended at Sandhurst. His assets include homes in London and the home counties and he is reckoned to earn a commission on Omani oil sales.

These figures were, however, immediately dismissed by an eminent London City source as 'a classic example of British understatement'. The source continued by putting Landon's liquidity at somewhere between four and five hundred million pounds, with the value of his property in Britain alone totalling some seventeen million pounds. Senior members of Oman's establishment also laughed at the figure given in the *Sunday Times* list. It was a quality of humour which stung the *Sunday Times* in the latest edition of its 'Rich List', published on 7 April 2002, to rethink its account of the Landon millions. Bringing him from 105th to 98th in the rich stakes, drily commenting: 'We raise Landon to £330 million this year as our sources indicate that his wealth is more than we thought. A former Army Officer, Landon, 59, made his fortune from close links to the Sultan of Oman, whom he befriended at Sandhurst. He is reckoned to earn a commission on Omani oil sales and has assets that range from yachts to a home counties estate.' It is, however, notoriously difficult to arrive at any accurate assessment of Landon's business activities, for as the *Rich List* has laconically commented in the past, 'Nothing appears about him in the press, nor is he listed as a director of any company.'

It is in the matter of the recruitment of such riches that the picture is not always clear. Many people in the Sultanate are concerned about the amounts of Oman's money which have, over the past 30 years, accrued to 'the Brigadier' through his access, work for and advice given to their head of state. In the latter case, the angst generated has more to do with jealousy but, nonetheless, adds considerably to the comprehensive resentment visited upon the man once described as 'the White Sultan' and the most powerful man in the country after its ruler. To seek substance to such claims, such enduring resentment, is to meet with a welter of 'evidence', some credible and verifiable, while much is born of personal animosity and as such does not bear close inspection.

What does clearly emerge as a constant is the anger generated in Oman and Britain at the way Landon has benefited from his close relationship with Sultan Qaboos. Landon's friendship, in the words of a former British diplomat in Oman, 'has always had the very high risk of rebounding'. But as Landon was subject to ultimate British control during his early years in Oman, why couldn't his post-coup, cash-inducing activities have been restricted by London? The one-time Muscat-based diplomat gives the most credible answer:

> Landon really is the one who got away, slipped the leash in fact. After the coup, he ceased to be a seconded officer and entered the personal service of Sultan Qaboos, became in fact a member of his household. He was his Equerry for a while, his military adviser and travelled on an Omani diplomatic passport. From that position he was able to wield enormous power and did so. While, later on, there were concerns that he was getting out of control, was, to be absolutely frank, out of order, there was little or nothing any British Ambassador could actually do about it because of his relationship with the Sultan.

And such a 'close relationship' did begin to pay dividends, of that there can be no doubt. The base of Timothy Landon's personal fortune was Oman's very high defence expenditure, paid for from the hugely-increased oil revenues that OPEC's oil shocks delivered to the industrialised world throughout the 1970s and 1980s. The bonanza enabled the Sultan's Government to spend an estimated six hundred million US dollars on arms purchases in 1980 alone, a staggering amount for a country with an indigenous population estimated at the time at 750,000. In his role as Military Adviser Landon was well placed to benefit from such expenditure, but there was nothing illegal or indeed contrary to local practice in this, it being expected that those in high places would naturally use their role as a functionary to garner personal gain along the way. Even before it was considered prudent for his close relationship with Sultan Qaboos to be given a lower profile, bringing about his return to Britain where on the Foreign and Commonwealth Office Diplomatic list he is named as 'counsellor', he had formed a London-based company. Its offices were in

Mayfair's Upper Brook Street and Green Street, dealing principally in the supply of arms to African and Middle Eastern regimes. He also opened an office in Washington, where he employed a one-time CIA operative, Chet Nagel. His main business partner in the arms trade is David Bayley, a British Arabist who had fought the Royal cause in North Yemen in the 1960s but who had moved to Oman shortly after the coup that brought Sultan Qaboos to power. In Muscat, Bayley set up shop as a defence resource adviser. What Landon lacked – business experience – Bayley brought to bear and what Bayley lacked – contacts at the top – Landon provided in good and ample measure. The two men are very different in nature, Landon being 'polar cold, calculating, ruthless even in pursuing his objectives', while Bayley is 'relaxed, jovial almost, someone who does actually care about people'. The partnership has proved to be hugely rewarding in financial terms with Bayley also being a very rich man indeed. As with Landon, the genesis of that wealth has been commissions from the huge amount spent on arms by the Government of Oman at the height of the oil boom.

While Landon's profile was deliberately lowered with his departure from Oman, his fortunes continued to rise, except for a disastrous spell in Hong Kong, where he quickly lost much of the fortune he had acquired in Oman, much to the delight of the city's Taipans who loathed his air of superiority. Sultan Qaboos principally replenished his wealth. As a frequent visitor to Muscat, he continued to keep his eye 'very much on the main chance', in the words of the former Muscat-based diplomat. By now he had cultivated the friendship of Margaret Thatcher, then in Downing Street along with her husband and son, Dennis and Mark. Landon, Bayley and Mark Thatcher did some arms and oil deals together in the 1980s, although the two partners apparently 'did not consider Thatcher up to the game'. So while the two men remained social acquaintances of the British Prime Minister's son, their business dealings were allowed to wither on the vine. But the association did produce a compensation of sorts for Landon. During Mrs Thatcher's visit to Oman in April 1981, Sultan Qaboos asked the Prime Minister if a British honour could be bestowed upon Landon. As a result of such an approach, Mrs Thatcher recommended to Queen Elizabeth that he be invested with a Knight Commander of the Royal Victorian Order (KCVO). However, the Order was gazetted as an honorary Knighthood, thus prohibiting him from putting the prefix 'Sir' to his name. The reason, according to London sources, was the continuing unease in certain departments of state at the nature of Landon's business activities (of which the Duke of Edinburgh is known to have expressed distaste); the way round this was to give him the award not as a subject of the Queen, but as an Omani, given that he often travels on his Omani passport, thus prohibiting him as a foreigner from using the title 'Sir'.

But it is not only his commissions from arms purchases by Oman that exercise and animate so many in the Sultanate whenever the name of Landon is spoken. It is his 'close involvement with Sultan Qaboos's private affairs that has been such a source of anger', a senior Omani comments:

> We believe him to have been closely involved in so many of His Majesty's decisions to purchase residences outside Oman. Most definitely, he was instrumental in HM buying his first property in Britain, Wargrave Manor in Berkshire and, later, the Castle at Garmisch in Germany.

The Sultan purchased Wargrave (just a few miles from Landon's manor house Faccombe), for £800,000 from a business associate of Landon's, Nigel Broackes, who was at the time Chairman of the Trafalgar House Company. More purchases were to follow,

> . . . all at Landon's suggestion. Grove House in London's Regent's Park, a property outside Vienna formerly owned by King Hussein of Jordan and, most recently, a chateau at Fontainebleau, outside Paris. We simply do not believe that Landon did not profit from these purchases by HM. I know, for certain, that during HM's visit to London in 1996, Landon kept urging the Sultan to buy a very expensive painting, which he said was ideally suited for the castle in Germany.

Not that Landon has ceased to acquire properties for himself. In the autumn of 1994 he paid ten million pounds for what has long been regarded as England's finest shooting estate, the 36,000 acre Gunnerside Estate in Yorkshire, formerly the home of the Earls of Peel.

The animosity towards 'the Brigadier' in certain circles of the Omani capital is, on occasions, disturbing in its intensity, particularly when it assumes a very personal nature. An example of this was a comment on his marriage to a lady from the ancient and aristocratic Austrian family, Esterhazy. It came to be believed in Oman, from which source no one really seems to know, that she was a Hapsburg of the former Austro-Hungarian

Empire, a belief which by all accounts, Landon himself did little to contradict, though he neither inspired the belief nor spread it . However, in the autumn of 1989, a member of the Hapsburg dynasty, Dr Warburger von Hapsburg, the daughter of Count Otto von Hapsburg, visited Muscat as an employee in Vienna of Oman's Ministry of Information. During the visit she made it forcefully known that Mrs Landon was not a member of her family. Since that time 'the Brigadier' has had the appellation among a small, select group of Omanis as 'Mr Perhapsburg'.

But it was an apparent concern for the plight of his colonial cousins in Southern Africa that, according to a distinguished Omani source, led Timothy Landon into a foreign adventure, conducted from Oman's soil. To many, this is the single biggest risk he has taken with their country's international reputation. As ever with the business reputation of 'the Brigadier', his tracks are somewhat complicated but in this particular case the trail is clearer and given that at least two senior Omani citizens were associated with him in the venture, it is well established.

During the opening years of the 1970s, the government of Ian Smith of Rhodesia, which had unilaterally declared its independence from Britain on 11 November 1965, was facing an increasingly desperate situation. Trade sanctions imposed by the British Government a decade earlier were comprehensively adopted by so many states and the United Nations. As a result, they were now beginning to bite into the beleaguered settlers' economy. Shortages of vital goods, such as machine tools, spare parts for military vehicles and oil were causing very real problems. The refinery at Feruka, in Rhodesia's Eastern District, which was connected to an oil pipeline running from the then Portuguese-controlled port of Beira on the coast of Mozambique, was all but starved of oil. This commodity, which was the lifeline of Rhodesia's economy, had to be purchased from wherever it could possibly be obtained and in a manner that would circumnavigate the British Navy's blockade of the Beira Channel. Landon, having family ties with both Rhodesia and South Africa (whose apartheid regime was itself soon to face an internationally arranged oil embargo), was, with his sympathies in place and his position of power in an oil-producing country, to come to both states like the legendary arrival of the cavalry over the hill.

An eminent Omani, who held ministerial office throughout the period, takes up the story:

The company was known as Transworld Oil, which had its offices in the Muscat suburb of Al Khuwair. The Zawawi brothers, Qais and Omar, were very much involved with Tim Landon in the operation, which for many years sent oil and other supplies to Rhodesia and South Africa, making huge fortunes for themselves in the process. Millions were made, even though the cost to Oman had the operation been discovered, in that United Nations-sponsored sanctions, which Oman was morally bound to uphold, were being violated, would have been very high in terms of the country's reputation.

Qais and Omar Zawawi are men whose family origins lie in Saudi Arabia and who were educated in India. They were, even before the arrival of Landon in Oman, successful traders in their own right. Both men were eventually given appointments in Sultan Qaboos's Government. Qais, whose death in a car accident in 1995 whilst the Omani ruler was behind the wheel made the international news, was first appointed Foreign Minister but later became the country's equivalent of the Chancellor of the Exchequer. His brother Omar has for many years held the post of Special Adviser to Sultan Qaboos and is reputed to be one of the world's richest men.

However the sanctions-busting operation run by Transworld Oil led to recriminations against those behind it in Oman, with the eminent source explaining:

> It was a high-risk venture for the country, even though it was a purely private enterprise. The oil shipped to Southern Africa left Oman by sea, with bills of lading made out for Japan, but these were changed several times on the high seas. They also had a cargo plane which secretly flew other supplies down to Rhodesia and South Africa. The financial returns were also enormous. Many of us believe that, even today, Landon still receives a commission on oil sales to South Africa, deals that he arranges, as well as commissions on the major arms purchases we make.

The land once known as Rhodesia, but which the world now knows as Zimbabwe, was also the scene of yet another foreign adventure in which, according to British and Omani sources 'the Brigadier' was principally involved. On 16 May 1983 the *Wall Street Journal* ran the headline in its *Brass Tacks* column: 'Ashland Oil Chief's Sudden '81 Departure is Linked by

Insiders to an Oman Payment.' The report centred on the sudden, and at the time unexplained, departure in 1981 of the President of the Kentucky-based Ashland Oil Company, Orin E. Atkins, which was brought about in part by 'a controversial payment and other transactions in Oman in 1980'. Atkins was actually the fall guy on this occasion and did not personally receive any payment. America's Securities and Exchange Commission was concerned with 'certain improprieties that may have occurred' in Ashland's purchase of crude oil from Oman in late 1980 or early 1981. The *Wall Street Journal* continued:

> How the company's Omani dealings began isn't clear. Last week's statement by the company says that 'in 1980 Ashland Oil purchased crude oil from the government of Oman. Sources inside Ashland say the company bought 4.8 million barrels of Omani crude, in eight shipments, between December 1980 and July 1981, when the purchases ceased. By that time internal concerns were raised that certain improprieties may have occurred with respect to such purchases.' One of the possible improprieties, say Ashland sources, was a 1,350,000 dollar commission payment. The payment was, however, returned.

The link with Landon, according to an American source, is that the commission payment was made to a Liechtenstein company, as the *Wall Street Journal* reports. The *Journal* did not report however that the company was 'Etablissement Landon', which the Brigadier used to finance many of his business deals. The *Journal* report also commented on another transaction involving Ashland. This was a twenty-six million dollar investment in a chromium mine in Zimbabwe, 'purchased from a group that included a prominent Omani'. Ashland subsequently commissioned a Pittsburgh law firm, Kirkpatrick, Lockhart, Johnson and Hutchison to investigate its Oman dealings. Their report was delivered to the Ashland board on 27 October 1981, which stated that 'no violation of US law has occurred'. The reason for such a conclusion? 'The recipients in the (Oman) transactions weren't foreign officials as defined by the 1977 Foreign Corrupt Practices Act.' An American Offical recently commented, 'The "after-taste" of the Ashland affair continues. Whenever Landon's name comes up certain bells ring at the FBI.'

In the summer of 1971, Sultan Qaboos paid his first visit to London since assuming power. Timothy Landon was prominent in his party. During their time in the British capital the Omani ruler presented Landon with a Rolex watch. One of the party remembers the occasion well, 'Tim was quite overcome. He said that he never thought that he would own a Rolex and that he was going to put it in the bank for safekeeping.'

It is perhaps, too easy to criticise a man who was given a certain task by his government; who then 'slipped the leash' once the job was done and subsequently seized the opportunities presented to him to acquire great riches. The essential question has to be who, in such a position, would have behaved differently? Not many, and in any censorious exercise on Brigadier Timothy Landon, such a human factor should be borne in mind. This is not to say that those Omanis who now increasingly articulate their fierce resentment of his conduct in their country are wrong to exercise such attitudes. It really is a question of degree and in that respect the man described in the British press as the country's 'most secretive man' does indeed owe an explanation to those in Oman who are critical of him.

It is of no small interest that his fascination with far away places with strange-sounding names continues, ever the hallmark of those with a colonial bent. In the late 1990s 'the Brigadier', through his association with the London-based International Security Company Executive Outcome, continued his long affair with Africa, this time the West African state of Sierre Leone, that war-torn and corrupt land which through its diamond mines should be anything but poverty-stricken. Landon sent Andrew Clark, son of the former Conservative Defence Procurement Minister Alan Clark, on a security mission for Executive Outcome. Even here there is an Oman dimension, for Andrew Clark is a one-time British seconded officer in the Armed Forces of Sultan Qaboos.

Today, there are reports, not widely believed in Oman, that Landon 'softens'; that he studies Buddhist ethics, which is an interesting rumour but an unlikely one, particularly because that would presumably prevent him from pursuing one of his favourite pastimes, 'killing things'. This reference is to his shooting parties at Faccombe Manor in Berkshire, at Gunnerside in Yorkshire and when he has time to get away, in the American southern state of Georgia. But he does have some concerns, mainly about his own personal security, a preoccupation which had led him to be driven around in London in his very own black taxi cab, a foil presumably, for would-be kidnappers from Oman, Timbuctoo, or wherever. As one establishment figure in Oman observes:

It could have all been so very different if he made some effort to put some of the money back into Oman, by donating a school or a hospital, it would have been so much better for him and for us.

A former Omani Ambassador to London comments, 'I found him extremely difficult to work with and felt he was arrogant, but we Omanis are patient people and we hope that he will, one day, make amends.' But 'the Brigadier', who rejoices in infuriating the politically correct (who so well deserve to be irritated in any case), continues to live in his own exclusive little world, one of his own creation and in which he alone makes the rules. He is quite impervious to the fact that what eventually did for the dinosaur, a change of climate, may well come to affect even him. In short, Brigadier (Honorary) Timothy Landon KCVO (Honorary) goes marching on.

# CHAPTER NINE

## The Woking Class

'He is crazed by the spell of far Arabia. They have stolen his wits away.' – Walter de la Mare

Oman has always been different and those Westerners, especially the British, who have beaten a path to her door, have long known it. Indeed, this very special region on the Arabian Peninsula was long regarded, correctly, as a place where officers dwell as opposed to the artisan class who actually ran the British Empire; those colonies, dominions and protectorates where, as Noel Coward observed, 'It isn't true that everyone expectorates.' In Oman it was most certainly true. No true Brit, living in the Sultanate, would ever engage in a practice so common or unhygienic as spitting. Professional killing (in a desert war), most certainly, a financial 'killing' (in the wake of an oil boom) most definitely, but spitting in public, never! That is left to the legions of expatriate workers from the Indian subcontinent, those who clean the streets, wait at tables, labour in the laundries of the land, black the boots of those they domestically serve, make the beds and, in short, make life tolerable for those who regard Oman as being their very own place in the sun.

In recent years, much to the consummate horror of so many in the British expatriate community, the Indians, Pakistanis and Bangladeshis have moved on to white collar jobs and in the process have taken to demanding more respect than that afforded them in the past by their former Imperial masters. This healthy social development has been brought about not just by the rapid rise in the number of subcontinentals with professional qualifications and abilities every bit as good as those of their British counterparts, but also by the fact that so many Britons, due to an inestimable sense of their own worth have, quite literally, priced themselves out of the job market. This has been a development greatly prized by many Omani businessmen who, understandably, rejoice in (sometimes) ensuring a job is well done by an employee who will not only be considerably less expensive in almost every way but, into an often excellent bargain, will be considerably more subservient; less likely to tell him things he really doesn't want to hear and, in the inevitable process, tell him things he most definitely does, even when they aren't true.

These, however, are recent developments. One is not obliged to hark back to the days of George Nathaniel Curzon and the high old days of Empire to recall a time when on the Muscat verandahs of the British, a denizen of Virginia Water, Cheltenham or Woking could clap his hands at sundown, shout 'Boy!' and have a pink gin appear at his elbow as if by an act of illusion. A British expatriate, whose time in the country commenced within weeks of Sultan Qaboos's assumption of power, recalled the domestic ease with which one 'cruised through the day', even though this was a time before the widespread arrival of air conditioning in the country. The months of summer may have been all but intolerable, but the availability of houseboys from the subcontinent considerably diluted the stress and strain of it all:

> My boy came from southern India, Kerala, and I must say was absolutely bloody marvellous. To tell the truth, I now feel a little ashamed at just how little I paid him, although he seemed happy enough and had lots of perks. Actually, it was really rather funny. When I arrived in Muscat I was, not to put too fine a point on it, well, fat. When he came to work for me he was as thin as a hat-stand. A year later, because of the heat, I had become three stone lighter, whereas he, because he now ate three European-style meals a day, had developed an enormous paunch and a bloody big behind. But from the moment he woke me up with a cup of tea and ran my bath, to the time he turned the bed down at night, everything, simply everything, was done for me. Breakfast, lunch and dinner appeared from the kitchen always on time, the house was kept spotlessly clean, as was the car. In time, when he knew what to buy, he even did the shopping, such as it was in those days. And my shirts have never been so beautifully washed and ironed as at that time. It was domestic bliss. And they all wanted to work for an English bachelor, because, of course, there was no Memsahib in the house to order them around all day. Or to stop them raiding the fridge. It was a perfect arrangement, from both sides. Now, well you can't always

trust them and they have taken to answering back. Too bloody cheeky nowadays. Still, I was almost afraid to return to Britain, not knowing how I was going to manage.

While the reasons that prompt someone from metropolitan Britain to leave home and hearth and live in a little-known corner of Arabia are many and varied the very special attraction the Sultanate of Oman has for a particular kind of Briton is not that difficult to define or, indeed, to understand. In a minority, but most notable among a really diverse and more often than not, unusual breed of men, is the Arabist: he whose commanding passion is a love of the Arab people and for the stark, austere beauty of their land, a geographical canvas which has shaped and developed the Arab character across the centuries. The true Arabist knows, and gladly acknowledges on all occasions possible, that Arab culture was the guiding force for so much of the Western world's intellectual development. He knows, for example, that the very first university on European soil was established by Arabs; that so many of the stars in the heavens were charted by Arab scholars; that they gave the world the game of chess; that in the *Oxford English Dictionary*, algebra and alchemy (the basis of the disciplines of mathematics and chemistry) are given as deriving from Arabic; that this most remarkable race hammered at the gates of Europe centuries before the people of Western Europe founded their own empires. For the British Arabist, whose very own self-proclaimed virtues of honour, integrity and loyalty remain icons of social conduct to be admired (but which are so rarely upheld today), it is hard not to forget that these are values to which Arab society continues to cleave. The Arab past is one from which inspiration, in an all too often tawdry world, can be gained. An example of this is the chivalry and valour of that great Arab statesman and warrior, Salah ad-Din Yousef: when Richard I's horse fell under him at the Battle of Jaffa in 1190, he sent the English monarch two fresh horses and, later, when he lay ill in his tent with fever, sent peaches, pears and snow from Mount Ascalon to cool him. Among Arabists, smaller in number but of equal significance, are those whose interest and commitment to the Arab ethos extends to the religion, Islam, and who have come to believe with no small justification that its spiritual imperatives have much to offer an increasingly morally-bankrupt world.

A close second in the eccentric cast-list is the Briton who serves not as a soldier of the Queen but of the Sultan, a man who so often epitomises all that was once so very good and so internationally admired in the British character. Few now remain of such men, who saw themselves as following the footprints in the sand of such luminaries of the desert as Captain Shakespear, described by that great Arab monarch, Ibn Saud, as 'this finest Englishman' and who met his end fighting for the Wahaibis in the sands of the Saudi Kingdom. Or that father of the Hashemite Arab legion Glubb Pasha, at the sound of whose name the heart of the British Arabist skips a beat; men who while no Colonel Lawrence (of *Lawrence of Arabia* fame), found their very own personal paradise on earth in serving alongside the noble Bedu, those best of men, sons of the desert, free of the spirit-sapping domestic tyrannies from which so many Britons fled to Arabia. While they would in the main deny such sentiment, these Britons (of what is usually referred to as 'the old school') are men who like nothing more than to serve the Gulf's royal rulers as officers, shoulder to shoulder with their soldier subjects; essentially men of a solitary condition, who are not just romantics in the classical sense but who shun their expatriate compatriots, the fleshpots and watering holes of the increasingly urbanised capitals of the Gulf states. Not for such individuals, holding at bay as they do an increasingly ignoble world, with its craven, vulgar appetites of greed and self-aggrandisement which, it is sad to report, both Omanis and expatriates alike are visibly prone to, or the doubtful and all too often dubious delights of the Al Bustan Palace Hotel's Disco, or the Intercontinental 'English' Pub's 'Happy Hour'. But for this small yet happy breed of men, the austere appeal of the desert maintains its magnetic pull, and so does the silhouette of a Beau-Geste-style fort at sunset, with the Omani tricolour flying from its ramparts in the oven-hot breeze of a saffron-coloured dusk. It is this which continues to fulfil all earthly and spiritual requirements.

But as with the dodo and the dinosaur, the British soldier of former character is, now, very much an endangered species. In the case of these two examples the former became extinct because of its inquisitive, inquiring and, most fatally of all, unsuspicious nature which led it all too easily to being clubbed unceremoniously to extinction by protein-starved settlers; the latter because its habitat dissolved in a new climate. The soldier's end, so cruelly and swiftly approaching, is attended by conditions and circumstances not unlike those which spelt the end of the dodo and the dinosaur; the final sunset of an imperial climate of noble paternalism, in which he was not only welcome but flourished; and the arrival on the scene of the brutal advice of the 'cost-effective', crusading, egalitarian-suited accountant. His many and varied warnings to those in authority in Oman concern the 'real world' which has to be lived in; the rapidly approaching post-oil age with its declining revenues which dictate that the expensive, expatriate British soldier can no longer be afforded. So while old soldiers of the old school do indeed fade away, their place, on the Oman stage at least, has been taken by their expatriate cousins. By their very appearance, nature and expectation, they herald the arrival of a new and very different cast-list of Brits in a land which, according to the pen of a former 1980s British Ambassador to the Court of His Majesty Sultan Qaboos, contains the very last vestiges of the Raj. Not for them the concept of 'service', of benign paternalism, allied to a mission designed to uphold and propagate the very best in British administration and good governance. This is not to report that this new breed of British expatriate in Oman does not have a role to play or indeed a service to offer, in the country's rapidly changing social climate. In an exquisite irony, given the 'old school' expatriates' unalloyed adoration of Margaret Thatcher and all her works, the crassly commercial attitude struck by so many of the new generation of British residents in Oman which, daily, is a cause for much flinching by those who remember when only 'Englishmen of respectability' resided in the land, is very much more in tune with the times than the imperial hymn of 'Pomp and Circumstance'. This anthem is still defiantly aired by the last of the British few remaining in the Sultanate. They now resemble an increasingly unhappy band of exiles caught on a sandbar, under siege from a rising and most unwelcome tide.

Thatcher's children are on occasions of greater honesty than those of their race that went before. The latter were unfailingly awash with all of the social graces they could conceivably muster, but all too ready if unwatched by their peers to sup greedily at the oil-laced chalice of enlightened self-interest. With the children of the 1980s so excitedly abroad, there is little or no pretence. They are in Oman, on fixed-term contracts, to bask in the sun awhile and given such a climate, make hay while that very same sun shines down upon them. It is an attitude that shows little willingness to conform, either to Islamic codes of dress or other forms of social conduct expected of them as Britons abroad. The very notion that they are 'ambassadors' for their country is regarded as a poor joke. In a reference to those who toil on Britannia's behalf within the whitewashed walls of the British Embassy on the Muscat sea shore, a British resident in Oman's capital remarked with caustic but refreshing candour:

> They are not interested in me and I am not interested in them. They
> are here to sell British goods, mainly arms, and I am here to earn as

much as I can in the shortest possible time and then go home. I work hard, in difficult conditions, and the pay-off is a tax-free salary, a rent-free house and a return air-ticket home once a year. After five more years of this I will have paid off my mortgage and given my son a good start by buying him a private education up to the age of 12. It is a good bargain. Oman wants my technical skills and I need the money the country is prepared to pay.

While it is an attitude which pains the purists, their objections are more to do with that well-fashioned British practice of snobbery than reservations that can be banked on. The shaking of grey heads and the chorus of clicking tongues at the conduct of the new breed of British expatriate in Oman, is generated more by the idea that in not upholding social standards maintained by generations of Britons in the Gulf, the 'side' is being grievously let down. No example is being set to the native population as to how things should be really done; 'standards' are wilfully being abandoned. All of which is true in a very real sense. But what so few of the dismayed and so-strident accusers really understand is that they, like their erstwhile colonial cousins in the former colonies, dominions and protectorates, have been overtaken and subdued by the cruel march of time. Time itself has ambushed them and the land from which they came, Britain, has irrevocably changed. Those who have been principal in reshaping and redefining Britain's social mores, have caught up with them and caught them out in their very own Arabian Eden: a hiding place from the real world, where the heat-burdened tedium is for many only relieved by interminable cocktail parties, official luncheons or dinners and the occasional visit by second-rate 'Dinner Theatre' productions, flown in from London in which, as soon as the curtain rises, the 'leading man's' trousers fall down. No small wonder then that visitors to the Sultanate have, over recent years, delivered harsh judgement on the country's social climate, the most frequently heard being 'a place in the sun for shady people'. The most cruel declaration was delivered by a former Conservative MP who, having totally failed to get what he came for, described the Sultanate as 'a second-rate country for third-rate people' and the Government of His Majesty Sultan Qaboos as 'the Oman County Council'.

However, it would be a particularly insensitive individual who did not feel sorry for those now besieged by Britannia's new standard bearers, with their short shorts, high hemlines, loud voices and whining mobile phones in Muscat's more discreet restaurants. But their fate has always been destined to be that of those stranded at the high water mark of history, fearing for the future where they are, but mightily fearful too of attempting to make a run for the shore; to return home to a country virtually bereft of servants and, the unkindest cut of all, no respect from the natives. The most interesting aspect of this social revolution introduced by the new breed of British expatriates in Oman, however, has been the welcome extended to it by so many among the country's better-educated. Remarked one young, professional Omani:

> When I go to Dubai I find that the Brits there are so much nicer, more relaxed than those in Muscat, where so many of them continue to behave as if they were gods. They behave in a superior way and it's all nonsense. So few of us Omanis believe that any more, or are prepared to accept it.

Fallen idols always cut poignant figures, yet it is the fate of those who fence off a part of the world in an attempt to preserve it for their very own self-appointed 'officer' class. That they upheld the social graces of an earlier age is undeniable and that they did so in an intolerable climate so far from home, can only be but admired. Undeniable too, is the irrefutable truth that many of them (but most certainly not all of them) had a well-developed, sustained sense of service and in exercising such attitudes raised their own reputation and that of their country. But equally undeniable is the fact that they deceive themselves in believing in their permanence in the scheme of things, even continuing with such an attitude when the warning winds of change, which herald a fundamental shift in the social climate, blow so exceedingly strong. Indeed, the 'officers' in a land so long considered by so many to be safe from the ever-turning wheel of evolution have been terminally ambushed and outnumbered, for good or ill, by those whose very existence they preferred not to notice, the 'other ranks' in Britannia's new and thrusting brood. But the latter's very presence in the Sultanate of Oman is proof enough that only one thing has changed since Noel Coward penned the self-mocking words, 'mad dogs and Englishmen go out in the midday sun'. Mad dogs have since learnt better, but Englishmen, of whatever class or social creed, continue just the same.

# CHAPTER TEN

## Mr Snooks of Streatham

'Servants take on the traits of their masters adjusted in scale and
in order to reflect their lower status' – Juvenal, *Satires*

In the early spring of 1997 a retired intelligence officer and Arabist par
excellence lay dying of cancer in Salalah. His love for and knowledge of the
people and politics of the Arabian Peninsula was legendary. He spoke not
only Arabic but several local dialects, including the notoriously difficult
Jebali, the tongue of those fiercely proud and independently spirited people
of the Jebal. For many years Oman had been his home, a country to which
he was entirely devoted and to which, in both war and peace, he had given
much of his working life. His service to the Omani state had been of such
consistent quality that Sultan Qaboos, with his usual generosity and
kindness, had ordered that a house be built on the Salalah shoreline for the
comfort and enjoyment of this truly remarkable Briton's retirement years.
Not for him, as he had long known, a return to a country he no longer really
knew or, indeed, understood. Not for a man shaped by the Arab ethos, a
wind-swept, litter-strewn dormitory town in England's Home Counties; or
a damp, isolated country cottage with dripping hedgerows in the shires
where, on long winter evenings, times past in Arabia would be recalled in
front of an artificial log fire. For him Arabia, Abu Dhabi, Aden and finally
Oman had been the life and it was to be his life forever.

While in recent years he had been something of a recluse, rarely
venturing beyond Dhofar let alone Oman, with his visits to Britain having
become ever more infrequent, he had in earlier years been more sociable,
although as befitted his career it was on a very select basis. But to those he
took to and who accepted him on his own somewhat eccentric terms, he was
generous, thoughtful and, that most admirable of human qualities, very

loyal. He was also unusual in that he had never fallen prey to that most insidious of expatriate pastimes, cocktail circuit gossip. He rarely spoke ill of either Omani or fellow expatriate, unless there was a good, proven reason to do so. A lifelong bachelor, he was popular with women, to whom he displayed a never-failing courtesy, never forgetting a name, a face, or anniversaries. He was, in terms both pure and simple, an Arabist and a gentleman of the 'old school': kind, loyal, courteous and, sadly, a representative of a rapidly vanishing breed of men. All the more extraordinary, all the more out of character then, that just days before his death in March 1997, when recalling times past on the Peninsula, this most extraordinary man delivered a scathing indictment at the mention of a former colleague. It is all the more remarkable given that the man in question, even then in his late 70s, continues in public office in Oman, a post from which he wields significant power and influence and to which so many in senior authority in Sultan Qaboos's administration have for so long deferred.

Anthony Clayton Ashworth was born on 28 July 1921, enlisting in the British Army at 20 years of age. He retired with the rank of major in the Queen's Own Hussars in 1962, entering what a former intelligence officer with experience of Oman describes with a grin as 'The Diplomatic Service' in that same year:

> It is interesting, this coterie of former cavalrymen which descended upon Oman in the 1970s. Landon was in the 10th Hussars as was a chap by the name of Dwerryhouse who subsequently became a merchant banker with Morgan Grenfell but who has had a long association with Oman where he operated as an 'economic adviser'.

Anthony Ashworth arrived in Aden in 1963, at a turbulent time in its history as the various nationalist groups fought both the British and themselves for political control. His post in the colonial administration was that of First Secretary (Information). With the departure of the British in 1967, he went to Hong Kong, with the same job title but, in actual fact he ran that group of Intelligence Analysts known as 'The China Watchers'. It was during his time in the Colony that he developed his keen interest in China, its history and culture, and is particularly well known for his extensive knowledge of the subject. Comments a former Muscat colleague:

China remains Tony's real passion, if you can use such a word to describe such a human reaction in one so cold! Actually, when in discussion about China he often used to give the impression that he preferred working with the Chinese rather than the Arabs. On one occasion, when comparing the two cultures, he described Omani silverware as 'junk', in relation to Chinese porcelain.

After four years in Hong Kong Ashworth returned to London, where he remained for a year before being posted to the British Embassy in Beirut, with the same job title of First Secretary (Information). In November 1974 he was seconded to the staff of Sir Gawain Bell, a distinguished diplomat and Arabist who, at the Sultan's invitation, was to study what best arrangements could be put in place for the long-term future of Dhofar Province. It was during this time that Ashworth's appetite for the official control, management and dissemination of information came to the attention of his former Hussars cavalry comrade, Tim Landon. The former Omani minister mentioned earlier remembers the occasion well:

> In those days office accommodation was still in short supply and I was summoned by Tim Landon to a tent, where he drew up a contract for Tony Ashworth's appointment. Tim was insistent that we needed someone of his particular experience to handle the press.

Ashworth was appointed Adviser to Oman's Minister for Information, Abdul Aziz bin Mohammed Al Rowas, a designation later changed to Consultant in order to make it appear less intrusive. He presented then, as now, the carefully crafted air of an English gentleman of Victorian manners, with an almost excessive courtesy and standard-bearer of, well, 'standards'. This was however but one aspect of his role as 'Oman's Doorman', in the words of an Austrian journalist. Others are less generous when making reference to the manner in which he conducted his wide-ranging and varied duties. These were more often than not a discreet telephone call to an often bemused Minister of the Omani Crown, and such conduct led to Ashworth being referred to as 'God'. Comments the former Omani Minister:

> Tony and his wife, Margaret, while being polite and what the British usually call 'sweet', did not have any real appeal for those Omanis they came into contact with. Arabs are good judges of character and while we place much value on courtesy we, among ourselves, knew

instinctively that they considered themselves very superior people. After all, they looked down on so many of their own people, they could hardly be expected not to look down on the ordinary Omani. Margaret comes from a colonial background, Trinidad I believe, where her family had owned estates and, in the past, had slaves. She is not so stiff as Tony but even with her you are left with the impression of haughtiness. Actually, I do feel just a little sorry for her. Tony organises who she should meet and what she should say. He controls things in such a way that she ends up by talking without saying anything.

It is not only in Omani circles, particularly in recent years, that concern has been expressed about the influence and power exercised in Oman by Anthony Ashworth, described by a current Omani official as an individual 'out of time and out of place'. In a *Guardian* newspaper article of 1997, headed 'British Advisers Fuel Gulf Anger', Ashworth was described as 'another former British Intelligence Officer'. The article continued, 'Tony Ashworth functions as adviser to Sultan Qaboos on the foreign press. Mr Ashworth's policies have made Oman one of the most difficult countries for foreign newsmen to enter.' While the article is an accurate reflection of the insurmountable hurdles Ashworth can raise against journalists he believes do not share his view of the world, it is not true that all journalists have the Sultanate's door slammed in their face. In a stable of Ministry of Information representatives overseas, who cover some 18 countries, journalists considered safe and reliable are treated to occasional 'freebies', cost-free visits to Oman designed, hopefully, to secure a good press. It is a system that for years has worked astonishingly well, even though it has meant that so many reports on Oman can only be described as 'news with a condom'. But such a tried and tested method can no longer be relied upon to always produce the desired result.

In the autumn of 1997 a journalist writing for the Dutch press was recommended to Ashworth's office as someone who could be trusted to file the desired 'broad, sunlit uplands' article expected from all those given a 'freebie' to the Sultanate. Following a series of visits and interviews with carefully chosen ministers who could be trusted to sing Ashworth's song, the journalist duly obliged Oman's 'Doorman' by presenting him with the expected article. But neither had taken into account the robust attitude of Queen Beatrix's Ambassador to the Sultanate who, fearing that 'a totally ersatz, misleading impression of Oman', would appear in the Dutch press, raised such a concern with the visiting journalist. This episode is worthy of comment for one reason and one reason only, the reaction of Anthony Ashworth upon learning of the Dutch Ambassador's conversation with his fellow countryman. 'He was extremely angry in his usual cold, controlled manner,' remarks an insider. 'It was an extraordinary performance even for him. The phone calls and visits to the more obscure offices in Muscat went on for days.' While, on this occasion, the Ashworthian grand design came to naught, it is astonishing that, in the words of a Western diplomat in Muscat: 'A foreign, civil servant in an Arab State, in the late twentieth century, can act in this way.'

Such episodes are far from few. On 17 August 1995 the *Sunday Times* reported the death of Oman's Minister of Finance, Qais Zawawi, in a car accident that had occurred while Sultan Qaboos was behind the wheel. The *Sunday Times* journalist, Marie Colvin, commented on:

> A group of elderly, former military and intelligence officers who help the Sultan run his country. A powerful figure is Tony Ashworth, a civilian with Whitehall connections, whose influence is crucial in the tight limits that are kept on the number of visitors to the Sultanate.

Marie Colvin, on the orders of Oman's 'Doorman', is now not welcome in Oman. The lady's prohibition is just another sad example of the totally counter-productive policies of a man described by a fellow British expatriate civil servant in Oman as:

> A real old Stalinist. Tony will go down and out fighting the Cold War and warning us all of the dangers we will face when the Empire collapses. It would be funny if the implications for Oman in having such a man represent it were not so serious.

But by continuing to wield his sword against imaginary dragons, Anthony Ashworth, the former British spy who in going to Oman came in from out of the cold with a vengeance is, at the very least, without discrimination.

In the May 1995 edition of America's celebrated *National Geographic Magazine*, which carried a detailed article on Oman, Peter Ross Range wrote that 'Ashworth, a high-ranking official in the Ministry of Information', had sought to discredit the opinions of some of those interviewed. The article continued:

The Ministry is, itself, one of the most powerful and feared in Oman. It exercises draconian control over press and television, which permits little open discourse on topics the Government does not want to discuss. The Ministry can censor advertisements and close down publications for any reason.

This was an episode which led to yet more (controlled) hisses of rage and to 'a whispering campaign against Peter Ross Range, the author of the *National Geographic* article', according to a Ministry insider.

On 9 August 1997, the London-based *Economist* magazine published an article entitled 'Where's Our Sultan?' which warned of the increasing disaffection among Omanis with the state of things. Shortly after publication Ashworth, not unlike a rattled janitor attempting to discover the source of an unpleasant and unwelcome smell in a house under his care and control, flew to London where he demanded to see the *Economist*'s editor, who was then expected to explain the temerity of it all. Later he flew to Switzerland, where he took the Swiss journalist Lizel Graz, who is an *Economist* writer, to an expensive restaurant for lunch, hoping that she could help uncover the name of the recalcitrant author of the offending article. It is, by any standard of conduct, an extraordinary state of affairs, one to which Omanis in rapidly increasing numbers now take very great exception indeed. A former Omani Ambassador laments: 'It is as if he knows what is best for us, that we cannot be trusted with the truth about our own country. His great interest is China and its people about which, to be fair, he is very knowledgeable.'

The one-time MI6 officer's China connection is well established. It was a connection that did not end with his departure from the Colony of Hong Kong in 1972. Following his Oman appointment Sultan Qaboos also appointed him as Oman's representative to Hong Kong, on a visiting basis. But even here, the presence of Ashworth and the evidence in Hong Kong and elsewhere of the degree to which Ashworth has benefited financially from Sultan Qaboos's extreme generosity has become a source of fierce resentment.

Such feeling has to be evaluated while taking into account the human appetite for resentment born of envy, however justified. There is much that is to Anthony Ashworth's credit. During his early years in Oman there is no doubt whatsoever that he made a pivotal contribution to establishing the good name of the country in the world's press. The fact that, along the way, he made enemies is but an indication of just how well he did his job. Most certainly to him must go the credit, in the words of a former minister of the Omani Crown:

> For establishing Abdul Aziz bin Mohammed Al Rowas in his post as Minister for Information. Rowas was inexperienced but Ashworth trained him well. Rowas, although he doesn't like to acknowledge it, owed his post, and the grip he had on it, to Tony.

What is equally without doubt is that as the years went by, his influence grew in proportion to the perceived success of all he did. His work was not confined to controlling current events but extended to controlling details of Oman's past. For it has become all too clear to both Omanis and expatriates alike that he has been imprinting upon the Sultanate his very own perception of the world, how things should be as opposed to how they actually are. Indeed, the very words he uses in conversation are patently designed not to inform, enlighten or educate, but to mask the true nature of the subject under discussion.

Arab rulers have long had Wazirs, special advisers on important, usually sensitive subjects. But Anthony Ashworth proved, not unlike the Curate's egg, to be a good Wazir only in parts. Not knowing when, of his own volition, to take his leave of His Majesty Sultan Qaboos, he has run the very real risk of reducing himself from the role of trusted adviser to that of someone who might have overstayed his sell-by date.

Obviously, the Omani ruler, kind, forgiving and generous to a fault, is apparently unaware of the excesses of his ever-active servant. But when he turned his attention to Tony and Margaret Ashworth, it was usually a time of singular benevolence. Both travel on Omani diplomatic passports and lived in one of Muscat's most palatial residences. There is much talk to which the Ashworths, with no small degree of justification, pay little heed. Yet given the rapidly changing social and political climate in Oman, it would perhaps be prudent for discretion, ever the better part of valour, to be exercised. For life in Oman, as elsewhere, has much to do with how things are perceived in the public domain.

For many a year Anthony Ashworth, when asked about a possible departure date, would say that he did not know when he would 'bail out' of Oman. But in the summer of 2000 a really quite extraordinary story, even by the standards of Oman, began to gain currency in the salons of Muscat. Prompted by a particularly long absence from the country, the belief gained ground that Anthony Ashworth had, at very long last, become subject to the Sultan's grave displeasure. It was most reliably thought that he had been made a Prohibited Immigrant and that the Ashworths were now marooned at their home on the Isle of Man. Neither he nor his wife were invited to that November's National Day celebrations, an absence so notable that messages were sent, from various places: the Isle of Man, Reid's Hotel on the Island of Madeira, Vienna, Switzerland. All said that their long absence was occasioned by 'Margaret's continuing health problems', a role the lady declined to play, taking to her garden on the Isle of Man and planting 'hundreds of bulbs'.

When presented by a journalist with an Oman storyline with which he did not agree, Anthony Ashworth had the habit of commenting, 'Yes, but would Snooks of Streatham find this interesting? I doubt it, you know.' This attitude alone demonstrated just how out of touch the man had become with the contemporary world, as it exists beyond the Sultanate of Oman. Of course, whatever may have passed between the Crown in Oman and the Ashworths should be, in an ideal world, a private matter for them and them alone. But such an expectation is an unrealistic abdication of the fact that in today's world it has become, as the British Royal family knows only too well, virtually impossible to separate the private from the public. As regrettable as this may well be, it is an evident truth that people will choose to ignore at their own eventual discomfort. Indeed this man, like so many in that tight, secretive, egocentric circle who work for one of the world's last absolute rulers, is by the very nature of his presence and power in an Arab state, in the twenty-first century, a source of abiding interest to many. Including, alas, Anthony Ashworth's old and trusted ally in the dubious art of counter-persuasion, Mr Snooks of Streatham.

# CHAPTER ELEVEN

## The Endgame

Palace coups, 'bloodless' or otherwise, are never neat affairs. The sanitised line drawn under the overthrow by those who comprise the new order escapes questions their actions have given rise to and which, in an inescapable appointment, are destined to be answered at the bar of history. Over the past 30 years, the Government of Oman's Ministry of Information has spent an inordinate amount of time, cash and effort in attempting to persuade a sceptical world that the events in the Salalah Palace on the late afternoon and early evening of 23 July 1970 constituted a peaceful 'abdication'. But the inconvenient truth has refused to go away or be erased by the passage of time. The bewildered pain and irritation so evidently expressed by some, if not all, Ministry officials at the stubborn nature of the facts of the matter has long been a source of astonishment. It demonstrates the dangerously naive belief held by so many in Muscat that the press beyond the borders of the Sultanate can be treated on an *à la carte* basis.

Such attitudes are based on a very doubtful premise indeed. For it is a fact that the most persistent question in the minds of so many is why the country's recent past has been shrouded in such excessive secrecy, including the events which brought Sultan Qaboos to the throne? This includes some inhabiting the stable of 'safe' journalists who, in the words of one of their number, 'have felt oppressed by the burden of Anthony Ashworth's hospitality during my Oman freebies'. It is a situation that, six years ago, prompted a London-based newspaper to plan a series which, in the event, never materialised, 'Inside Oman — The Sultanate of Secrets'. There is a point of view which suggests that the spinning of such a web of deceit, particularly by those around Oman's ruler, has been entirely counter-productive and in itself raises questions which otherwise may not have arisen even in the minds of the naturally inquisitive. Comments the same 'safe' journalist:

> It really is a policy based on a supreme arrogance and cynicism, one fed and watered by the belief that if journalists, especially those who are being used to get across the never-absent 'good news' aspect of Oman's affairs, are kept in five-star hotels during their visits to the country, then awkward questions will not be asked.

It does, however, come down to one basic fact. What is this secrecy all about? What has prompted it? Who has been dictating that it is so necessary? Has Oman discovered the meaning of life on earth? Has the fountain of eternal youth been discovered in the country's deserts? Has the government a secret nuclear programme? Is it vitally involved in the only big story in the Middle East: the Israeli-Palestinian conflict? The answer to all of these questions is a resounding no! So what has this secrecy been all about? What is being covered up? These are questions to which many Omanis are themselves demanding answers in increasingly vocal tones, as the new century unfolds.

The Oman story is an enigma, wrapped in a mystery and shrouded with secrecy. One of the more bizarre events of the twentieth century it is, by design, far from easy to piece together. It is indeed an extraordinary tale, at once complex and beguiling; not unlike an intricate, colourful Arabesque mosaic, the multitudinous pieces of which have been scattered to the winds in an intentional attempt at total obfuscation. But in any piece accomplished by an Islamic artist, he must work in an imperfection because only Allah is capable of total perfection. So it is that this strategy of secrecy has one essential flaw, that being the willingness to talk of those who were there at the time, and in on 'The Grand Design', and consequently, 'know where the bodies are buried'. These people are now unwilling to take such information with them to their graves for a variety of personal reasons. So with assistance that has been as provocatively brave as it has been conscientious and honourable, it has been possible to painstakingly fill in the formerly concealed areas, hitherto marked as 'unexplored', on the map of the Sultanate of Oman.

To begin to remove the shroud of secrecy which for over 30 years has concealed from public scrutiny the enigmatic and mysterious nature of events which propelled Oman into the contemporary world, it is necessary to ask one central, straightforward, fundamental question. It has often been asked but never satisfactorily answered. Why did the Conservative Government led by Edward Heath, which came to office on 18 June 1970, decide within 35 days to conspire in the overthrow of a Middle Eastern monarch who for the previous 38 years had closely worked with successive governments in Whitehall and who was bound to them by treaties of friendship and mutual interest? An Arab monarch who, so unceremoniously heaved aside in favour of his son on 23 July 1970, had been Britain's closest ally in the Gulf for almost two generations, both in war and peace?

We have seen earlier in this book the concern and mounting irritation (not to say alarm) displayed by the British at Sultan Said's attitude of spirited independence, dating from the mid-1950s. The first indication was the treaty with American oil companies, granting them exclusive exploration rights in the south (Dhofar's Midway Row, for example, having been built in 1955 for the American Mecom Oil Company). There was his adamant refusal to adopt and implement a British agenda in the matter of 'developing' his feudal state with the oil revenues that were soon to roll in; a fact which, again as we have seen, concentrated some British minds so mightily. But such facts have never been given as the reasons why Britain conspired in an act of treachery against an old and trusty friend. The official reasons given for Sultan Said's overthrow (in addition to his son's alleged, unprompted dismay with his father's slow pace in modernising Oman) were said to be primarily military strategy. They were led by a fear that if the PFLOAG rebels won the Dhofar war, the Sultanate would fall under Soviet and East German control via their client state, South Yemen, with the attendant reason that the shipment of oil through the Straits of Hormuz would then be put at risk.

For a detailed examination of such official reasons for the Palace coup in Salalah, it is best to turn to a source who was associated at the time, albeit in the backrooms of power, with the political and financial strategy behind removing the Omani ruler from his throne by force:

> The background to the whole exercise were suspicions held by many in Whitehall that what vested interests – represented by a coalition of military, financial and political forces – were pushing them towards in Oman, came under the heading of a very private enterprise, led by some exceptionally greedy but plausible and not untalented conspirators. Principal in such a group were members of Britain's military intelligence community, who had strong links with

the country's arms manufacturers and who could see huge financial gains to be made from sales in oil-rich Oman, provided of course that the right man was in charge. And poor old Sultan Said was most definitely not the man they had in mind! Important, also, in the grand design, were senior figures in Britain's military establishment, especially in the SAS, men who were fearful that unless a bigger role could be found for the organisation and pretty damn quick, they would, in the face of defence cuts, be substantially dismantled and would, as a direct result, be facing redundancies. In fact, during the two years leading up to the coup, redundancy for many in the SAS was a very real prospect. Sir Peter de la Billiere and General Johnnie Watts, both of whom did tours of duty in Oman, went on the record, with Sir Peter confirming it in his books published in the 1990s, that they were desperate to find a new role for the SAS and that without the organisation's involvement in the Sultanate it would have been out of business in the Gulf and the Middle East for good. Even such delicately uncovered shards of truth, which only begin to approach the Oman saga, continue to be bitterly resented by some of those who were intimately connected with the coup. This was demonstrated in 1997 when Sir Peter was banned by the Ministry of Defence in London from attending an annual SAS knees-up, because of his honest and candid assessment of the organisation's past strategies and varying fortunes in his books. Whenever Oman's name surfaces in such circles, it is for certain that much madness and paranoia will soon appear! On the diplomatic front, the words of Sir Anthony Parsons, well before his Foreign Office career took him off to the British desk at the United Nations, also serve as evidence of the disquiet with which so many in official circles in London viewed the 'private enterprise' nature of what was planned for Oman by a small, scheming group in Britain. Parsons, as a former British Political Agent stationed in Bahrain, from where Muscat and Oman was closely monitored for many years, not only had a legitimate concern for the Sultanate but an intimate, comprehensive knowledge of its affairs and an honourable, healthy concern about the character and motivation of those plotting Sultan Said's downfall. He, as the British representative at the UN, was obliged to take an awful lot of stick from the so-called progressive, nationalist Arab states following the Sultan's forced removal. Parsons had, in actual fact, to defend a policy about which, in private, he held very real misgivings, principally because of those involved and his suspicions of their long-term, selfish motives. Sir Anthony was what he had been throughout his distinguished career, a British diplomat of the highest integrity and instinct, a man with a sense of history, an understanding of its irrepressible nature and, therefore, a keen awareness that his country would be judged by future generations by its past conduct on the world stage. Not for him the constant counting of coins in the palm of one's hand. His approach has always been the bigger canvas of history. It was natural, therefore, for him to have been suspicious about the real, self-serving intentions of those winking and whispering away for Sultan Said's removal, but he was, of course, just one of many and by the time of the overthrow was no longer immediately involved in the dubious mechanics of the plotting by the few for the Palace coup.

With regard to the involvement of the SAS in the Dhofar War, once the coup had taken place and with it a role for the organisation in the country, there came a new dimension for the Ministry of Defence in London and, of course, for Britain's arms manufacturers. The whole arrangement was unique in Britain's post-colonial history in that every kind and item of military assistance provided to Oman was charged for at the going rate; Western market rate. There were also times when Oman was obliged to pay for services and supplies in advance! These hard facts are of considerably greater relevance in any truthful assessment of what the coup was, in part, about; more than the fact that to conceal SAS involvement in what some sections of the media termed 'Britain's Secret War', its members on active service in Oman were described as the 'British Army Training Team'. That was primarily a device for passing the whole enterprise safely through the hands of MPs and the press! An equally crucial factor in the equation was the justification for the coup as being the safe supply of oil to the West and that this was linked to a military strategy to defeat the insurgents from the Marxist-orientated People's Democratic Republic of Yemen. Frankly, such alleged justifications don't bear too close a scrutiny. If, as has for so long been said, the purpose of mounting the coup was a central plank in a policy designed to make Oman and the Gulf safe from Communism before, during and after the 1971 withdrawal from Britain's east of Suez role and, even more crucially, military assistance was essential to protect supplies of oil which did not involve passage through the

Straits of Hormuz, then the prize was surely worth a straightforward military support Treaty, similar to the one Britain had with Kuwait, which was promptly activated in 1961 when the socialist-inspired General Kaseem of Iraq threatened to seize the oil-rich state! In any event, the well rehearsed litany of Oman's oil being particularly crucial in that it could be made accessible without the need to go into the Gulf, thus making it strategically enticing, is palpable nonsense. In 1970 Iran, under the Shah, both militarily and politically, was the 'Policeman' of the region as far as Western interests were concerned. Actually, Oman didn't have a defensive Navy to speak of at the time with which to guard the Straits. And who remembers now, the dire predictions that if, following Britain's withdrawal from Aden, the communists came to power and influence, then the 'Gateway to the Indian Ocean', via Suez, would be closed to the West? Well, the Russians and the East Germans did arrive in Aden after the British left but their arrival didn't inhibit the passage of Western shipping one jot. Actually, in the harsh light of realpolitik, the policy makers, those devoid and divorced from self-interest, didn't give a damn if Oman, like Southern Yemen, fell under Soviet and East German influence, given that Iran and Saudi Arabia produced more oil in a day than Oman did in a whole year. The policy makers in London looking towards the North Sea where, by 1970, it had become clear that Britain had potentially far more oil than Oman and, crucially, far more recoverable high-grade oil and would become not only a net exporter but one of the world's biggest exporters of high-grade oil, didn't give a stuff about Oman being a source of long-term supplies to the West? Actually, there were those who would have welcomed the Soviets or the East Germans, both of whom became so active in Aden following the British withdrawal in 1967, becoming expensively bogged down in the debilitating sands of Oman, not unlike Ronald Reagan's and Margaret Thatcher's secret rejoicing when Leonid Brezhnev so disastrously bogged down the Soviet Union in Afghanistan in later years.

While there was no direct American involvement in the Oman coup, it was an event with a Washington dimension, as there always has been with Britain's foreign policy since the Second World War. There was for sure mounting, and as was proved in 1973, warranted concern in Washington throughout the late 1960s at the stability of the regime of Emperor Haile Selassie, the ruler of Ethiopia. This was a particular worry for America's intelligence community in that the CIA had a listening post at Massawa on the Red Sea, home to the Ethiopian Navy, in the then Ethiopian northern province of Eritrea, and was fearful that if, as actually happened with the fall of the Emperor, a Communist-led government came to power, it would lose it. However, after the 1973 Marxist-inspired revolution, the Mengitsu regime was too clever to attack the post itself. It left that to the Eritreans who were fighting Mengitsu's army for the establishment of a separate, sovereign state of their own. On one occasion the Eritreans actually captured, and held hostage, three Americans from the post. These were events long feared and anticipated by the Washington policy makers, which had the CIA boys at Langley, Virginia, studying their maps for an alternative site to replace Massawa. Even before the overthrow of Sultan Said such a site had been identified as being in the northern area of Oman known as the Musandam. So while, again, America took no physical role in the removal of the Omani ruler and had, in actual fact, more or less abandoned attempts to get a stake in the country via American oil companies, through which, by their wooing of Sultan Said from the mid-1950s, they had attempted to establish themselves, as they had done, via Aramco, in neighbouring Saudi Arabia, they did continue to have a strategic interest in what happened there, given their intention to eventually establish a listening and over-the-horizon scanning facility in the Musandam.

Which was why, just five months after the July coup, in December 1970, the British were obliged, in an attempt to eliminate a further internal threat to the Qaboos regime which they had so recently put in place, to mount the air, land and sea operation 'Intradon', which had the cover name 'Breakfast', arranged, in the words of an 'Appreciation of the Situation' British Army document of 19 November 1970, 'to eradicate dissidents from the Musandam Peninsula'. The dissidents, members of the Shihu tribe, were not only hostile to the new regime in Muscat but resentful of any Western presence in their remote, rugged mountain terrain, such as an American intelligence-gathering post would represent. The Shihu were described in that same document in the following terms: 'The Shihu occupy the whole of the mountainous area of the Northern Peninsula. They are fiercely independent and aggressive when their independence is threatened. Although normally widely scattered they move easily on the hills and have the ability to concentrate rapidly. Although armed only with rifles, primitive swords and axes, unfriendly Shihu could make operations by our troops extremely difficult.'

Earlier in this 'Appreciation Report', the numbers of the dissidents were given as 93. Yet so desperate were the British to secure the Musandam and by so doing prove to the Americans the total territorial viability of their new and greatest asset in Oman, Sultan Qaboos, that they mounted this formidable military exercise, Intradon, or, if one prefers, 'Breakfast', involving operations by land, sea and air to 'eradicate' the dissident Shihu and pacify the remainder. It is also of interest to note that the SAS were in on the act, although in an Intradon document dated 11 December 1970, 'Instructions in the Event of Press and Publicity Enquiries', the order was given that 'the presence of the SAS and an interrogation team in this operation is to be denied throughout'. Intradon, a sledgehammer to crack a nut was, of course, successful, with the dissidents being quickly eradicated, with those that got away fleeing over the border into the tiny Sheikhdom of Ras Al Khaimah. And the desired result was thus achieved. The Musandam was made safe for Qaboos and the American Government. In due course, Washington's intelligence-gathering, over-the-horizon listening post was constructed in the Musandam by the CIA-styled 'Collins Communications Corporation', where it remains to this very day. During the Cold War it played a significant role in monitoring Soviet naval activity in the Indian Ocean and indeed beyond.

But the complexities of the overall deal struck between London and Washington over the establishment of Oman's 'New Dawn' did not begin and end with the installing of Sultan Qaboos and making the country safe for Western interests. Indeed, the Shihu were not the only 'little men' obstructing the big idea, 'The Grand Design', as we shall now see.

In the annals of the British Empire, the islands of the British Indian Ocean Territory do not loom large, with the name of Diego Garcia, a part of the Chagos archipelago, hardly surfacing for public attention. Yet in 1966 in an ultimately disgraceful and shameful act, the Labour Government, by the simple expedient of an exchange of notes between London and Washington, dated 30 December 1966, abdicated Britain's colonial responsibility by handing Diego Garcia to America for 'defence purposes', for 50 years without payment; there was an option for a further 20. Lord Chalfont, on behalf of the Foreign Secretary George Brown, signed London's acceptance of the arrangement. There was no parliamentary debate and no publicity of a deal done in the dark corridors of power. In 1972, when the Conservative party had returned to power, the American Navy was given permission to establish a 'limited communications facility' on Diego Garcia. In 1974, with Labour back in office, the Secretary of State for Defence, Roy Mason, hastened to calm the Government of Mauritius, alarmed by the establishment of a superpower's military facility in their region of the world. Mason went on the record, telling the Government in Port Louis, 'Diego Garcia will not be used as a military base.' In 1976, with Labour Prime Minister James Callaghan in No.10 Downing Street, his Minister of State, Roy Hattersley, completely abandoned the assurances given to Mauritius by Roy Mason and put London's final seal of approval on Washington's intention to turn Diego Garcia into a military base of very considerable significance. The 'limited communications facility' sanctioned by the Heath Government was now, under Callaghan, to become:

> A support facility of the United States Navy . . . the facility shall consist of an anchorage, airfield, support and supply elements and ancillary services, personnel accommodation and transmitting and receiving services. Immovable structures, installations and buildings for the facility may be constructed.

In short, Diego Garcia was now to become a fully-fledged American military base, from where the West's interests in the Indian Ocean and in the Gulf, with its vital oil supplies, could be safely monitored and controlled. In fact, the first American forces had arrived on Diego Garcia in March 1971.

All of which was, by Western imperatives, good enough in the light of the Cold War. But for one consideration: the Islands of the Chagos Archipelago, and particularly the island of Diego Garcia, were not without indigenous inhabitants. Clearly, they were in the way and could not be permitted to remain in their island homes. The Ilois people, who numbered some 2,000 (more than the total population of the Falkland Islands in whose defence Britain went to war in 1982) had homes, villages, smallholdings, schools, shops, churches. As evidence to the centuries they had lived there in isolated contentment, with the British Crown as guarantor of their way of life, they also had graveyards. But in a disgraceful, shameful act, the Ilois were removed by force from their homes (including the young, the aged and the infirm), put onto ships and sent to Mauritius. There, frightened and bewildered and with a derisory, one-off compensatory cash payment, they were told to begin a new life in what was an alien land.

But there were American voices raised in their defence. In 1975, the United States Senate, alarmed by the cost of establishing this new and expensive military base in the far-off Indian Ocean, questioned the State Department about the arrangement. In an attempt to placate Senators, a State Department official said, 'There are no inhabitants on Diego Garcia.' By this time it was a truthful statement. They had all been sent into exile, in an exercise not unlike that carried out by the Soviet leader, Josef Stalin, who had the Tartars sent into exile from their native Crimea. To emphasise the pointlessness of Ilois hopes of eventually being allowed to return to Diego Garcia, the British Government ordered the closure of all the islanders' means of livelihood, such as their once flourishing copra plantations. The Foreign Office in London, alarmed when the expulsion of the Ilois surfaced in the American press, issued a statement which was on that particular occasion so economical with the truth that it was howled out of court by at least one member of the American Congress. 'All went willingly,' the Foreign Office statement had intoned, 'no coercion was used.' Replied the Congressman, 'No coercion was used? After you had cut off their jobs? What other kind of coercion do you need? Are you talking about putting them on the rack?'

It was thanks to American concern, and principally through the American press, that in 1975 the dispossessed Ilois did eventually, albeit briefly, have the world's spotlight turned upon them. The appeal for redress was led by Senator Edward Kennedy, who described the forced removal by Britain of the Ilois people from Diego Garcia as 'this clear lack of human sensitivity'. The Washington Post, more directly, termed it 'this act of kidnapping' and belatedly, The Times reported that the expulsions made 'depressing reading for anyone who wants to believe in the essential decency and honesty of the British Government'. But it was the hearings in the American Senate, during which the compensation for the Ilois was demanded, which finally brought them some redress of substance. They were awarded, as a community, a sum equivalent to four million pounds.

But alas, not even to this day have they received the essential comfort of a promised return to their island homes, even though in 2000 the Ilois mounted a legal challenge to the British Government. The case went through the London courts, which ruled that their expulsion had been illegal. What the Ilois were not aware of was that the tragedy represented by the forced depopulation of Diego Garcia was just one more piece, a crucial one in fact, of the scattered mosaic that was the overall 'Grand Design', in which Oman by its very geography, was regarded as a very significant part indeed. The former official witness to the Sultanate's story relates why:

Yes, Diego Garcia, as an American base, was directly linked to what happened in Oman, in terms of making sure that there was a ruler on the throne there who would comply with Anglo-American military and intelligence requirements. The only development that could have saved Sultan Said from being overthrown by the British, and replaced by his son, would have been the discovery of oil in Dhofar in commercially viable quantities, by 'His Americans', that is the Americans he gave concessions to in the 1950s and the '60s. Of course, this did not happen. Once that possibility was out of the way, the principal American concern became having intelligence facilities in Oman and this the British were only too willing to more or less guarantee once their nominee, indeed the only nominee available to them, Qaboos, was safely on the throne. The proof of the importance of Oman to the Americans, in relation to their base on Diego Garcia, was seen as recently as the Iraq-Kuwait conflict in 1991, when during Operation Desert Storm, B-52 aircraft, flying from the island, were given landing and fuelling rights in Oman on their way to bombing raids over Baghdad. This was, of course, another consideration in the 'Grand Design', the construction of runways in the Sultanate suitable for use by American military aircraft. The British Royal Air Force runways at Bait Al Falaj, Salalah and on Masirah Island were considered woefully inadequate by the Americans, which for their requirements they were of course. This was the background to the really quite extraordinary story of the construction of Thumrait Airbase, in Dhofar, in 1974.

It was during Sultan Qaboos's visit to Tehran in March, 1974, during which he sought further military assistance from the Shah with which to fight the Dhofar war, that the question of the construction of a new military airbase was raised. The reason given by the Shah for such a base to be built was that it would be needed if he were to send Oman the requested squadron of Phantom aircraft, capable of attacking rebel bases in South Yemen. Qaboos returned home and ordered that the construction of a 4,000 metre runway commence immediately, regardless of cost, at Thumrait in central

Dhofar. It was an incredible exercise and actually broke all known construction records. The runway is not only 4,000 metres long but 13 feet thick! Prodigious amounts of cement were flown into the country and the cost of construction soared. In fact, the costs grew so alarmingly that some Omani ministers did voice their concern. However, by December of that year the job was done and the base was fully operational. It had cost a staggering one hundred and forty-five million dollars, which added considerably to the financial difficulties Oman was then beginning to experience. Yet, incredibly, the Iranian Air Force only ever used it for one strike against South Yemen! What, however, was not known was that the Shah, in insisting upon its construction, had merely been acting as an American proxy. The construction of Thumrait, far from being needed to fight the Dhofar War, was regarded by Washington as a long-term necessity for the protection of Western interests in the Gulf region. It was built essentially for that purpose and to specifications which would enable it, for a very long time to come, to fulfil such a role. Thumrait was an important aspect of the design, one of the reasons why it has the world's longest operational, military runway outside the Edwards Air Force Base in America. To produce conditions in which such designs could be carried out was, in essence, the endgame which began to be played out by the forced removal of Sultan Said in his palace, in July 1970. Of course, the design almost came to grief when Qaboos's uncle, Sayyid Tarik, was appointed Premier. His demands that Qaboos become a constitutional monarch and that Oman proceed towards becoming a parliamentary democracy were a very real threat, because had they been put into place the manifestations of very private, political, commercial and military interests, which have so dominated Oman, would have been quite impossible to pursue. So the campaign began. Tarik had to be stopped! And that is exactly what happened. In the face of Tarik's independent line, the whispering campaign of denigration began until, in an orchestrated chorus in the ear of Sultan Qaboos, it rose to a crescendo. Tarik must go! And, principally by expatriate scheming, it was made quite impossible for him to remain as Oman's Prime Minister. So he went and the endgame was, once more, resumed.

In a world in which distractions abound, the overthrow of Sultan Said of

Oman has long been regarded as an historical footnote in a region of the world where palace coups and associated acts of violence are but the norm. Yet, remote, transitory and inconsequential as the 1970 coup may have appeared to the Western world, it demonstrated just how terribly easy it can be for a nation considered by others to be 'small', and in the case of Oman in 1970, inexperienced, to be manipulated by 'larger' states with very private agendas; with concerns and priorities not always in sympathy with those of the nation at their mercy. The background to the planning of the coup was one of diplomatic intrigue and evasion: Cold War strategies; rivalry between Britain and America for supremacy over a nation's natural resource, oil; and the possibilities for financial exploitation by an extraordinary coalition of commercial and political interests, in which the sale of arms loomed large. As such the Oman story is, by any yardstick, of considerable international significance. Central to the story is, of course, how single individuals can direct the path down which Third World countries are so often led, a path that is essentially followed in order to pursue the plans of those charting the course. To name just two (and there are others): Timothy Landon and Anthony Ashworth. Both separated by time, circumstance, expectation and temperament, they were delivered onto the shores of the Sultanate at a time, and in a manner, which gave them considerable power. And the nature of how such extraordinary power was used is an essential element in the Oman equation. It was a power enjoyed by some expatriates of which they can now only dream in places such as Spain, Portugal, and the windswept, litter-strewn towns of metropolitan Britain to which they eventually dispersed.

There will be many, looking at the Sultanate of Oman today, with its reasonably efficient civil service, the apparent absence of crime or mass civil dissent, its police force which is almost certainly one of the finest in the whole of the Arab world, its unfailing pro-Western stance and, so often remarked upon by visitors, its suspiciously clean streets, and ask, 'So what?'

Well, yes, all of these would be legitimate points to make. Indeed, by comparison with Somalia or the Congo, Oman is an exceptionally well-run, efficient state and the credit for this has to go to His Majesty Sultan Qaboos and to those, Omani and expatriate alike, who, during the past 30 years, have assisted him in the task of governing a nation which his forebears did not always regard as a particularly easy task. There are those too, who will say that had it not been for the overthrow of Sultan Said, the Dhofar War would have been lost and Oman would have endured a long night of Marxist-inspired mismanagement; that the country would have become a client state of the Eastern Bloc regimes. But as legitimate as such points would be, they fail to take one fundamental aspect of the Oman story into account: human nature, man's insatiable appetite for detailed information about the past and, in particular, the abiding resentment of so many Omanis, of both the pre- and post-coup generations, regarding the atmosphere of state secrecy woven around the beginning of the country's 'New Dawn'. Many feel it is an official ploy to disguise the fact that it was very much a Western-sponsored affair that, while delivering the promised modern state, has had the effect of distancing themselves as a nation, as far from the Arab mainstream as they were under Sultan Said. To compare Oman with the strife-torn, poverty-stricken, corrupt states so common to the rest of the Third World, would be to compare a peach with a crab-apple. While often used as an argument to deflect critical comment, such comparisons can only be regarded as being born of an assumption that Omanis are quite unable to think for themselves, despite the country's rapidly increasing educated class. But this they most certainly do and while exercising sentiments of loyalty to their sovereign, they are increasingly unhappy about those Omanis and expatriates who have for so long besieged him in their craven pursuit of personal riches.

Omanis have a well-documented history of remaining silent, passive for only as long as their requirements of the hour are being delivered by those who govern them. Such a national characteristic will be ignored only at considerable, future cost and the early warning signs are there for all those with eyes to see. For as the *Economist* article of 9 August 1997 reported, 'wealth is not trickling down as comfortably as it once did'. Ally such a reality to the *Guardian* article, 'British Advisers Fuel Gulf Anger' and, as leaner times loom, it is far from difficult to understand the disquiet now surfacing and the questions that are being asked. At the heart of such questions is the future role for the oligarchy of businessmen-cum-politicians, again both Omani and expatriate alike. They are perceived to have been the principal beneficiaries of the country's comporatively modest oil wealth, allied to the power they have had to make policy perceived not to have been in the real interests of the state by so many Omanis.

Comments one senior Omani:

> His Majesty has come to a point in his reign in which he can have
> the continuing loyalty of the greater majority, or he can stick with
> those who have done him so much damage in the eyes of his own
> people. He has a choice. But he cannot have both. Basically, we want

to know, even given the current low oil price, why, with a population of under two million, we now face austerity.

Another troubling factor for so many Omanis is the hijacking of the country's foreign policy, by the exporting of oil to Rhodesia (now Zimbabwe) and South Africa in the 1970s and 1980s, in defiance of United Nations sanctions. The senior former state official again:

> There were two, private oil exporting countries who did this. Both of them were of critical importance to South Africa and Rhodesia in terms of the supply of oil and other goods, flown out of Seeb International Airport in a DC aircraft, goods they were barred from purchasing on the open market. The UN and British sanctions monitoring people kept tripping over these companies when cargoes of Omani oil were switched twice and sometimes as much as four times while at sea. The oil was, theoretically, going to legitimate destinations, such as Japan. Let us assume an average profit of a dollar a barrel and an average trade of half a million barrels per transaction, and the profit, which I've set in light of the fact that neither of these companies actually paid so much as a dollar towards the cost of the oil's production, then you can see that it made a few people spectacularly rich, very, very quickly. The problem for us Omanis is that the whole exercise was illegal and while it was a private scheme, carried out for personal gain, the blame for it goes to Oman.

As ever with Oman, its history and so much of its recent past, is characterised by secrecy. Yet again this prompts the question, 'Over what exactly?' As the country proceeds into a new century, which promises to be one of particular challenge, it is increasingly unlikely that the questions currently being asked by so many Omanis will evaporate into thin air. It is a particular irony that the questions now being put are coming from those who have received a superior education as a direct result of the domestic policies pursued by Sultan Qaboos. They could in certain circumstances, be expected to remain silent, in the interests of that elusive and often misinterpreted goal 'national unity'.

But the world is an uncertain place and gratitude rarely falls where it is due. Indeed, as Sultan Said said to the British Undersecretary of State for War, Julian Amery, all those years ago in Salalah, 'You ask me to build schools. But look what happened to you British in India! You did that and then they threw you out!' History is not only of a cyclical nature but an aspect of the human experience that actually has no end, only a sense of direction. In the opening years of a new century, when a new sense of direction is sought by so many, it would appear that the full consequences of the shots fired in anger in the private apartments of Sultan Said's palace in Salalah 32 years ago, are destined to continue to reverberate not only around Oman but far beyond her shores.

# CHAPTER TWELVE

# Full Circle?

History, contrary to common statement, does not in actual fact repeat itself. That is a too simplistic belief by far. What it does is imitate the past, which is an altogether different matter. But even given that the tide of history is indeed a recurring imitation of past events there is, in the Oman story, a very definite cyclical nature in the tidal rise and fall of its fortunes. Four examples of this serve to illustrate the point.

The practice of material consumption as opposed to investment for the future, so evident in the nineteenth century when Muscat's merchants used their revenues from slave trading to embark upon a programme of palatial house building, as a result of which the country was starved of essential, productive investment, was continued by their late twentieth-century counterparts. The affluent have used much of the easy money generated by the oil boom of the mid-1970s and early 1980s for conspicuous consumption, witnessed by the proliferation of private 'palaces' in Muscat's capital area and which, as the country approaches leaner years, is a cause for much resentment by so many Omanis. It is a situation that in itself can only give rise to the distinct possibility of future social unrest.

Secondly, there was the practice of 'buying' peace and public acceptance, so evident in 1874 and 1885, when Sultan Turki and Sultan Faisal respectively paid the rebellious Al Harthy tribal leaders to lay down their arms and return to the interior. This mirrors to some considerable extent Sultan Qaboos's expensive, and in some instances counter-productive, rush to modernise during the early years of his reign, a strategy designed to show Omanis that he was indeed different from his slow-moving father and, through such a process, gain rapid, public acceptance.

Thirdly, the practice of using the military representatives of foreign states to maintain a grip on power has also been a recurring theme in Oman's past, witnessed by the use, between 1806 and 1820, of British and Persian troops to evict the Wahaibi invaders. Also of note is Sultan Taimour's resort to British officers to beat off the 1915 attack by Imamate rebels on the barracks at Bait Al Falaj and in the 1970s, Sultan Qaboos's use of British, Iranian and Jordanian forces to win the Dhofar campaign.

Fourthly, the suffocatingly close British presence, alternately endured and, presumably, welcomed by Oman's rulers, is of a recurring nature. It is witnessed by the constant attendance of Political Agents of one sort from 1837, when Captain Robert Cogan was in the suite of Sultan Said bin Taimour, to 1970 when a similar presence in the suite of Sultan Qaboos bin Said was one Timothy Landon.

The practice of relying, basically, on a mercenary-led army (and the term is most definitely not used in a pejorative sense) to maintain a grip on power must have been cast in doubt for Sultan Said on 23 July 1970, when British officers in his service were instrumental in removing him from his throne. As must have been the trust in the word of the intrusively close representative of the British Government who, in 1932, gave an assurance to his father, Sultan Taimour, that if he complied with the demand to abdicate, they would take good care of his son. It was the very nature of the collusion and intrigue which attended the forced removal from the throne of Sultan Said by a British Government barely a month in office, which gave principal rise to the basic and fundamental question, why? Why did the British decide to abandon him and, in the process, abdicate past commitments to which it was bound by Treaty to honour and, therefore, uphold?

While he would most definitely have moved at a more gradual pace, Sultan Said had, as we have seen, commenced the development process and, what is more, had announced his intention to do so as early as January 1968. That was within five months of the commencement of the flow of substantial oil revenues. Much of the planning for the development projects initiated by his father was already at an advanced stage by the time Sultan Qaboos came to power in the wake of Said's overthrow. For example: the building of the first school for girls had been completed before the coup; work was well ahead on two hospitals; the contract for the road from Muscat to Sohar had been signed; blueprint plans for the construction of a modern port at Muttrah along with an airport of international standard at Seeb had already been drawn up.

The 'why' factor in the Oman equation, to which this book has in substantial part given an answer, is given a further dimension in a restricted and unpublished document titled 'A Short History of the Sultan's Armed Forces', written by Lieutenant-Colonel Colin Maxwell, deputy commander of the Sultan's Army in August 1967. The document passes succinct comment on the exact nature of the predominant British interest in Oman: 'Since the First World War British interests have been largely territorial . . . to uphold the Sultan's Government against foreign influence . . . the security of air bases and overflying rights . . . and the safeguarding of oil interests.' It is of no small interest to record that, again at official demand, Colin Maxwell's private diaries were, like 'Mac' Maclean's, destroyed at the end of his life and, in the sad process, an important account of the nature of the Anglo-Omani relationship together with much of its detailed history, was lost forever.

It is an appropriate place in this political narrative to acknowledge, with Colin Maxwell's integrity so evident, the enormous contribution made by so many individual Britons to Oman's development, progress and good governance. Their numbers are legion, their selfless commitment to Oman and its people, delivered in arduous conditions, has on occasions, reflected the very best that the British race and nation has to offer a people working towards the establishment of their country as a well-governed, progressive and independent state. Neither should the facts presented in this book be regarded as negative comment on the rule of His Majesty Sultan Qaboos, who has an enviable record of quite extraordinary achievement, arising from his personal and sustained courage in taking upon himself the role to which birth, history and circumstance committed him. That he was brave enough to take his people by the hand and lead them into the modern world, a journey which was, and indeed remains, hazardous in its social implications for the future, cannot be denied. It is a journey far from being completed.

In November of 1996 he announced his intention to introduce a Basic Law, a written constitution that will provide Omanis with a Bill of Rights, guaranteeing them freedom of the press, religious tolerance, an equality of race and gender and the appointment of a Supreme Court to interpret the Basic Law and act as its guardian. This is an initiative without parallel in the Gulf and Oman's ruler deserves the widest possible support in order that in his own, inimitable style he can bring such a development into being. The opportunity is taken, via this book, to suggest that left alone to fashion national policy in concert with his own people, Sultan Qaboos will emerge as one of the first constitutional monarchs on the Arabian Peninsula, sooner rather than later.

The essential burden of the facts presented here centre on the all too often intrusive nature of the British connection during the past 200 years, which has not always been to Oman's advantage. It has too often trespassed upon the sovereignty of the state and has forced strategic decisions, such as who should occupy the throne of Oman, on a number of occasions. Even closer to the point is the conduct of a coterie of Britons who, since the emergence of the country as an oil-producing nation, have, via the trust afforded them by Sultan Qaboos, regarded Oman as very much a private preserve even if this meant going as far, in the case of arms sales and sanction busting, as affecting vital aspects of national policy. It is this domineering aspect of some British 'Advisers' conduct, particularly by those close to the Sultan, which is of greatest concern to so many, as a former Minister of the Omani Crown now describes:

> From his very early days, right through to the first 20 years of his reign, His Majesty has been surrounded, in more ways than one, by British people with very limited opinions. By that I mean extremely right wing and of a militaristic nature. It is almost as if it was planned that he should not have a mind of his own, an independent point of view. He has been bombarded with their opinions and this has had an effect. The problem is, he's just too kind to let people, to whom he thinks he owes something, know that much of what they say he recognises to be in their own private interests. He's very loyal to his so-called friends, British and Omani, and frankly this has long been a problem because of their influence over him. They won't let go and give him a break, which they should do if they really are honourable people, as they pretend to be. But for them, enough will never be enough.

A senior officer in the Sultan's Armed Forces expresses similar concerns:

> This small group's power is no longer acceptable. It has had a negative effect for many years. In 1974, for example, I have been told that it was one of them who persuaded the Sultan that we had to have a particular integrated Air Defence Missile System, manufactured by British Aerospace. This almost bankrupted the country. More recently, in November 1990, His Majesty was persuaded to host a meeting of a secretive, right wing group known as 'The Circle' run by former intelligence agents, senior Western politicians, arms manufacturers and bankers. We know

this from the diaries of Alan Clark, the former Conservative Defence Procurement Minister, who wrote that the disgraced former Conservative Minister, Jonathan Aitken, was present at the meeting and was in the country as a guest of His Majesty. This organisation, by meeting in one of the Sultan's palaces, and with people like Mr Aitken present, is, I tell you, simply not in Oman's interests. It gives a wrong impression of the country to the outside world.

Such concern and resentment, increasingly expressed, at the continuing influence on the governance of Oman by the small, secretive group of Britons, dates from the early days of Sultan Qaboos's reign. Comments a former court official:

> It was always the custom in Oman for Sultans to have the additional title of 'His Highness'. Certainly, as official documents prove, this was the title used by Sultan Said, Qaboos's father. The title of 'Majesty' is not actually in accordance with Arab Islamic custom. King Fahd of Saudi Arabia, for example, does not permit such a title to be used. We believe it came into use here after Sultan Said's downfall. I, myself, well remember the day I received the written instruction that all official correspondence had, in future, to end with 'Your Obedient Servant', again a British practice! Not, most certainly, the Arab Islamic way of doing things.

But it is in the presentation of Oman's face to its own people and to the world beyond, via the country's most 'feared' Department of State, the Ministry of Information, which recruits the most vocal opposition. An example of such hostility was the banning in the country of the *Financial Times*. This was because of an article carried in its edition of 7 November 1994 by its Dubai-based correspondent, Robin Allen, who reported that a World Bank study had come to the conclusion that Oman's financial policies, and particularly its levels of state expenditure, were 'unsustainable'. In particular, the article detailed the Bank's concern at the Sultanate's 'repeated budget deficits, current expenditure trends and the decline in investment'. Quoting the report, the article continued:

> If these and other problems are not corrected and the reforms proposed ignored, Oman is heading for a major economic and social

upheaval, as the oil and gas era comes to an end and Omanis are forced to give up accustomed standards of consumption.

Allen's article went on, 'The Bank's analysis also represents a comprehensive rebuke to officials at all levels who have developed the plausible and positive platitude almost to a fine art form, even when confronted with unpleasant realities.' The report, the *Financial Times* concluded, also expressed concern at Oman's 'exceptionally high levels of defence and national security expenditure', which it reported, 'is among the highest in the world'.

The most telling aspect of the article is not how it was received by Omanis generally but by Anthony Ashworth in particular. A Ministry of Information staff member reports:

> The decision to ban that edition of the *Financial Times* in the Sultanate was an insult to Omani people everywhere. It did us, and our country, much damage because it made us look as though we couldn't cope with the truth of our own situation. The banning of the paper was a humiliation for us and for the country's reputation abroad, a public relations disaster.

Such comment is pivotal in any assessment of Oman's recent past and indeed of its future. There is a growing awareness by many in the country of the connection between the country's very high defence expenditure, reliably believed to consume 40–44 per cent of the annual budget, and its current climate of austerity. In the words of a former defence official:

> We now realise that most of the arms we have been persuaded to buy, we did not really need and most certainly could not afford. And more of us point to the disaster of Kuwait in 1990, when the Iraqis invaded. Despite all the billions of dollars they had spent on Western arms, they were of no real use in stopping the invasion. Kuwait, in the end, had to pay yet more millions to Britain and America so that they could kick the Iraqis out. It was a lesson for us here in Oman.

It is an eternal truth that a country's political direction is driven by the state of its finances. Just as Sultan Said embarked upon a political strategy in 1932 to relieve his state of debt and, hopefully, restore at least some of its lost sovereignty, so did the promise of imminent riches bring him down in

1970. It was this new, easy wealth generated by oil revenues which principally made it possible for Sultan Qaboos to lead his people from the dark valleys of poverty to the broad, sunlit uplands of prosperity. But now, as the revenues continue to shrink, he is faced with a completely different, far more difficult, political journey: that of taking the Omani people down to the plains of a modest existence, a journey that will be akin to walking through a minefield. That he has the political will and courage to make such a journey is not in doubt if, that is, he has a matching will to confront those around him who have become part of the problem. In short he must have the political appetite for personal confrontation with those individuals who have been responsible for creating the worst of the state's difficulties. He set a precedent some years ago, in a Royal Decree which forbade his ministers and advisers to have business interests. But a subsequent series of 'interpretations' made the Decree virtually null and void. It is in the interests of the Omani monarch, his state and his people, that such a Decree be reissued and strictly implemented and by so doing demonstrate an understanding of Aristotle's celebrated warning that 'the avarice of mankind is insatiable.'

Sultan Qaboos has shown before that he has the will and talent to astonish the world. He can do so again. His policy of diversifying the national economy away from a dangerous dependence on oil and gas revenues is well in hand. Although a policy with limitations, given Oman's small population and therefore the need to export at least some of its limited range of manufactured goods in a fiercely competitive regional market, it can succeed in the long term because of the Sultan's ability to galvanise the Omani people. Fisheries, due to the corruption of permitting industrial over-fishing by principally foreign fleets, are more problematic but here too, policies to redeem the situation are well advanced. Of greater promise is tourism, and those who do travel to Oman for that purpose will find an astonishingly beautiful land and a people, with their unique culture and Arab courtliness, a delight to be amongst.

General Timothy Crease's remark that 'Oman brings out the best and the worst in both men and machines' does have some truth. But Lawrence of Arabia predicted that if the Arabs were forced into Western ways they would succumb, like any savage race, to its diseases, meanness, luxury, cruelty, crooked dealings and artifice; and that, like savages, they would suffer them in an exaggerated form for lack of inoculation. This has, in general terms, happily not come to pass in Oman. On the vexed question of arms sales and the defence not just of Oman but of the other states in the region, the Omani Monarch's initiative at the meeting of the six-state Gulf Cooperation Council, held at Muscat in December 1989, offered a potential way out of the costly and far from effective means of maintaining national security. Sultan Qaboos's suggestion that a pan-Gulf Force be established of 100,000 men drawn from the existing forces of Bahrain, Kuwait, Qatar, Saudi Arabia, The United Arab Emirates and Oman, one that would have, like NATO, a rotating command, deserved greater support than it received. The Gulf States have in the past been able to purchase a formidable array of Western military hardware, but they will only be able to give such costly purchases a strategic purpose when a united regional strategy has been adopted and applied.

However, Oman's high defence expenditure, with its negative financial effects (and the potential to eventually bring the country full circle, back to the state of debt from which, without the benefit of oil revenues, Sultan Said rescued it), is but one contributing factor to the overall climate of increasing social unrest now facing the Sultanate. It led, in the summer of 1994, to the widespread arrests and the subsequent secret establishment of an Oman Civil Rights Committee, some statements of which are reproduced in the Appendix. The manifestation of such strains can best be described as a generation gap within the country's current structures. The educated class, now increasingly public in their criticism, regard the entrenched oligarchy of businessmen and politicians, an apparently insoluble marriage between private commercial gain and the governance of the state, as being responsible for the perceived corruption among this 'old guard'. Without doubt they do, most decidedly, hold the reins of political power, with state appointments being made, principally, from within their group. The post-coup generation therefore feel alienated from both the economic life of the country and the decision-making process at a time when they have rising expectations for greater involvement. In 1991 an attempt was made to meet such rising expectations by the creation of an assembly, known as the Majlis Ashura, a consultative body comprised of elected members from the regions. The fact that it is restricted to only suggesting laws and regulations and prohibited altogether from discussing such crucial issues as the state's finances, defence expenditure, foreign policy and the running of the country's oil and gas industries, has resulted in comprehensive disillusionment. In the words of the *Economist* magazine of 9 August 1997, the assembly has become 'ineffectual'. But the expectations not only remain but continue to rise. Thus is it apparent that the growth and functioning of Oman's systems of government do not match the nation's intellectual growth and therefore, they fail to meet the aspirations and legitimate expectations of its people for greater influence in the government of the land. It is a situation which, as the twentieth century drew to its turbulent close, promised for Oman the sad possibility of internal dissent from which the country has been free since the end of the Dhofar War in 1975. In the words of one young professional Omani:

> As a people, as a nation, we now have to turn our back on past practices and face the future, for if we do not it will face us with levels of confrontation that will put in danger all that has been achieved since His Majesty came to power. To prevent such a situation arising, Oman, with the continuing leadership of Sultan Qaboos, must begin to modernise the institutions of government, that the machinery of government must be reformed.

It is an appeal that should be heard and should be allowed to be heard. For if it is suffocated, or muted, none of the security arrangements currently in place will be able, in the event, to preserve the status quo, prevent further domestic dissent or, in the final analysis, protect the Sultan's governments from the destruction of all that has been achieved. The best that the current system can obtain is the buying of time in which change can come through peaceful, directed evolution. The future success of Oman, as a united and well-governed land, free of dissent and civil strife, will increasingly depend on this fundamental reality and indeed on the dispatch with which those who comprise the current power structure come to realise it. The time when the power of rhetoric can pass for reality is rapidly drawing to a permanent close. In the words of a senior member of the Omani establishment:

> The nationally encouraged practice of confusing rhetoric with reality has confused many and must now stop. We think more of His Majesty than to read of him in the local press in terms which would not have been out of place in Chairman Mao's China. His Majesty deserves better than that and so do the Omani people. And as we are not afraid of the future, neither are we afraid of the past. To have our past hidden from us has been a negative exercise, a policy which has actually done Oman damage in that it has led to speculation about our affairs not just here but abroad. In the words of Shakespeare, from *Macbeth*, 'Confusion now has made its masterpiece.' But we do not want any more confusion. We are, now, and as Sultan Qaboos

promised, a modern country and we need modern policies which can take us safely into the future.

To seek the truths of the past has long been a trusted remedy for assisting a nation into the future. This is not so that its past should dominate its future direction, but to enable it to chart a course that will guide it away from past pitfalls and give it a sense of having come to terms with itself. In the Oman story, such a process is as necessary for Britain as it is for Oman. Through this, the true nature of Britain's relationship, over the centuries for good and ill, with the people of this extraordinary land can be openly acknowledged and set to rest. Not just the imperial flourishes and consequent excesses in the early years of the association but, of even greater relevance, the circumstances in which Britain's last hurrah as a Middle-Eastern, military, colonial power was played out in Oman's very own backyard, when in an aberration prompted by an essentially privately sponsored enterprise, it engineered the downfall of one of Arabia's last grand old men. But his fall from British grace did, at the very least, herald a new dawn in a place in the sun, where shadows will, hopefully, no longer be permitted to fall from a country whose friendship, it was once written, shall continue until the sun and the moon have finished their revolving career.

# APPENDIX 1

## Manumission Certificate

*No 21 of 1929*

**BRITISH GOVERNMENT**

**MANUMISSION CERTIFICATE**

*Be it known to all who may see this that the bearer* <u>Adb Ali   son   of   Chawash</u> *aged* <u>20</u> *years has been manumitted and no one has a right to interfere with his / her liberty.*

*Dated* <u>Muscat</u>   *this* <u>6th</u> *day of* <u>November</u> 1929.

*Signature & Designation*
*of*
*British Representative* }

<u>Major, Political Agent and</u>
<u>H.B.M's Consul, Muscat</u>

Copy of a 1929 Manumission Certificate, issued by the British Political Agency, guaranteeing the freedom of slaves held by Omanis.

# APPENDIX 2

## 'The Word of Sultan Said bin Taimour'

We consider the first period to run from pre-1914 to 1920. The Government in the era of our grandfather, Sultan Faisal bin Turki, and in the era before him had only a simple way of despatching all the affairs of the country; no budget, no planning and no organisation. Improvisation was the basis of all that was done and said. This was the situation prevailing at that time in most Arab countries.

In 1913 (1331) our beloved father, Sultan Taimur bin Faisal succeeded to the throne on the death of Sultan Faisal bin Turki. He inherited a legacy of many debts and a Government burdened with loans due to be repaid to the merchants of the country. This situation continued and the debts increased until 1920, when, realising it was not easy to rule the country with its finances in such a state of weakness and disorganisation, he determined to improve the State finances by introducing modern methods. Finally it was clear that his Government could make little progress until it was freed of its burden of debts, which, as we have said, were to a number of merchants in the country. He realised that it would be best to negotiate one major loan which would enable him to liquidate the old debts and still leave a surplus which could be used to achieve the desired reforms. The only body able to meet his request was the Government of British India, which agreed to lend him the money necessary to free himself from his debts on the understanding that it would be repaid in ten years. He decided at the same time to ask the Egyptian Government for officials to reorganise the Customs. The Egyptian Government agreed and sent him three Customs experts who set about their work with a will. He also engaged an English official, Mr D.V. McCullum, to supervise the reorganisation of the Finance Department. Thereafter the finances of the Government slowly recovered; there were no deficits in the annual budget and the loan instalments were paid off regularly. The English official engaged in 1920 stayed for only six months, however, and, in the absence of a successor, Sultan Taimur appointed Mohammed bin Ahmed Al Ghashn, then Wali of Matrah, as his Minister responsible for financial affairs. This situation prevailed until the end of 1924, when there was a deficit due to the negligence of the responsible officer and the maladministration of the Treasury Officer, as a result of which, the State's finances were so shaken as to make it impossible to continue to repay the instalments of the loan at the proper time.

The second period begins in 1925 when, in view of the poor state of

Government finances, Sultan Taimur bin Faisal, decided to engage a new official to reorganise them. He selected an Englishman, Mr Bertram Thomas, whom he appointed as Finance Minister on a five-year contract, with a view to his improving the financial position of the Government. (Mr Thomas was the first Westerner to cross the Empty Quarter, doing so from Dhofar to Qatar in 54 days.) At the outset he exerted considerable efforts which produced a measure of improvement in financial affairs but unfortunately this improvement was not maintained for more than three years, after which the financial situation again deteriorated and the Government ceased to repay the instalments of the loan. This was due to the maladministration of the official referred to in the previous period for he allowed Government spending to exceed the approved Budget. This led to a deficit and disorder in the State's finances. The balance of payments was upset and unpaid instalments of the loan, and other expenditure, piled up, constituting a new debt, additional to the balance of the previous one.

In 1930 an economic slump struck the world. This affected the trade balance, resulting in a sharp fall in Customs revenues, which were virtually the Government's only source of revenue. While great hopes were pinned on Mr Thomas to repair what others had destroyed, he in fact brought the finances to ruin and left them in an even sorrier state.

Thereafter Sultan Taimur bin Faisal considered engaging a financial expert to put right what was wrong. In 1931 he engaged as his Financial Adviser, Mr Hedgecock, an Englishman and a senior official of the Iraqi Finance Ministry, who immediately set to work with great vigour and determination to rescue the finances from the state they were in as a result of Bertram Thomas' maladministration. He reduced salaries and cut expenditure and was eventually able to put the financial records in order and to organise proper Budgets. We reveal no secrets if we say that at that time the Government's Budget was no more than Rps. 700,000 (£50,000) from which the Sultanate had to pay the cost of the Government machine, repay the balance of the loan and meet various other items of expenditure, including the customary gifts and presents to the tribal Sheikhs and delegations, since, outwardly, the Government appeared very rich. Mr Hedgecock deserves admiration and respect for what he did to reorganise the finances of the Sultanate. Unfortunately, however, he did not stay long, resigning for private reasons after eight months.

At that time we were Prime Minister with oversight of the Sultanate's financial affairs. After the resignation of Mr Hedgecock it was decided to appoint Mr R.J. Alban, an Englishman, as Financial Adviser. And then, on 2 Shawal 1350 (11 February 1932), we succeeded to power upon the abdication, for reasons of health, of our beloved father, Sultan Taimur bin Faisal.

We gave our special attention to finance but found that because of the effects of economic pressure on world trade we were compelled to reduce expenditure in various sectors, our first economy being to halve the Sultan's Privy Purse. The reader may be surprised to learn that when we took over the reins of power the Sultanate's Treasury was completely empty. No doubt many of our contemporaries will recall what the financial situation was like in those days.

However, thanks to painstaking efforts and close supervision of finances signs of improvement became visible, and, as 1933 neared its end, debts had been liquidated and the sums due to the merchants paid off. At the end of 1933 the Financial Adviser resigned whereupon we assumed complete personal control of the Sultanate's finances and the preparation of its annual Budgets. The improvement in Customs revenues continued (the Sultanate having no other income to speak of) enabling us to raise officials' salaries and to give attention to the welfare of the Sultanate. The financial position has continued to improve until the present day.

The third period runs from 1939, with the outbreak of the Second World War, until 1945. During this period prices rose and consequently so too did Customs revenues. We further increased officials' salaries and undertook much needed reforms in various parts of the Sultanate. From 1933 to this day there has been no financial deficit in the Government's Budget and the Government has been able to build up reasonable financial reserves against emergencies, as well as meeting necessary expenditure in various fields, especially that of defence, which swallowed up about half the Budget. We were anxious to introduce various urgently needed reforms for the welfare of the country, but found that there was not enough leeway either in the Budget or in the reserves to support any sort of planning, for we did not want to overburden the Sultante's finances and weigh them down with new debts, after having paid off all the old ones. Doubtless it would have been easy to obtain money in various ways, but this could only have been by a loan with interest set at a percentage rate. This amounts to usury, with which I completely disagree, and the religious prohibition of which is not unknown.

By now the financial position of the Sultanate will have been made plain to you by the facts we have set out for you, and which account for the inability of the Government of the time to bring the country up to date. We were fully aware of the many reforms which the country needed, but whilst the eyesight was long, the arm at that time was short. Despite all this, however, we were never at a loss to undertake any work which brought general benefit to the county whenever we found a way to do so. For example, when the opportunity occurred in 1940, during the war, we built the Saidiya School in Muscat, the first Government building constructed after getting over the difficult period. Similarly we made a number of improvements to Government centres and forts in various Wilayets.

In 1958 our friends, the British Government, offered us financial assistance to strengthen the Sultanate's Army; to introduce improvements in education; to set up Health Centres in some of the Wilayets along the coast and in the interior; to build Experimental Farms to raise the standard of farming in the country; to construct roads and other improvements. We accepted this with deep gratitude. There was a time limit to it in that it was to continue only until the finances of the Sultanate improved. It continued until the end of March last year, i.e., four months before oil exports began at the end of July 1967. During this interim period we depended upon such financial reserves as we had. Had it not been for our economy and for our reserves, we would not have been able to bear the burden of expenditure during these months. In particular the allocation to the Sultanate Army took up a large part of our resources until the Government obtained its share of oil revenues.

Now the oil flow from the fields at Fahud and Natih through the pipes to the tanks at Mina Al Fahl in Saih Al Maleh (which ought now to be called Saih al Huluw). Soon the product of another field at Jibal near Fahud will flow to join the output of the first two fields supplying the tanks at Saih Al Huluw whence the oil is pumped out to the tankers anchored at Mina Al Fahl to be carried away. Thus our dear country becomes among the exporters of oil and we can insert a new subhead in our Budget: 'Oil Revenues'. Yes, only now that we know that revenue from oil will be coming in steadily can we consider and plan and estimate how to put into effect the various projects which the country needs. We hope these revenues will continue to increase each year.

We ought at this stage to mention the relationship between the Sultanate and the oil company. The first agreement was concluded in the middle of 1937. The Company paid a rent for the right to search for oil in Sultanate territory and this helped to strengthen the Budget somewhat. In 1964, when oil was discovered in commercial quantities in the Sultanate, the present Company suggested a revision of the agreement signed between the Sultanate and the previous oil company, the new agreement to correspond with several agreements signed recently between the various oil companies and the Governments of the oil exporting countries of the Middle East. The Sultanate agreed and asked the Company to put forward a suggested revision for the Government to study.

In March 1967, after talks between the Sultanate and the Company, Agreements were concluded giving the Government 50 per cent of the oil profits, and the right to 12.5 per cent of all oil exported. This accorded with the decision of OPEC, an organisation formed of some of the Middle East oil exporting countries. The Agreement included many other matters bringing advantage and general benefit to the county.

All of this took place during the period in which Mr F. Hughes was the Company's General Manager and Representative. He was appointed by the Company to negotiate the detailed revision of the Agreement and we found a complete understanding of the situation on his part. Agreement on terms was reached with great ease, thanks to the efforts displayed by him so that the Agreement should benefit both sides.

God willing, 1968 will be the start of a new era for our country which will see the beginning of various plans which will be executed under the supervision of qualified technicians and experts. Firstly we shall begin building offices for various Government Departments; then houses for officials who will come from abroad; then step by step will come various projects such as hospitals, schools, roads, communications, and other necessary works including the development of fisheries, animals and agricultural resources etc. until modern projects spread over the whole of the Sultanate, to each area according to its needs. So long as oil flows the Government will match its flow with continuing development for the welfare of the country. Naturally projects involve much effort and hard work. The progress we see in other countries was not the work of a day, but the result of efforts over long years. It takes time for the results of projects for improvement to be seen and there will be an unavoidable gap between the receipt of oil revenues and the appearance of benefits for the populace. We are straining every nerve to improve the lot of the country both in general and in particular.

An initial task is to increase the salaries of Government officials which we consider need to be increased and to establish a cadre to regularise promotion. We shall reinforce the Government machine by adding to it a number of experts and technicians. This will ensure that the Government has a modern administrative machine. The present situation requires changes in the existing Government set-up.

There are urgent schemes to which we consider we must give priority.

- APPENDIX 2 -

1. Water – work on this project is being pressed ahead, and we hope that a water pipeline to Muscat and Matrah will be laid within 21 months of the date of contract, making pure water available to all.

2. Electricity – all the preliminary stages have been completed and work is going ahead briskly. It is hoped that the Company to which the project has been entrusted will supply electricity to consumers in Muscat and Matrah next summer.

3. Matrah Port – because of Matrah's outstanding natural location, secure commercial position and reliable communications with the various parts of the Sultanate, which make it the commercial capital of the country, we consider that we should make a start on the construction of port facilities in the near future, to which the general Customs Department will be transferred, and where steamers, sailing craft and motor boats may moor to load and discharge. Sufficient warehouses will be provided for the storage and protection of incoming and outgoing goods.

4. Saidi currency – another project which will be given priority and special study is that of currency. The Saidi currency will be based on the Saidi Riyal, subdivided into 1/2 Riyal and 1/4 Riyal. Baizas will be minted to meet the requirements of the people, denominations being of 100, 25, 20, 10, 5 and 1 Baiza. The necessary announcement about this will be made at the appropriate time.

When we talk about planning we must not forget the oil-bearing area and the Duru tribe who live there. They must be given special attention and must get the projects they need and which suit them.

Other plans will follow later, in order of importance. We must not forget the area of the Sultanate is more than 100,000 square miles, that its coastline is no less than 1,000 miles long and that its population is estimated at more than half a million.

We shall appoint a body, known as the Development Board, to execute such plans as we decide upon. This body will be responsible for drawing up a Budget for each project and for keeping in touch with experts, technicians and others whom it is necessary to consult in connection with any desired project.

We shall also appoint a special Board for the water and electricity schemes. It will oversee the progress of work and will ensure that the schemes conform with the regulations fixed by the Government to safeguard the needs of the people.

We are now passing through a preliminary planning stage for the projects which enjoy priority because they are for the benefit of all. We are looking forward to a bright future by which we guarantee raising the standard of living of the inhabitants of the Sultanate and increasing the income of the individual. We shall develop the country so as to keep pace with the cavalcade of present-day civilization. We shall ensure every benefit and advantage for the populace and we shall pursue those developments which bring us that which is best and preferable and is consonant with our people's heritage and ancient history. However much we progress and move forward we must keep before our eyes our true religion on which we place our reliance and traditions which are our heritage. There are prohibitions of our religion which are inviolable for ever and there are customs which can be altered without infringing the basic traditions of the country which are among the glories of our worthy ancestors, which are a source of pride and which protect our very existence. The Almighty said in his Book: 'Say "work" and God will see your work.'

We ask the Almighty whose works are great to inspire us to do that which is right, to crown our efforts with success, bring us success in our enterprises and grant us victory in our desires. We are humble towards him whose power is sublime and brings us success in what is for the good of our Omani people and our country.

The statement issued by Sultan Said bin Taimour on 1 January 1968, explaining to his people the county's past financial condition and clearly setting out his plans for natural development when Oman is in receipt of revenue from oil.

*Opposite Page*: The Foreign Office Minute illustrating Britain's involvement in the forced removal of Sultan Said bin Taimour from his throne. The Minute refers to the 'coup . . . last night', and is dated 23 July 1970. Yet the coup did not take place until the afternoon of that day. The minute was actually written before the palace coup had been staged.

# APPENDIX 3

## Secret British Foreign Office Minute

Mr Hayman

### COUP IN THE SULTANATE OF MUSCAT AND OMAN

This is just to summarise the arrangments which are being made Sayyid Qabus' successful <u>coup</u> against his father, the former Sultan, last night:

(a)   the former Sultan, although wounded in four places, is apparently out of immediate danger and appears to be in good heart, is now in Bahrain where he will receive further medical attention at the RAF Hospital Muharraq.

(b)   the Political resident proposes to evacuate him to the UK tonight on RAF Britannia Flight 6394, ETA Brize Norton at 08.25 hours our time tomorrow.

(c)   the Ministry of Defence have arranged for the former Sultan to be taken straight from the airfield, by ambulancem to the RAF hospital at Wroughton in Wiltshire for further medical treatment. They are laying on appropriate security precautions and liaising with the local police.

(d)   the Private Office have agreed that you yourself should welcome the fomer Sultan on arrival at Brize Norton and convey to him a short oral message on behalf of the Secretary of State.

(e)   Mr Mayall and Protocol and Conference Department are making arrangements for cars to be at Brize Norton, together with Mr Seaton Deardon or some other Arabist from GHF, in order to transport the dependants accompanying the former Sultan to a hotel near to the hospital. Protocol and Conference Department will make hotel bookings for the dependants when their number is known (MOD have as CBFG to let us know this number as soon as possible).

2.   I am dealing separately with the question of recognition of Qabus in the light of Muscat telegram No. 294 to Bahrain Residency.

c.c   Private Office
      Mr Renwick
      Mr Daunt
      Mr Tesh
      Mr Mayall
      News Department

(J.M. Edes)
in Department
23 July, 1970

# APPENDIX 4

# Statements by the Oman Civil Rights Committee

THE OMAN CIVIL RIGHTS COMMITTEE
MUSCAT, SULTANATE OF OMAN

May, 1995

To all concerned,

This note, together with many that are to follow, is a sincere attempt at explaining recent developments in our beloved country. Many believe these developments will prove to be a turning point in our country's history. They will undoubtedly influence the way the people and the Government of Oman conduct their affairs and interact with each other from now on. We feel it is important therefore that every citizen and resident of this country understands clearly what has happened so he or she can make a sound judgement based on facts. The Government, which is the sole source of information in the country, has not been forthcoming with information about these matters, with the exception of a couple of cryptic press releases to its news agency. Even these were only made after foreign news services, notably the BBC World Service, started to run the stories in their bulletins.

Lack of clear information has obviously resulted in a lot of rumours in the country, many of which originating from government sources as part of its campaign to misinform the public and to character assassinate the individuals concerned. In these notes, we hope to shed more light on the matter and uncover the truths and expose the real motives behind these events.

During a three-month period starting late May 94, the Government Security Forces raided homes and offices and violently arrested more than 400 Omanis. These individuals were then interrogated and some were tortured in trying to force them to admit to false and baseless charges. Those who came to know about the arrests were shocked at the ways the security forces conducted the raids and the arrests and how the privacy and sanctity of people's houses were violated with no regard or respect to women and children. Some of the arrested were tied and put in sacks. It was an inhumane and degrading episode and should be condemned by all fair-minded people.

– 216 –

Over the following months, many of the detainees were released without charges or were given suspended sentences, the remaining 146 people were sentenced to prison terms ranging from 3 to 20 years.

These individuals come from all walks of life. Many are well educated and were holding important jobs including Under-Secretaries of Ministries, an Ambassador, judges, doctors, engineers, Senior civil servants, businessmen, teachers and students. They consist of both Ibadhis and Sunnis and are come from all regions of the Sultanate. In fact they form a microcosm of an Omani society. They dearly love their country and they gave all what it takes to serve it. They were hard working in their jobs and were fair to all. They are people of high moral character derived from a strong Iman and they respected everybody and were respected by all who know them or had dealings with them. They always prayed in Mosques and involved themselves in good works in the community. None of them was involved in drinking, womanising or any other corruptive behaviours. The reader is hereby asked to inquire for himself about the personal character of any of those still in jail.

Like the majority of Omanis, they were concerned about the direction their country is heading; the lack of social justice, the ever increasing gap between the rich (few) and poor (many), corruption, deterioration of education standards, unemployment, proliferation of outlets selling alcohol and the resulting drunkenness and drug addictions and in general the erosion of Islamic moral standards. Their concern stems from the deep love of their country and its people. Despite all this, they did not do or even intend to do anything to undermine the authority of the Government in any way. Therefore, there is no logical explanation for their imprisonment apart from sheer injustice and for the self-satisfaction of a corrupt security system.

However, the accused believed the solutions to all these problems and as security against catastrophe in future is for everyone to return to Islam and re-assert its values and this will only be achieved through Daawah and Islah as Allah say in the Qur'an

كنتم خير أمة أخرجت للناس تأمرون بالمعروف وتنهون عن المنكر وتؤمنون بالله

*Ye are the best of peoples, evolved for mankind, enjoining what is right, forbidding what is wrong, and believing in God . . .*

We can see that these individuals are important assets this country cannot afford to waste by incarcerating them in jails. They are young and over the years they have proven to be good and sincere in everything they did and have served their country sell. Putting them in jail will not solve anything. On the contrary this will exacerbate the political situation, polarize the society and further destabilise an already fragile country. We believe there is still an honourable way out of this mess for all parties concerned. We believe those in jail are mature people and are capable of negotiating their release and in resolving this problem and this has to be done soonest before there is a hardening of feeling on both sides.

# - OMAN -

OMAN CIVIL RIGHTS COMMITTEE
SULTANATE OF OMAN

URGENT CIRCULAR

With sadness, astonishment, anger and deploration we are obliged to inform you recent actions of the Omani Security Forces at Al-Rumais Prison. Fifty of the 146 unjustly jailed for over a year, have been poisoned. They were then left to suffer in this atrocious conditions for more than four days and were denied access to any medical services.

This incidence took place early May 1995. This situation became apparent only when the inmates were visited by their close relatives on June 1995. These visits were supposed to have taken place in May to coincide with Eid Al-Adha (The Muslim Major Celebration Day), but were delayed because of this incidence. The relatives were shocked and alarmed by the state of their close ones who appeared as tired, weak and some unable to stand on their feet.

This still could have a straight-forward food poisoning due to the unhygienic food services at the prison. But if it's purely that, then, it's appropriate to question the intentions of the Security Forces for denying the medical assistance to these individuals. These people, who were just few months ago some of the most reputable individuals in the Government, and still most respected by the mass.

It's important to indicate to all those concerned that, atrocities like these produce instability and violence in the normally stable and peaceful state. We hereby call upon to the international human rights organizations and the countries that are friendly to Oman, such as USA and UK to advise the Sultan of Oman to exercise reasons and responsibility in the affairs of the countries. Washing his hands from the bad incidence in the country and attributing them to the directors does not fool the masses. Oman is now entering a new period where freedom of expression and human rights are the aspirations of every one. The Government forces can not delay the waves of mass awareness which was already building up even prior to these arrest and tortures.

# BIBLIOGRAPHY

Akehurst, J.B. *We Won A War* (Russell, 1982)
Allen, C. *Savage Wars of Peace: Soldiers' Voices 1945–1989* (Michael Joseph, 1990)
Allfree, P.S. *Warlords of Oman* (Robert Hale, 1967)
Arkless, D.C. *The Secret War* (Kimber, 1988)
Boustead, H.R.D. *The Wind of Morning* (Chatto and Windus, 1971)
Carter, J.R.L. *Tribes in Oman* (Peninsular, 1982)
Deane-Drummond, A.J. *The Arrows of Fortune* (Leo Cooper, 1992)
de la Billiere, P. *Looking for Trouble* (HarperCollins, 1994)
Fiennes, R.T.W. *Where Soldiers Fear to Tread* (Hodder & Stoughton, 1975)
Fiennes, R.T.W. *The Feathermen* (Bloomsbury, 1991)
Graz, L. *The Omanis: Sentinels of the Gulf* (Longmans, 1982)
Halliday, F. *Arabia Without Sultans* (Penguin, 1974)
Hawley, D.F. *Oman* (Stacey, 1977)
Hawley, D.F. *Tropic Storm and Desert Wind* (Michael Russell, 2000)
Hoskins, A. *A Contract Officer in the Oman* (Costello, 1988)
Innes, N. *Minister in Oman* (Oleander Press, 1987)
Jeapes, T. *SAS Operation Oman*, (Kimber, 1980)
Joyce, M. *The Sultanate of Oman* (Praeger, 1995)
Lucas, I. *A Road to Damascus* (Radcliffe, 1997)
Lunt, J.D. *Imperial Sunset: Frontier Soldiering in the Twentieth Century* (MacDonald, 1981)
Morris, J.H. *Sultan in Oman* (Faber & Faber, 1957)
Perkins, K. *A Fortunate Soldier* (Brassey, 1988)
Perkins, K. *Khalida* (Quartet, 1991)
Peterson, J.E. *Oman in the Twentieth Century* (Croom Helm, 1978)
Peyton, W.D. *Old Oman* (Stacey, 1983)
Skeet, I. *Muscat and Oman: The End of an Era* (Faber & Faber, 1985)
Smiley, D.de C. *Arabian Assignment* (Leo Cooper, 1975)
St Albans, S. *Where Time Stood Still* (Quartet, 1980)
Thesiger, W.P. *Arabian Sands* (Longmans, 1959)
Thwaites, P.T., Sloan S., *Muscat Command* (Leo Cooper, 1995)
Tinson, A.R. *Awards of the Sultanate of Oman* (Spink, 1985)
Townsend, J. *Oman: The Making of the Modern State* (Croom Helm, 1977)
West, N. *The Friends: Britain's Post-War Secret Intelligence Operations* (Weidenfeld & Nicolson, 1982)

# INDEX